Collected Works of Sebastian Kappen

Volume I

Jesus and Freedom and Related Essays

Collected Works of Sebastian Kappen
Volume I

Jesus and Freedom and Related Essays

Compiled and Edited by
Sebastian Vattamattam

2020

Collected Works of Sebastian Kappen, Volume I: Jesus and Freedom and Related Essays, Ed. Sebastian Vattamattam — published by the Indian Society for Promoting Christian Knowledge (ISPCK), Post Box 1585, Kashmere Gate, Delhi-110006.

ISBN: 978-93-88945-76-9

Cover design: Manush John

Laser typeset by

ISPCK, Post Box 1585, 1654, Madarsa Road, Kashmere Gate, Delhi-110006
• *Tel:* 23866323

e-mail: ashish@ispck.org.in • ella@ispck.org.in
website: www.ispck.org.in

Sebastian Kappen (1924 - 1993)

Sebastian Kappen, an Indian Jesuit theologian, doctored in 1961 from the Gregorian University, Rome, with a thesis on 'Praxis and Religious Alienation according to the Economic and Philosophical Manuscripts of Karl Marx.' His subsequent studies had been geared to the requirements of transformative social action in India. This led him to an investigation into the liberative and humanizing potential of the original teachings of the historical Jesus as well as of Indian religious traditions, particularly the tradition of dissent represented by the Buddha and the medieval Bhakti Movement. He wrote and lectured extensively on the cultural restructuring of Indian society.

In 1977 appeared Kappen's major work in English, *Jesus and Freedom*. It was followed by *Marxian Atheism* (1983), *Jesus and Cultural Revolution - an Asian Perspective* (1983), *Liberation Theology and Marxism* (1986), and *The Future of Socialism and Socialism of the Future* (1992). His posthumous publications are *Tradition Modernity Counterculture* (1994), *Hindutva and Indian Religious Traditions* (2000), *Divine Challenge and Human Response* (2001), *Jesus and Society* (2002), *Jesus and Culture* (2002), *Towards a Holistic Cultural Paradigm* (2003), *Marx Beyond Marxism* (2012), *Ingathering* (2013), *What the Thunder Says* (2013). His books in Malayalam are *From Faith to Revolution* (1972), *A Sexual Morality for Tomorrow* (1973), *Ecology and Culture* (1988), *An Introduction to the Philosophy of Marx* (1989), *Prophecy and Counterculture* (1992), *In Search of the Non-Christian Jesus* (1999), *Liberation of Jesus from the Churches* (2012), and *Death of God and the Birth of the Human* - tr. of *Marxian Atheism* (2015)

Sebastian Kappen had been visiting professor to the Pontifical Seminary (Pune), Vidyajyoti (Delhi), The Catholic University of Louvain (Belgium) and Maryknoll Seminary (New York). Mother Earth called him back on 30 November 1993.

Contents

Introduction

Fr. Sebastian Kappen started publishing his writings in the 1960s. Probably, his first work in English is the essay "The Eucharist and the Quest of India for a New Vision of History" (Chap.11), written in the context of the International Eucharist Congress in Bombay. In this, he appears as deeply rooted in the Church dogmas about Jesus Christ and at the same time trying to take the Church to the midst of the world. But, he finds his Church in Kerala, his native place, moving in the opposite direction with its capitalist leanings and internal divisions into caste-like rites. These are the issues he takes up until 1969.

Next, we see Kappen confronting Jesus of Nazareth in the historical background. His essay, "Jesus Today", written in 1975 denotes a turning point in this direction. He sees Jesus as a prophet, taken hold of by God and anointed to preach the coming of the Kingdom of God on Earth. Meanwhile, Kappen wrote two books in his mother tongue, Malayalam: *From Faith to Revolution* (1972) and *A Sexual Morality for Tomorrow* (1973). We can see his thoughts on Sexuality developing together with aesthetics, culture, and ecology in the 1980s.

In 1977 came out Kappen's first book, *Jesus and Freedom*, in English. It was censored by the Vatican in 1980. "Censorship and the Future of Asian Theology", the last chapter of this volume, is Kappen's open response to censorship. The Vatican took no further action on him. One reason may be that in the last two decades he was living independently in rented houses, outside the Church establishments.

This first volume of the Collected Works of S. Kappen contains his book *Jesus and Freedom* (Orbis Books, 1977) and related theological essays.

Let me express my gratitude to Mercy Kappen, and artist C F John, both closely related to Fr. Kappen, for their consistent support and encouragement in completing this volume. The cover image of this book is John's artistic creation.

Sebastian Vattamattam

Part - I
Jesus and Freedom

Preface of the First Edition

Though written down only in the course of the last year (1976), the basic vision underlying *Jesus and Freedom* is the fruit of more than a decade of anguishing search for relevance, a search inspired largely by the many groups of students, seminarians, and intellectuals whom I had the privilege to address at seminars or in classrooms. It is they who made me ask questions that I had not dared to pose till then and embark on the arduous path of a radical criticism of the Christian faith. Their positive and often enthusiastic response to my all too tentative interpretation of the message of Jesus assured me that I am on the right track.

However, no claim is made that the views expressed here constitute my last word on the matter. Representing as it does a search that is not yet ended; the work contains quite a few statements that are exploratory regarding, if not content, at least formulation. Nevertheless, I firmly believe that only an interpretation, along the lines I have indicated, does justice to the witness of the Gospels and the requirements of our age.

The present work is addressed not to specialists but to the educated youth in India who may seek in the Gospels inspiration for radical commitment. The stress, therefore, is on projecting a vision, rather than on providing a mass of information. In keeping with this aim, I have tried to make the text as readable as possible. I have also avoided confronting the reader with the maze of the conflicting interpretations offered by biblical scholars. Instead, I have put forward what seemed to me the best interpretation in each case without trying to justify them on exegetical grounds. Footnotes too have been reduced to the minimum. A select bibliography is given at the end as help for further study.

I am deeply grateful to Francois Houtart, Director of the Centre for Socio-Religious Research, University of Louvain, Belgium, whose deep humanity and profound concern for the underprivileged all over the world have been a source of constant inspiration to me, for agreeing to write an introduction to my book. I should like to thank also M. S. Menon and Mary Samuel for going through the manuscript and suggesting improvements in style and presentation, and Josee Cleymans, who offered to type out copies for print.

The book will, I hope, be of help to the youth in other countries also who are grappling with the problem of the relevance of faith for the liberation of humanity.

Sebastian Kappen

1

The Quest and the Questions

Our age is marked by a heightened awareness of the many forces that oppress humans and prevent their spontaneous unfolding into rich and meaningful existence. Many find in religion itself a force for oppression and are convinced that the sooner it disappears, the better for the future of humankind. Others, while granting that many historical forms of religion have played, and are still playing, a reactionary role by legitimizing and reinforcing systems of unfreedom, believe that authentic religiosity can be a potential for liberation. It is this latter conviction that impelled us to conduct an investigation into the relevance of Jesus for the integral liberation of humans.

Every investigation proceeds from its own assumptions, which determine its general approach and method. Our basic assumptions are twofold: that it is necessary to go back to the original message of Jesus, and that it is equally necessary to reinterpret it in the context of the self-understanding of contemporary human. The validity of these assumptions will, we hope, become clear in the course of the investigation itself. In this chapter, we make a few preliminary remarks to help the reader to participate better in our search.

It is necessary to go back to the historical Jesus because his original message is much more relevant for us than most subsequent interpretations, which have either rendered it innocuous or even distorted it. To grasp this it is necessary to dwell on the history of Christian alienation.

Jesus Alienated

The alienation of Christian faith and practice from the historical Jesus took place along three principal lines — cultic, dogmatic, and institutional. For an adequate grasp of this process, it would be necessary to go back to the very sources of Christianity and from there to trace its development right up to our day. This is not possible within the limited scope of this book. What is attempted here is only a schematic and, admittedly, simplified outline of the more salient features that stand out even on a cursory analysis.

Cultic alienation was the first to set in. The historical Jesus devalued cult by subordinating it to justice, mercy, and love. He did not project himself as an object of worship. He did not institute any rite that can be called cultic in the traditional sense of the term. But soon after his death, there developed a cult centered upon him. However, its focal point was not the Jesus of history but Jesus risen from the dead and seated at the right hand of the Father. Jesus who was a part of our history was replaced in Christian piety by the risen Christ, regarded as above history, as eternal and immutable. The same piety removed him from our midst, from the common run of everyday life, and installed him in the tabernacle. It built a separate home for him furnished with flowers, candles, holy water, and incense. It projected him as a stickler for ritual purity, who avoided publicans and sinners and looked down upon the 'profane' world of everyday life. Cult also started a process of abstraction. The death of Jesus was dissociated from his historical life or reduced to a mere prerequisite for resurrection. Jesus was further fragmented into many formal aspects, each of which in its turn became the object of a new 'devotion'. Thus we had a plethora of devotions having for their objects the 'Precious Blood', the 'Crown of Thorns', the 'Five Wounds', the 'Sacred Heart'. By the Middle Ages, Christianity had become a cult-centered religion. Mercy, justice, and love became secondary to the Eucharistic cult and the devotions. The circle was complete. A non-cultic prophetic movement had ended up as a cultic religion.

The history of dogma and catechesis shows a parallel process of alienation. Jesus, as pictured in the Synoptic Gospels, is a human among humans, a member of the family of humans. He was less word made flesh than flesh become word, matter endowed with a tongue. The flesh of our flesh, the blood of our blood, he learned to love by being loved by others, gained knowledge of himself in being acknowledged by others. It was in meeting his kind that he learned kindness and compassion. He loved humans. He struck root in others to such an extent that they became a need for him, especially in moments of crisis. Exquisitely attuned to everything human, he valued the friendship of women; loved children, wine, and the lilies of the field. He could rejoice with those who rejoiced and weep with those who wept.

Like any human, he too had to grow in wisdom and favours with God and humans (Luke 2:52). He was a quester after truth, after the God who made him. And he found him on the banks of the Jordan River. On the day of his baptism at the hands of John the Baptizer, he was taken hold of by God. He was swept off his feet, uprooted from his familiar world, and transplanted into the realm of the divine. There he was given a new mind and a new heart, and he began to see the world in a new light, in the light of the reign of God. But his search did not end there. He had still to come to terms with God and reach a point of clarity regarding his mission in life. The consequent inner struggle with light and darkness is represented in the Gospels as the temptations in the desert.

Jesus was also fully conscious of his limitations. Asked about the final coming of the Kingdom, he replied, "But about that day or that hour no one knows, not even the angels in heaven, not even the Son, only the Father" (Mark 13:32). So too he admitted openly that he could not dispense the blessings of the age to come just as he liked. The sons of Zebedee who sought the favour of being allowed to sit in state one on his right, the other on his left, were told bluntly that to sit at his right or left was not for him to grant, that it was for those to whom it had already been assigned (Mark 10:40). Though the Divine was in him radiating his power, he did not think to snatch at equality with God (Phil. 2:6). When a stranger called him 'good master' his answer was, "Why do you call me good? No one is good except God alone" (Mark 10:17-18).

Like any other human, he was subject to varying and conflicting emotions. The woes he uttered against the hypocrites of his day betray a spirit that was quick to flame with indignation. He was filled with anger at the sight of the trafficking that went on in the temple, the house of his Father. The destiny he was to meet in Jerusalem set every fiber of his being in tension. "I have a baptism to undergo, and what constraint I am under until the ordeal is over" (Luke 12:50). The prospect of death was to him a source of infinite sadness that he wanted to share with his friends, "My heart is ready to break with grief" (Mark 14:34). It filled him with fear and anguish. To quote the writer of the Letter to the Hebrews, "In the days of his earthly life, he offered up prayers and petitions, with loud cries and tears, to God who was able to deliver him from the grave" (Heb. 5:7).

Jesus is so much like us and yet, in his very likeness, stands out as the wholly other. What a far cry from this Jesus is the Christ of dogma! The latter is Jesus transmuted as he was made to pass through the Greco-Roman mould of thinking. He came out of this mould fragmented into abstractions such as person, nature, hypostasis, body, soul, substance, quality, quantity, essence, and existence. What cult did at the level of action, theology did at the level of thought. Jesus was reduced to a mere sum of formal concepts. Seen from the human plane, he is a human with two natures subsisting in one divine person. Seen from the divine plane he is the second person of the Trinity, identical in nature with the Father and the Holy Spirit. Controversies raged as to whether the Spirit proceeds from the Father only or the Father and the Son. What is worse, in this process of sterile philosophical reflection, the humanity of Jesus was downgraded. Of course dogma as well as theology affirmed his human nature but not without denying him the status of a human person, a mode of reasoning that sounds very odd to us. This had its repercussions in popular catechesis. For the mass of believers, Jesus appeared as God under the guise of a human. In their eyes he did not grow in wisdom; for, being God, he knew from early infancy all there is to know. Though they recited the official creed, which said that he suffered under Pontius Pilate, they knew well enough that he could not have suffered, endowed as he was on earth with the beatifying vision of God. If ever they read the Gospels, they slurred over the passages that affirmed his human condition or, if clever enough, managed to put dishonest interpretations on them. In short, if cult segregated him from the company of humans and settled him down in churches on the fringes of the real world, dogma banished him to the world of ideas. In this process the Jesus of history became a forgotten person.

Institutionalism distorted the image and the teachings of Jesus, more than cult and catechesis. The Gospels picture him as one who, right from the outset of his public life, rejected power whether economic or political, as a means to usher in the New Age. And the historical movement he set in motion was one predominantly of the poorer classes in Palestine and the Greek-Roman world who had no political ambitions. But with Emperor Constantine, who declared Christianity the state religion, the leaders of the Christian community began to enjoy economic and political privileges. The temptation Jesus overcame in the desert, his disciples succumbed to all too easily. The Church began to exercise control over every sphere of life. This led to a proliferation of institutions. Though in course of time political life regained its autonomy vis-a-vis the Church, the latter held on to its institutions — schools, colleges, hospitals, and orphanages — and even started new ones. Every local church has today its institutional empire. What is still more saddening is that most of these institutions have not even an umbilical bond with the gospel of Jesus. By and large, they embody the values of capitalism — private interest, competition, aggression, and lust for power. Besides, insofar as they violate the legitimate autonomy of secular spheres of life, they have become even instruments of domination.

Thus, by a curious development, the good news of liberation preached by Jesus gave rise to structures of unfreedom. Institutionalism has in this manner disfigured his image and neutralized the revolutionary, disruptive force of his teaching.

The tragic consequence of all this is that Jesus of Nazareth is the most forgotten person among the very people who claim to be his disciples. He lies buried under the weight of accumulated layers of rituals, rubrics, laws, concepts, legends, myths, superstitions, and institutions. He lies bound hand and foot by innumerable cords that tradition has cast around him. His voice is smothered, his spirit stifled. If he still acts and makes his presence felt in history, it is more through honest dissenters among Christians than through the official Church. Therefore it is the duty of all who cherish the vision and hope of Jesus to set him free from the prison-house of cult, dogma, and institutionalism so that he can freely go about pointing, as of old, his accusing finger at the scribes, Pharisees, elders, priests, and Herods of today. To this end, it is necessary to remove the many veils that historically conditioned faith and tradition have put on him, and let his visage shine forth in its original splendor, and his words ring out in their untamed incisiveness.

What we have said thus far should not be interpreted to mean that the history of Christianity until now has only been one of progressive alienation. The development of Christian theory and practice in the West contains also positive elements in harmony with the teachings of Jesus. These elements have to be distinguished from those that are at variance with it. Such a critical study may be useful, and even necessary, up to a point, but should never be made an absolute for people who do not share the Western tradition. If we Indians have no other way to meet God as revealed in the life and teachings of Jesus than by mentally reenacting the history of Western Christianity we are of all men the most to be pitied.

We have seen that it is necessary to go back to the historical Jesus. But is not the attempt doomed to fail considering that the Gospels are not historical documents in the usual sense of the term but the expression of the faith of the early Christians? This is a serious problem on which an adequate discussion, though useful, is not possible within the scope of this chapter. This much, however, may be said. The nature of our sources indeed renders futile any attempt to write a biography or psychology of Jesus. It is impossible to reconstruct the sequence of events in his life. But to go further and say that no understanding of the historical Jesus at all is possible is unwarranted. The Gospels are the concrete embodiment of the response of the early Christians to an historical reality: to the life, words, and deeds of Jesus of Nazareth. Hence we can have a real encounter with the historical Jesus in and through the Gospels. Using the criteria provided by contemporary biblical criticism we can arrive at an adequate grasp of the person and teachings of Jesus, which are themselves events in history, and perhaps also, of a very broad outline of his life.[1] Nothing more is presupposed in this book. However, this is no plea for rediscovering the historical Jesus to mimic him or to repeat parrot wise his teachings. His message needs to be reinterpreted in a spirit of creative fidelity.

Jesus Beyond Jesus

The need for such a reinterpretation was prevented by the traditional approach, which all too one-sidedly emphasized the divinity of Jesus to the neglect of his humanity. To those who saw him primarily, if not exclusively, from the plane of the divine, it was but natural to conclude that his teaching in all its details was eternally and immutably true.

But this whole approach is to be called in question. It was not from above nor from the angle of preconceived notions that his contemporaries saw him. They saw him from below as a human among humans, as the carpenter from Nazareth. It was in observing his ordinary human behavior — his words, gestures, and actions — that they gained a glimpse into the divine dimension in him. Their approach should be normative for us too. The recognition of Jesus as a member of the human family must be the point of departure of all our reflections. But to recognize him as a human is to regard him as rooted in the soil, as inserted in the current of history. And as part of history, he shared the mode of thinking that prevailed among his people.

Now, the ideas and beliefs of any people bear the imprint of their social system constituted by the mode of production, the stratification of classes, and the structure of political power. Any significant change in the social base implies also a corresponding change in the system of ideas and beliefs. The self-understanding of a human in a tribal society is not the same as that of a human in a feudal society or that of a member of the capitalist society. It is therefore evident that Jesus, who lived twenty centuries ago, viewed nature, human, and God differently from us.

This does not mean that his teachings contain nothing of perennial value. Even people of earlier ages could have gained profound insights valid for all times, though cast in outmoded conceptual molds. This is all the more true of prophetic individuals who emerge in periods of cultural crisis. They give articulate expression to the revolt against the past and the longing for the new, which exist in an inarticulate, confused manner among the masses. They are essentially heralds of the future, humans who dream new dreams and see new visions. Their destiny is to leap into the unknown ahead and carry the masses with them. They are gripped by the ultimate concern of life and, therefore, their message necessarily has something of the unconditioned. Both in their revolt against the status quo and their commitment to the not-yet, there is much that is valid for humans of all times. Yet in the very breakthrough, they achieve at the level of the total vision of human, they remain conditioned by the status quo they revolt against. The new they can envisage only in the language of the old. Even the very content of their message exhibits this tension between the not-yet and the already, between the absolute and the relative. Though lonely in the sweep of their vision and the passion of their commitment, they remain very much humans of their age.

Jesus of Nazareth was one such prophet — so transcendent in his vision, yet so immanent in his world; so perennial in his appeal, yet so rooted in his age; so absolute in his demands, yet so conditioned by his environment. His message comes to us, cast in a cultural mold we have long left behind. Hence the need to reinterpret it in the light of our contemporary experience by distinguishing its perennially valid elements from the historically conditioned, and by bringing to light its deeper implications for the humans of today.

But, in trying to reinterpret Jesus for the contemporary world, are we not committing the same mistake as did the early and subsequent generations of Christians? Are we not distorting his image to suit our tastes and safeguard our interests? That there is such a danger cannot be denied. And the only way to avoid it is to see that our interpretation is not naive but critical. But what are the criteria that should guide such criticism? They are twofold: fidelity to the original Jesus-phenomenon and responsiveness to the God who reveals himself to us in history.

Christians of the first centuries could not have applied the first criterion. For they lived in an age in which the boundary between myth and reality was blurred. Reality tended to be mythicized; and myth, to be looked upon as history. Consequently, it was natural for the early Christians to raise Jesus to the status of a mythical person. Criticism in our sense of the term was therefore not possible for them. Quite different is our situation. We have gone beyond the stage of primitive myth. We know that any valid interpretation has to be like a response to historical phenomena as we encounter them. This obliges us at every stage to subject our subjective prejudices and preferences to criticism, lest they colour our interpretation of reality.

Let us now come to the second criterion. In the message of Jesus, there is an absolute and a relative dimension. The absolute dimension can be explained only based on his encounter with the Absolute, with God. But precisely because this encounter was enfleshed in a historical situation, it is possible and even natural that the total significance of it overflowed the limits of what as explicitly perceived by Jesus himself. This is, in fact, true of all aesthetic and religious encounters with truth. That is why the truth of a work of art is often perceived more fully by the viewer than by the artist himself. Similarly, it is only subsequent generations that understand the total meaning of a great thinker or religious genius. However, any subsequent interpretation has to be in line with the fundamental thrust and implicit dynamism of the original datum. Now the fundamental dynamism of Jesus' message pointed to God working in history. If our reinterpretation of Jesus is to be authentic, we must encounter in history the same God whom he encountered two thousand years ago. It is our responsiveness to the God of today that guarantees our fidelity to the Jesus of yesterday. The demands that God in history makes on us help us understand the deeper meaning of the teachings of Jesus. Conversely, the teachings of Jesus help us interpret the signs of the times and decipher the divine challenges inscribed in history. In this way, the Jesus of history enters into dialogue, in and through us, with the God of today.

However, the encounter with God in question is not to be understood solely in a mystical or esoteric sense. Any human gripped by an absolute concern for his/her fellow humans has encountered God. It is possible, even likely, that the extreme radicals who are in prison today for the sole crime of having opposed an unjust society had a more authentic encounter with God than many professedly religious people who devote themselves to prayer and penance. For the same reason, the former may understand the significance of Jesus much better than the latter.

If therefore, we retrace our steps back to Jesus of Nazareth, it is not to pitch our tent with him but to go beyond him. We go beyond him when we free his message from its historical conditioning and translate it into today's language. In other words, we make it possible for him to go beyond himself and discover his true identity in our age. We let him slough off the past to come alive in the present, but not without carrying with him whatever in his past has an abiding value. Thus we raise him from the dead and give him a new name and habitation. Seen in this light, the resurrection of Jesus is a continuing process achieved through our reinterpretation of his message and our commitment in response to it.

A reinterpretation of the entire message of Jesus along these lines is an urgent need of our time. This, however, is beyond the scope of our investigation. We confine ourselves to just one question: What is the relevance of the message of Jesus for human liberation today? In seeking an answer our primary source is the Synoptic Gospels. Though they too are expressions of the faith of the early Christian community, in their case, as contrasted with the fourth Gospel, the veil of interpretation is not so thick as to prevent our gaining an insight into the salient features of the life and teachings of the historical Jesus.

The self-revelation of God in history is the light in which we have to reinterpret the message of Jesus, and, as such, should be the point of departure of all theological reflection. We shall, therefore, begin with an analysis of the Indian situation to focus on the challenge of liberation it poses. The subsequent chapters will deal with the response, in word and deed, of Jesus to the varied forms of human bondage. In the concluding chapter, we shall derive from our study some fundamental guidelines for action.

2

The Challenge of Liberation

The forces of oppression in contemporary India are many and varied. Some have their roots in feudalism, which in one form or another persists, especially in rural areas; others stem from capitalism which, though originally imposed from outside, has become deeply entrenched in the soil and today controls the entire economy. Some are found at the level of the economic, social, and political life of the people; others at the level of beliefs, ideas, and values. Some exist as objective factors that are relatively autonomous concerning individual options; others are lodged in the subjectivity of humans as a personal and unique center of decision. In what follows we shall try to describe briefly the basic structures and forces of oppression in our country.

Slavery Reborn

[Note that the financial statistics presented in this section are of the 1970s]

By far the majority of the Indian population is workers employed either in agriculture or industry. Landless laborers alone make up roughly 40 percent of the rural population. Many among the small peasants including tenants and sharecroppers, who form 45 percent of the rural population, are forced by economic necessity either to sell their land and join the ranks of landless laborers or to take to wage labour as an additional source of income. Urban workers of all types and their families amount to roughly 40 million.[1] The working classes, to whichever category they belong, are the real creators of wealth and form the backbone of the country. And yet, work for them is a process in which they fashion their fetters and strengthen the hands of their oppressors. To realize what this means we must reflect on the existing system of production.

Work, where it is truly human, is a process of the humanization of nature, of the environment. Workers take the stuff of the earth into their hands, breathe their spirit into it, and fashion it in their image. Thereby they give it a new form, unity, and meaning — all drawn from the wealth of their being. The products of labour are therefore the embodiment of their spirit, the extension of their being in time and space. Seen in this light, the civilization that is being constructed around us is nothing but the physical and mental energies of the working class, dead and buried in the matter and risen again in the form of things useful and beautiful. If this is true, the conclusion imposes itself that the products of work must belong to the producers.

But the opposite is what happens in the present economic system. The products are expropriated from the producers. It is not those who till the soil who eat the fruits of the soil. It is not those who make cars that travel in them. It is not those who produce costly foods that consume them. Those who make sophisticated garments go about clad in rags. Those who build mansions are condemned to live in slums. Those who build luxury hotels and posh restaurants are unable to afford even one full meal a day. Those who produce antibiotics and costly drugs are denied even the minimum of medical care when they fall ill. In short, those who create wealth are reduced to utter poverty. They are denied not only luxuries and utilities but also the bare necessities of life. All this is a matter of common observation. It is also borne out by the studies of experts in the field. According to one such study, 40 percent of the rural poor and 50 percent of the urban poor live below the poverty line both in terms of calories and of quality of nutrition, as of 1960. The increase since then in consumer expenditure (one-half of one percent per annum) has benefitted mainly the rich. During the past decade, while the condition of the rural poor has remained stagnant, that of the urban poor has deteriorated.[2]

It follows from what we have said so far that the most intensely felt bondage of the Indian masses consists in the fact that they do not have what they produce. They do not have what they produce because they are deprived of the means of production, agricultural as well as industrial. Land, the means of agricultural production, is concentrated in the hands of the big peasants and landlords, either because land reform laws are inadequate or have been poorly implemented. Taking operational holdings in the country as a whole, roughly 36 percent of the rural households either did not cultivate any land or cultivated only less than half an acre each; 57.9 percent of rural households cultivate either no land or less than 2.5 acres each. They operate no more than 7 percent of the total land. On the other hand, we have a privileged 2.09 percent of households that cultivate more than 30 acres each, which, when added, comes to 23 percent of the total land.[3]

No less glaring is the concentration of the means of industrial production. The big bourgeoisie consisting of about 75 to 100 business houses own 50 percent of all private company assets in India.[4] The policies pursued by the Government in respect of licensing and financial and technical assistance have themselves contributed to the concentration of wealth and income in restricted groups.[5] Even the so-called public sector has worked to the benefit of the private sector. Contrary to popular belief, the interests of private business do not usually come into conflict with those of the public sector, which consists mainly of big industries where private investment is not forthcoming. The public sector feeds the private sector by providing it at cheap price with the goods it needs, by entrusting to it much of its construction works, and by buying up its products.[6]

That the mass of producers is deprived of both the means and the fruits of production is the aspect of economic bondage that is most acutely felt. But, objectively, the most dehumanizing aspect is less the expropriation of products than the depersonalization of the producers. For the worth of a human is to be judged more in terms of what one is in reality than in terms of what one has. Consumerism has so shaped our thinking that even when we criticize capitalism we often do so with criteria derived from the same system. All the greater, therefore, is the need to highlight the existential degradation of the working class in contemporary Indian society.

A human is essentially a worker. In a sense, one is one's work. Work is not something added on to one's essence, already complete and rounded off in itself. One's essence is what one makes of oneself in the process of work. If so, to be deprived of work is to be denied the possibility of being human, of realizing what one ought to be. It is in this light that we have to view the problem of unemployment, which is steadily increasing. According to one estimate, one out of every ten Indians is unemployed.[7] Still more staggering is the problem of underemployment. Forty percent of the rural population lives below the national desired minimum of a per-head income of Rs.240 per annum as of 1961 prices. Leaving out another ten percent whose lot can be improved only through social services, we still have 30 percent of the rural poor numbering roughly 128.5 million who are poor because they are underemployed.[8] This means that millions of our brothers and sisters are denied even the minimum of participation in economic life and have been brutally marginalized.

In the case of those partially or fully employed, there is no freedom in the choice of work. The choice of work is subject to the law of supply and demand in the labour market. People are forced to take up jobs for which they are not suited, just because they have no other way to make a living. For them, work is not an expression of a spontaneous urge. The same unfreedom is experienced also in the place of work, whether it is field or factory. There they engage in the production of goods which they cannot afford. They work for goals in the choice of which they have no say, and for the satisfaction of other people's needs. Once they enter the place of work they belong not to themselves but to their employers, who dispose of them as they would things. Barred from employing their intelligence and initiative in determining goals and choosing means, they are reduced to the position of mere cogs in the wheel, of so many units of muscular energy expended to make machines run. They are like things that can safely be thrown away once they have served their purpose. What is worse, in producing goods they are in truth fashioning their shackles, providing their masters with ever new instruments of exploitation. Wage labour of this type is slavery reborn in a new form. It is a process whereby the masses, in humanizing nature, dehumanize themselves. It is, in the words of Karl Marx, a process of 'spiritual self-castration', of self-prostitution. Thus while the present economic system promotes conspicuous consumption among a few, it contemns the many to a stunted, crippled existence.

We have already noted that the masses are not the ones who set goals for economic activity. They have no control over the system, which, however, can maintain itself only with their sweat and blood. It is not they who decide what to produce where to set up factories or how to distribute the products. They are thus reduced to being mere byproducts of the system. They are not subjects of history but its objects. As objects, they are formed or deformed by the privileged classes, who alone hold in their hands the reins of the economy. This is a process that goes on both inside and outside the place of work. In the place of work, the natural and spontaneous needs of the working class find no outlet and therefore atrophy. All their needs are reduced to the need for wages. Even this minimal need goes unfulfilled. For the wage structure is determined not by the quantum of service one renders to society but by certain unjust criteria inherited from the past. One such criterion is the superiority of intellectual over manual work, which is to be traced back to the caste-ridden feudal system in which the Brahmins, in virtue of their monopoly over learning, also enjoyed economic and social privileges. Yet another criterion is the amount one has invested in receiving training or initiating enterprises. But it is all too often forgotten that such investments were made possible by unjust laws of inheritance. Thus one injustice is used to justify another. [9]

To sum up, the present economic system is essentially unjust. It expropriates from the mass of producers not only the products of work but also the means of production. It condemns them to what is equivalent to slave labour. It denies them the possibility of creating their future, of shaping their destiny. The reverse side of this economic servitude is social fragmentation and inequality, whose main elements we shall now discuss.

Man Divided

The social fetters the Indian masses have to break are of two types: those originating in feudalism and those others created by the capitalist mode of production.

CASTE INEQUALITY

The traditional form of caste is still a force to be reckoned with, especially in rural India. We have a pointer to it in the frequent newspaper reports about the burning of Harijans by caste Hindus in different parts of the country. But, on the whole, caste has undergone a significant change in recent decades. The vertical solidarity of caste based on ritual superiority has largely disintegrated. In its place, new horizontal solidarity is taking shape as a result of the joining together of various sub castes which traditionally fought one another. This form of solidarity has become a source of economic and political power where it enjoys numerical strength. It has led to the emergence of the so-called dominant castes like the Nairs of Kerala, the Gounders, Padayachis, and Mudaliars of Tamil Nadu, the Lingayath and Okaligas of Karnataka, the Kammas and the Reddis of Andhra Pradesh, the Marathas of Maharashtra, the Patidars of Gujarat, the Jats, Ahirs, Rajputs, and Kayasthas of Northern India. [10]

The dominant castes have a vested interest in maintaining the economic backwardness of the lower castes and the outcasts. They control most of the Panchayats and government agencies for rural development. For instance, in Andhra Pradesh, the Panchayat Samitis consists almost entirely of the dominant landowning castes.[11] What makes the situation still worse is the fact that often the dominant castes and the exploiting classes are the same people. From the ranks of the former are drawn a large percentage of the landlords, moneylenders, merchants, industrialists, and bureaucrats. It is the members of the dominant castes who, with the connivance of government officials, appropriate the greater part of the resources set apart for the uplift of the poor.[12]

CLASS EXPLOITATION

More iniquitous than caste inequality is the class exploitation introduced by the capitalist system. In the industrial sector, the main agents of exploitation are the big businessmen and entrepreneurs who monopolize the means of production and exploit human labour solely for profit. Then comes the commercial elite, who have been playing an increasingly dominant role in Indian economic life. Instead of using money capital for productive use, they indulge in hoarding, in black-marketing, and in creating artificial scarcity to maximize profit.[13] To these oppressor classes, independent professionals such as doctors, lawyers, and engineers play a supportive role. They depend very much on the patronage of the industrial and commercial community. The large majority of technicians and applied scientists trained in India or elsewhere look to businessmen as their potential or actual employers, whose interests, consequently, they are forced to protect.[14] The urban privileged classes have entered into a sort of tacit alliance, on the one hand, with the bureaucrats and the politicians, and, on the other, with the rural elite.

Among the exploiting classes in rural areas we may mention, first of all, the feudal type of landowners who still survive in many parts of India — absentee landlords and peasant landlords. Next come the moneylenders who charge exorbitant interest rates and in case of default of payment dispossess the debtors of their property.[15] Still, a third exploiting section in the rural areas consists of merchants and middlemen. After every harvest, they buy up the agricultural produce at very low prices and resell them at higher rates. They naturally ally themselves with the landlords and the moneylenders. Often the same people play the roles of moneylenders, merchants, and landlords.

The confluence of interests has created a close bond of mutual support and collaboration between the rural and the urban elite. The urban capitalists find in rich peasants and landlords not only buyers of conspicuous consumption goods but also suppliers of the necessary raw materials for industrial production. Like the urban, the rural elite function in close collaboration with bureaucrats and politicians. Their oppressive hold on the rural population consisting of small peasants, landless workers, and ruined artisans is tightening every day.[16]

It follows from our analysis that there exists in India an axis of oppression constituted by the rural and urban elite as well as by bureaucrats and politicians. This axis has to be broken if the masses are to achieve economic freedom and social equality.

Power Versus People

An oppressive socio-economic system can beget only an oppressive state. Exploitation at the level of economic and social life finds its support, sanction, and legitimacy in the political system. The Indian State, whether we consider it in its legislative, executive, or judicial functions, has become the enemy number one of the people.

Political power today is vested in the privileged classes. This has been the case right from independence when power was transferred by the British to the Indian National Congress, which alone had a sufficient organizational basis and popular appeal. The backbone of the party consisted of the educated middle class, which, despite the vague socialist ideology of its leaders, was deeply committed to the defense of private property. This class bias has since then become accentuated and is vitiating the legislative, executive, and judicial functions of the State.

Let us first consider legislation. Only the members of the dominant castes or classes are in a position to stand as candidates for election to the legislative bodies whether in the states or at the center. They alone have the financial resources to meet election expenses, which often run to lakhs of rupees (in the 1970s). They alone have the benefit of the higher education needed both for election propaganda and for fulfilling their role in the legislatures. To win votes, they exploit the feudal and economic backwardness of the people. Where feudal attitudes of hierarchy and personal loyalty prevail, the rich candidates can count on the votes of the masses, especially in rural areas. Where such attitudes have died out, they can still buy votes or extort them through various kinds of intimidation. Consequently, the state and central legislatures are dominated and controlled by the privileged classes. For instance, in West Bengal, rural leadership in the legislative assembly consists of people from the upper income groups.[17] The poor candidates look to big merchants and businessmen for election funds, which the latter willingly provide, since thereby they can influence political decisions. Thus economic power goes hand in hand with political power.[18]

Since the class structure of the legislatures weighs heavily in favour of the rich, it would be vain to expect the so-called representatives of the people to bring about the necessary amendments to the Constitution or pass progressive economic and social laws. That would be expecting them to cut off the very branch on which they are comfortably seated. In public, they mouth socialist slogans but in private they identify themselves with the exploiters of the people. This judgment applies also to political parties. Not the good of the masses but lust for power and money is the mainspring of political activity today.

The same class bias also vitiates the judiciary. This is true not only of the system of laws in terms of which justice is administered but also in terms of those who administer the law. The Constitution and the law reflect the interests of those who framed them, namely, the upper and the middle classes. Besides, the legal system itself is a relic of colonialism and is unsuited to the needs of a developing country. It was formulated to maintain stability rather than to promote change. Since the existing social order is unjust, the laws that seek to perpetuate it are equally unjust. Finally, the very class composition of the judiciary renders it a useless instrument for the administration of justice to all. The judges, on the whole, come from the urban elite, whose ideology and interests they naturally share. What is worse, the very persons entrusted with the administration of justice resort to corrupt practices. An official committee appointed by the Government reported in 1964 that corruption exists in the lower ranks of the judiciary all over India and that in some places it has spread to the higher ranks also.[19]

Finally, the masses are kept ignorant of their legal rights and this ignorance is exploited by the privileged classes and the bureaucracy. Even when their rights are manifestly flouted, the people are unable to move the court and get justice done. They are barred from doing so by the corrupt practice of lawyers who demand exorbitant fees for their professional service. In such conditions, to have recourse to the court is equal to opting for economic suicide. If in despair the people take the law into their hands, the iron hand of the police and the army come down upon them in the name of justice! Legal justice in our country is an article of conspicuous consumption which only the very rich can afford.

Much of what we have said about the judiciary applies equally well to the bureaucracy as a whole. The Indian bureaucracy has become largely dysfunctional in respect of the promotion of justice and economic development. It has to function within the framework of rigid rules and regulations inherited from the British. Where these are strictly adhered to, they pose insuperable obstacles before the common people. Bureaucracy suffers also from over centralization, making it impossible for lower officials to make responsible decisions. The farther removed from the social base is the center of decision the greater is the delay involved and the less adequate the decisions taken. The bureaucratic system has become almost autonomous vis-a-vis the people. Responsibility not towards the people but higher officials or to the impersonal system is what determines the conduct of officials. These inherent defects are aggravated by the class composition of the bureaucracy. Eighty percent of the officers in the Indian Administrative Service, the Indian Foreign Service, and the Indian Police Service is drawn from the top ten percent of the population, i.e. from the privileged classes to whom they are in loyalty bound. Officials use their discretionary power in favour of the big businessmen whom they consider as potential employers of their sons and daughters. Not infrequently they, on retirement, seek employment in big business.[20] Assimilated within the exploiting classes, the bureaucracy has also assumed the characteristics of a caste. They are what the Brahmins were in traditional India, and before them, the common people sink to the level of untouchables. They have only rights and no obligations to the people, who, on the contrary, have only obligations and no rights!

For government officials, corruption has become almost a way of life. According to the report of the same official committee referred to earlier, in all transactions on behalf of the government, a regular percentage is received by officials in the form of bribes that they share among themselves in agreed proportions. In the constructions of the Public Works Department, the amount received is anything between seven to eleven percent.[21] Such appropriation of public funds must be viewed against the background of the fact that the greater part of the revenue of each state is paid out to government officials in the form of salary. Seen from this angle the bureaucracy is the cancer of the body politic.

If the state in its legislative, executive and judicial functions is geared to the promotion of the interests of the privileged classes, it can in no true sense of the term be called democratic. What we have in reality is a form of classocracy, i.e. a government of, by, and for the privileged classes.[22]

Ideological Fetters

The present oppressive social system finds an accomplice in ideology. By ideology, we mean the system of ideas and values that determine the pattern of behaviour of a people. Ideology in India is a complex reality and is going through a period of crisis caused by the transition from feudalism to capitalism. While feudal ideas and values are either dying out or assuming a new content, those of capitalism are on the ascendant. Ideology, whether feudalist or capitalist, acts as an obstacle to progress by legitimizing the status quo and thereby dampening the spontaneous urge of the masses to revolt against it.

THE LEGACY OF FEUDALISM

In the sphere of religious beliefs, there is, first of all, the traditional emphasis on the pursuit and realization of the spiritual in humans. Underlying this mentality is a dualist conception of a human as a soul imprisoned in a body. Liberation (*mukti*) here means the liberation of the soul from the body. Since the body is the principle of one's solidarity with the material world and of one's insertion into the flux of time, liberation necessarily demands flight from the world of time and space, from the course of history. A sort of dualism is discernible even in Advaita, which claims to be non-dualist, since it enjoins on man to supersede the realm of empirical truth and attain to that of the transcendental truth. Naturally where such attitudes prevail, there is an inevitable devaluation of all temporal activities, whether economic, social, political, or cultural.

More than the dualist mode of thinking, it is the belief in *karma* and samsara that functions as opium for the people. The doctrine of *karma* could be understood in a positive sense as signifying the vocation of humans to create their future through the right mode of action. Quite different, however, is the popular understanding of it as the inevitable and necessary working out here and now of one's deeds in a previous life. Viewed from this angle, it breeds fatalism, pessimism, and resignation. The same attitudes find further nourishment in the sacral conception of the world, which sees every aspect of life as governed by rules and taboos ordained and sanctioned by the gods.

Similarly, undue stress on individual salvation and the total absence of any idea of collective destiny stand in the way of the emergence of a social humanism, which alone could provide an adequate basis for a truly socialist society. Individualism reigns also in the domain of morality. The primary moral concern is the practice of personal virtues such as austerity, self-control, detachment, and chastity and not man's social obligations.

The masses are held in bondage also by certain traditional social attitudes and values which serve either to reinforce the capitalist system or to smother the urge to revolt against it. Psychologically attuned to the collectivism of the traditional institutions of joint-family and caste, both of which subordinated the individual to the group, the people have little difficulty in adapting themselves to the collectivism of firms and factories. They find it natural to work for goals in the choice of which they have no say. Centuries of psychological conditioning by caste hierarchy facilitate the transition to the hierarchy of functions and authority inherent in capitalist production. Accustomed to considering wealth and status as associated with birth, the working class sees nothing unjust in seeing a few people concentrating in their hands the means of agricultural and industrial production. The division of labour characteristic of the caste system finds a counterpart in the capitalist division of labour. Traditional conceptions regarding the superiority of Brahmins as repositories of knowledge and bearers of economic privileges dovetail with the capitalist assumption of the superiority of intellectual over manual labour. Thus through a process of transference, feudal attitudes and values go to reinforce capitalism, at least in its initial stages of development. Finally, loyalties derived from kinship, caste, and community divide the exploited masses into so many opposing groups that they become unable to present a common front against the guardians and legitimizers of the existing social system.

THE VIRUS OF CAPITALISM

Deprived of its economic base, feudal ideology is either dying out or undergoing profound internal changes. Not so the capitalist system of ideas and values, since it is firmly rooted in an ever-expanding system of the capitalist mode of production. Hence it poses a greater threat to the true development of humans than the vestiges of feudal ideology.

The fundamental value of capitalism is private interest, which has its economic basis in private property. Private interest implies a negation of the social dimension of humans since it reduces society to a mere means to individual ends. Where it reigns supreme, one's neighbor takes on the character of either a threat or a rival. The threat has to be eliminated, the rival overcome. Thus competition becomes the order of the day. In any competition only one, who asserts himself aggressively, can survive. In consequence, force, whether physical, moral, or psychological, becomes socially respectable, and the law of the survival of the fittest determines economic life. Within this frame of reference, freedom means the chances a person has to pursue his ends unhindered by others. In reality, such freedom amounts to a license for the few to exploit the many. Similarly, equality in capitalism resembles the 'equal' opportunity that physically unequal competitors have in a race. It is a type of equality in which some are more equal than others.

Private interest manifests itself in the pursuit of profit and production for the sake of profit. As a result, production and efficiency rank high in the system of values. Production may become even an autonomous value, where it is viewed as a symbol of social power. Usually, it is geared to profit, and profit to consumption. The end-result is consumerism in the form of the fever for more and more comforts, more and more gadgets. With this, a new concept of happiness emerges. One's happiness consists in having something which one's neighbor does not have. And one's unhappiness consists in not having something which the neighbor has. One's value is judged in terms of what one has and not what one is. And one can have whatever one wants if one has money. Thus money becomes the mother of all values, the value of all values.

It is this system of values that is the principal determinant of economic, social, and political life in contemporary India. From the upper classes, it is percolating to the lower classes; from the urban areas, it is spreading to the rural. It is being progressively internalized by the masses. However, this process is not always a spontaneous one. It is largely manipulated. To sell their products the capitalists artificially generate needs in the people. This is done with the help of advertisements, posters, exhibitions, and the like. To this end, they prostitute sex, womanhood, family, religion, and even God. They weave myths around commodities and project them as symbols of status. Thus the economic system produces not only consumer goods but also consumer classes.

The values of capitalism have shaped the minds of people to such an extent that even when they revolt they do so in the name of these same values. The student agitations in the country, for instance, are not so much against the capitalist system as against their being denied the benefits of the same system. So too it is largely private interest that motivates strikes and demonstrations on the part of the organized working class. What is still more distressing is that even political parties professing socialism have become infected with the virus of capitalist ideology. Most politicians and legislators representing left-view politics do so merely as a means for promoting their economic interests. Thus we have the paradox of Communists fighting capitalism in the name of capitalist values.

It follows from the preceding analysis that the Indian masses can achieve liberation only through a total revolution, consisting in a restructuring of both society and ideology. What is needed is nothing less than the creation of a new society in which the human person will be the highest value, one in which the good of all will consist in the full flowering of each, in which cooperation will replace competition, love will replace aggression, quality will have primacy over quantity, the aesthetic will subsume the useful. It will have to be a society in which freedom will be realized not despite, but through one's fellowmen, in which commodities will take on the character of gifts, and the materialism of consumption will be replaced by the humanism of communion.

The Bondage Within

Thus far we have considered only those forms of human bondage which affect society as a whole and enjoy a certain autonomy concerning individuals. There are also others, which affect individuals in the deepest core of their existence, such as ignorance regarding the ultimate meaning of life, the ambivalence and vulnerability of freedom with its concomitants of sin and guilt, and finally, the problem of survival after death.

Besides, there are psychic determinants in the form of subconscious or unconscious forces that curtail one's ability to determine one's future. These problems are largely part of what we may call the human condition and, as such, are universal. No human, to whichever historical stage or culture he/she belongs, is exempt from them. The rich as well as the poor, the exploiter as well as the exploited, the educated as well as the illiterate, have to come to terms with them at one time or another in their lives. However, there are periods of historical crisis when these problems make themselves particularly felt. Our country is witnessing the initial stages of such a crisis of culture.

Unfortunately, too little research has been done in this field to enable us to make valid generalizations. All that can be said is that these existential problems do exist and are experienced differently by different people, depending on whether they belong to the urban or rural areas, to the affluent or the middle and poorer classes. One thing seems certain: It is neither the extreme rich nor the extreme poor but the middle classes — more precisely, the middle class youth — that are today raising questions regarding the deepest problems of human existence. The very poor still cling to solutions offered by the traditional world outlook and religious beliefs. The very rich, on the contrary, are caught up in the initial euphoria of consumerism and are not yet disillusioned enough with it to pose questions regarding life and death. Contrasted with these, the middle class youth have neither safe moorings in the past nor security regarding the future. It is they who are gripped by the problems of a culture in transition. Even among them, it is only a minority that succeeds in articulating what their peers experience existentially.

However that may be, with the progressive disintegration of traditional culture, the existential problems of humans are likely to become more and more accentuated. They have to be taken seriously for the following reasons: First, they are in themselves expressions of human's estrangement from his/her true being, from what he/she ought to be. Second, they contribute in their way to the perpetuation of the unjust social system and even give birth to ever new forms of the oppression of human by human. The creation of a new society is not possible without creating anew the minds and hearts of the people.

The challenge of integral liberation in India, of which we have tried to describe the salient features, is one that confronts all the citizens of the country, to whichever creed, community, or political party each one belongs. It is also one that calls for unconditional commitment. All those who do not refuse to be their brothers'/sisters' keepers are asking themselves how they may respond to the challenge in the light of their total vision of human. The disciples of Jesus are likewise bound to ask: What answer does Jesus give to the historic challenge of the total liberation of the Indian masses? Does his answer meet the needs of today? In what respects is it in need of revision and reinterpretation? What follows is an attempt at answering these questions.

3

The Prophet of the New Humanity

Historically, all religions have played a role in society either by protesting against its evils or providing it with norms and sanctions. This is particularly true of the religion of the Hebrews since they regarded God as revealing himself primarily in historical events and situations. Originally the focus of their faith was the past intervention of God in liberating them from slavery in Egypt and leading them to the Promised Land flowing with milk and honey. In course of time, with the emergence of prophecy, the emphasis shifted from the past to the future, namely, to the definitive intervention of God in the end-time. This did not, however, mean that the prophets ignored the actual problems of society. On the contrary, the more intense their longing for the future, the more vehement was also their criticism of social evils. For, in their view, the future had meaning only as the final overcoming of the evils of the present. Thus, in the great prophets — Hosea, Micah, Isaiah, and Jeremiah — the expectation of the future and the denunciation of the status quo draw nourishment from each other and combine to form but one powerful religious current. It is in the line of these great prophets that Jesus stands.

And it is his mission as a prophet that is of particular relevance for us today. For prophecy is not a thing of the past but an essential dimension of individual and collective life in all stages of history. When we revolt against whatever is dehumanizing and commit ourselves to the construction of a worthier future for humans we are doing what the prophets did of old. There is, therefore, no surer common ground between us and Jesus than prophecy. Unfortunately, Christian tradition from very early times devalued the prophet in Jesus and thereby obscured what was most challenging and significant in his life and teaching. Now the time has come to reaffirm the centrality of his prophetic role as attested by the Synoptic Gospels themselves.

The Prophet from Nazareth

That he claimed to be a prophet is beyond doubt. Unable to work miracles in his hometown because of the unbelief of its folk, he complained, not without a tinge of sadness, "A prophet will always be held in honor except in his hometown, and among his kinsmen and family" (Mark 6:4). He claimed to possess the Spirit of God, which in his days was taken as a mark of the prophetic call (Luke 4:18). As his life unfolded with all its tensions and conflicts, it became increasingly clear to him that like the prophets of old he too would be put to death. Hence his reply to the Pharisees who came to advise him to flee from Herod who was out to kill him, "I must be on my way today and tomorrow and the next day because it is unthinkable for a prophet to meet his death anywhere but in Jerusalem" (Luke 13:32).

His disciples too took him to be a prophet. Soon after his ignominious death on the cross two of them spoke of him as a "prophet powerful in speech and action before God and the whole people" (Luke 24:19). It was as a prophet that he was recognized by the common people. Those who saw him raise the widow's son to life could not but exclaim, "A great prophet has arisen among us" (Luke 7:16). The same was the reaction of the crowd when he entered Jerusalem, "This is the prophet Jesus, from Nazareth in Galilee" (Matt. 21:11). As a prophet, his mission was to confront his contemporaries with the will of God as revealed in history and to call upon them to respond to its demands through a personal decision.

The New Humanity

What was the divine purpose he saw inscribed in history? The answer is contained in the central theme of his message as recorded by Mark, "The time has come; the kingdom of God is upon you; repent, and believe the Gospel" (Mark 1:15). As is to be expected, Jesus does not give us any systematic exposition of what he meant by the kingdom of God. However, his teaching contains sufficient data based on which we can describe its salient features. The Sermon on the Mount is particularly revealing,

> "How blessed are those who know their need of God; the kingdom of Heaven is theirs.
>
> How blessed are the sorrowful; they shall find consolation.
>
> How blessed are those of a gentle spirit; they shall have the earth for their possession.
>
> How blessed are those who hunger and thirst to see right prevail; they shall be satisfied.
>
> How blessed are those who show mercy; mercy shall be shown to them.
>
> How blessed are those whose hearts are pure; they shall see God.
>
> How blessed are the peacemakers; God shall call them his sons.
>
> How blessed are those who have suffered persecution for the cause of right; the kingdom of Heaven is theirs (Matt. 5:3-10).

An attentive reading of this passage will show that the structure and movement of Jesus' thinking reflect that of our basic human experience, which is essentially ambivalent. All our experience is at once negative and positive: negative, since it reveals elements that diminish our knowing, thinking, and being; positive, since it contains elements of truth, beauty, and goodness. At least implicitly we reject the former and affirm the latter, and that too in an absolute manner. Rejection and affirmation are but two sides of the same coin. The rejection of evil is the affirmation of the good. Both are instinct with hope, are themselves acts of hope. We live in the hope that we shall overcome the evil and realize the good. This hope is the background against which our life unfolds. It is this absolute horizon of hope that Jesus had in mind when he spoke of the kingdom of God, with this difference, that for him its realization was not only a possibility but also a certainty, not only a project but also a promise.

In the Sermon on the Mount, he proclaimed that God will come to root out whatever is opposed to the fullness of human - sorrow, injustice, and estrangement from oneself. He will come to affirm and fulfill whatever is truly human - the gentleness of spirit, concern for right, purity of heart, commitment to peace, mercy to one's fellow humans. The kingdom of God, therefore, is, on the one hand, the liberation of humans from every alienation, i.e. from everything that renders them other than what they ought to be, and on the other, the full flowering of the human on our planet. In other words, it is not only freedom from but also freedom for - freedom for creativity, community, and love.

Seen from another angle, the kingdom may be described as the definitive reconciliation of every human with nature, with other persons, with God, and with oneself. Its coming means that humans will take possession of the earth. As lord of the earth, they will no more be subject to blind cosmic forces. Created anew, the earth will put forth all its riches at the service of humankind. Everything around humans, whether already given or refashioned by them, will be a symbol and instrument of human togetherness instead of being tools in the hands of some to exploit others. In the kingdom, each human will rejoin his/her fellow humans. Reconstituted sons of God, everyone will be a brother/sister to one's neighbor. One's need for one's kind, for love and recognition of others, will be fully satisfied. The New Age will thus mark the end of inequality, injustice, and exploitation. The realization of universal love will be at the same time human's final reconciliation with God. In communal love, each human will meet God, and in meeting God discover his/her oneness with all. Rooted in God, each human will achieve unity, harmony, and peace with oneself. In the language of the Seer, God "will wipe away every tear from their eyes; there shall be an end to death, and to mourning and crying and pain; for the old order has passed away" (Rev. 21:3-4).

The Not-Yet and the Already

When Jesus spoke of the reign of God, he did not mean by that term the action of God whereby he brought the world into being and maintains it in existence. He, of course, believed, as every Jew did, that the world owes its origin to God, that it is he who feeds the birds of the air and clothes the lilies of the field. Jesus had something else in mind when he announced that the reign of God was at hand. He meant that God was going to intervene definitively in history to sum it up and bring it to fulfillment. His eyes were focused on the future of the human community, not on just any future but the absolute future free even from the possibility of alienation.

It was this hope in the future as absolute freedom that he expressed in symbolic language when he said, "Many, I tell you, will come from east and west to feast with Abraham, Isaac, and Jacob in the kingdom of Heaven" (Matt. 8:11). He wanted his disciples too to plant their gaze on the kingdom yet to come. This is borne out by the nature of the prayer he taught them. If the disciples asked their master to teach them to pray it was not because they did not know how. Every Jew did. The real motive was their desire for a prayer that would express their distinctive faith as his disciples as distinguished from other religious sects who had their distinctive prayers. Significantly, the prayer they were taught had for its central motif the coming of the reign of God, "Father, thy name be hallowed; thy kingdom come" (Luke 11:2). The disciples are called not to sit around their master and enjoy his company, but to look forward to the coming reign of God. They are to march with him to meet God who is about to arrive.

Though the reign of God as a future event was the primary concern of Jesus, it would be wrong to conclude that for him that future began where our history ended. The age of freedom is not something that comes to fill the vacuum created by the death of our age, by the disappearance of our world. Rather, the future he looked forward to was seen by him as already present, though only germinally, in the here and now of his experience. He saw the future as impinging on the present, as new and different dawn over the realities of history. To put it differently, he saw the present not as something closed in and rounded off in itself but as open to the future and its fullness, as pregnant with promises for the full revelation of man and God.

What was that present in which he saw the irruption of the future? It was above all, his present, his presence in word and deed. "But if it is by the finger of God that I drive out the devils, then be sure the kingdom of God has already come upon you" (Luke 11:20).[1] He saw God at work in the exorcisms and cures he performed. To the messengers of John who approached him with the query whether he was 'the one who is to come' or some other, he answered, "Go and tell John what you have seen and heard: how the blind recover their sight, the lame walk, the lepers are made clean, the deaf hear, the dead are raised to life, the poor are hearing the good news - and happy is the man who does not find me a stumbling block" (Luke 7:22-23). Whether Jesus believed himself to be the 'one who is to come' is a moot question. But it is beyond doubt that he saw in the cures he worked so many signs of God's saving presence. In and through his word and deed the reign of God became a matter of human experience. This seems to be the meaning of his saying, ". . . for in fact, the kingdom of God is among you" (Luke 17-21).[2]

Jesus used many and varied symbols to express the germination of the new age in the womb of the old. The light of the age to come shines forth and dispels darkness whenever the disciples do good to their fellowmen who, seeing it, praise their Father in heaven (Matt. 5:14-16). The wine of the New Age is already active and is bursting the bounds of the old wineskin of Judaism (Mark 2:22). Just as a pinch of salt sprinkled over food purifies and preserves it, the creative power of the kingdom purifies the world and preserves what is good and true in it (Matt. 5:13). It is active in history in the manner of the little yeast that leavens a huge quantity of dough (Matt. 13:33). Again, God's reign is "like the mustard-seed, which is smaller than any seen in the ground at its sowing. But once sown, it springs up and grows taller than any other plant, and forms branches so large that the birds can settle in its shade" (Mark 4:31-32). The seeds of the future are breaking the soil, putting forth leaves and bearing fruit. And the harvest of the end-time is already begun (Mark 4:4-8).

Did Jesus think of the reign of God as present exclusively in his mighty word and deed? No. We already saw that the light of the kingdom shines forth through the conduct of the disciples. It is radiated by all those who come to the aid of their brothers and sisters in need. This is the deeper truth contained in the parable of the Good Samaritan. The New Humanity is present wherever humans lovingly reach out to their neighbors, wherever there is concern and responsibility for one another, wherever humans gather together to share what they are and what they have, and, in their togetherness, experience oneness with the ultimate ground of all. The visage of the New Age may be discerned wherever the blind see, the deaf hear, the lame walk, the leper is rendered whole, the prisoners set free, the unloved receive love, and the hopeless regain hope. It announces his presence wherever fetters are broken and human-made walls are demolished to let each human be all humans.

A Gift and a Task
How will the New Age come into being? Will it be the fruit solely of the action of God? Or solely of human endeavor? Or will it be the work of both God and humans? These are the questions to which we shall address ourselves now.

That Jesus conceived the New Humanity as a gift from God, none may doubt. The very term 'reign of God' means primarily the action of God whereby he brings things under his dominion. This aspect of Jesus' message is particularly stressed in the Beatitudes as recorded by Luke. There, participation in the blessings of the New Age presupposes nothing more than the vacuum of human need, the vacuum of poverty, hunger, sorrow, and infamy (Luke 6:20-22). The same truth finds expression in the words, "Let the children come to me, not try to stop them; for the kingdom of God belongs to such as these" (Mark 10:14). What is held up here for imitation is not the humility and the innocence of children, but their being receptive and expecting everything from the bounty and goodness of others. Only those have access to the kingdom who expect everything from God and cast all their hopes on him. Humans cannot construct New Humanity solely with their resources. They can only sow the seeds of the New Age. It is up to God to make them grow and fructify. "The kingdom of God is like this. A man scatters seed on the land; he goes to bed at night and gets up in the morning, and the seed sprouts and grows — how, he does not know. The ground produces a crop by itself, first a blade, then the ear, then full-grown corn in the ear; but as soon as the crop is ripe, he plies the sickle, because the harvest-time has come" (Mark 4:26-29). The same truth underlies Jesus' teaching on prayer. The disciples can do no more than pray, 'Thy kingdom come'. But to come and reveal himself - that is a matter of the free decision of God.

To understand the deeper meaning of the gift character of the kingdom, an analogy from ordinary human experience may help. A young boy meets a girl. He eventually develops a liking for her. And in course of time liking grows into love. He expresses his new-born love in many a fashion - through looks, gestures, words, gifts, and so on. Yet he knows full well that none of his initiatives can necessarily make her love him in return. If she does reciprocate it is not a necessary outcome of his attentions but a free self-giving. Nothing less than a gift on her part can transform their relationship into a true communion, into the nucleus of a community. Similarly, humankind cannot merit or take possession of God through its efforts. If every love is a gift, such pre-eminently is God's love for humans. The love whereby he gathers humanity into his heart can therefore only be a gift born of infinite freedom.

Does this mean that what we have to do for the coming of the New Age, is to remain quiet and do nothing? Has human initiative and commitment no relevance for the realization of the New Humanity? Not at all. The message of the New Age as a gratuitous gift of God has for its reverse side the call for human response. Jesus demands from his disciples an active response in the form of faith and repentance (Mark 1:15). Repentance here means something more than a mere expression of sorrow for past sins. It consists rather in a reorientation of one's whole life, with the implied acceptance of new norms and goals. It calls for a qualitative change in one's system of values and mode of life. If the community itself is the subject of repentance, the adequate response can be nothing less than a restructuring of the entire social and cultural system. Those members of the community who choose to repent will consequently have to live in a situation of conflict and tension with those who do not. This explains why the disciples of Jesus had to face opposition from the religious establishment.

The need for human response comes into clearer relief in the Matthew's formulation of the Beatitudes. Unlike Luke, Matthew makes entry into the kingdom conditional upon one's showing mercy to one's kind, one being an instrument of peace in the community, keeping one's heart pure, and hungering and thirsting for justice (Matt. 5:7-9). Of all, the most important prerequisite is love, a love that is more than mere wishing well, a love that must show itself in doing the will of the Father, in giving, in forgiving and, above all, in service (Matt. 7:21; 5:43-48; 6:14; Mark 10:42-45). It must take the form also of fighting the forces opposed to the reign of God. That was why Jesus sent his disciples not only to preach the good news but also to work cures and to cast out demons.

Then, the coming of the New Age presupposes not only the initiative of God but also the obedient and creative participation of humans. But how can it be at the same time a divine gift and a human task? Are these not mutually exclusive and incompatible? By no means. Deeper reflection will show that the character of the New Age as a gift does not make it any less a human task. To grasp this we must return to our analogy of human love. We saw that the lover neither merited nor effected the love his beloved had for him. This love was a pure gift, present right from the beginning of their relationship. It was, in fact, the openness of the girl to the boy, which was in itself a preliminary self-giving, that emboldened him to shed his inhibitions. In other words, it was her incipient self-giving that made him capable of responding. It came to him like an invitation, a challenge, and a promise: an invitation to give himself further, a challenge to work out the possibilities inherent in their relationship, and a promise that his response will meet with success. In sum, her gift of love became for him a task to be accomplished.

So is the reign of God. It is God's self-giving embodied in things, events, persons, and experiences that lie at the root of human response, individual and collective. It too comes to a human in the form of an invitation, a challenge, and a promise: an invitation to leave behind all the safe moorings of the past and march forward, a challenge to break all fetters and construct the future and, finally, a promise that this striving will come to a successful issue. Thus God's self-giving in history becomes, for those whose hearts and minds are open, a moral task. The New Heaven and New Earth is something mankind has to create, not by its resources but in response to the horizon of absolute hope, not in the monologue but dialogue with God.

Though Jesus believed that the New Age demands active human response, the stress is, manifestly, on its being the work of God. He speaks of the 'coming' of the kingdom, of people 'entering' it or even 'possessing' it. But nowhere does he speak of it explicitly as something to be constructed by humans. He does not call upon his disciples, in so many words, to commit themselves to its creation. How to explain this one-sidedness in the teaching of Jesus?

The reason can be none other than that Jesus lived two thousand years ago and shared the thought patterns of pre-scientific humans. At that age humans could not have thought of their collective future as something to be fashioned by human effort. The conditions for planning the future —science, technology, industrialization, collective production, transport, mass media, etc. — had not yet been realized. And what humans at any given period of history cannot do, they naturally attribute to God. And Jesus was no exception to this.

Living as we do in the scientific age, we cannot, should not, identify ourselves with every aspect of his world outlook. That would amount to living in the past and abdicating the present. And our age demands that we stress, more than Jesus or our forebears did, that the New Humanity is something we have to construct in response to God, who beckons us from beyond. To do so is to be creatively faithful to Jesus, the only mode of fidelity that does justice to his basic concern.

The Manifesto of Jesus

If Jesus preached the New Humanity reborn in freedom not merely as a divine gift but also as a task, the question naturally arises: How did he respond to the divine invitation? How did he fulfill the task of sowing and nurturing the seeds of the New Age? In the present context, we shall confine ourselves to indicating the general tenor of his response. Luke narrates an event that takes us right into the heart of the matter:

So he came to Nazareth, where he had been brought up, and went to the synagogue on the Sabbath as he regularly did. He stood up to read the lesson and was handed the scroll of the prophet Isaiah. He opened the scroll and found the passage which says, "The spirit of the Lord is upon me because he has anointed me; he has sent me to announce the good news to the poor, to proclaim release for prisoners and recovery of sight for the blind; to let the broken victims go free, to proclaim the year of the Lord's favour." He rolled up the scroll, gave it back to the attendant, and sat down; and all eyes in the synagogue were fixed on him. He began to speak, "Today, in your very hearing this text has come true" (Luke 4:16-21).

Here we have what we may call the manifesto of Jesus, the clearest expression of what he understood to be his mission in life. His task was not only to announce the age of divine favour but also, and above all, 'to let the broken victims go free'. God's purpose in history had to be realized through the human effort for the liberation of humans. This involved for Jesus, as it does for all who share his faith and hope, saying no to everything that oppressed humans, and yes to everything that accorded with the interests of the New Age of theandric (God-human) fullness. This 'no' and 'yes' determined his whole life from the day the Spirit invaded his soul on the banks of the Jordan to the fateful day he met his destiny on the cross.

It remains for us now to see how Jesus translated his 'no' and 'yes' into word and deed. We shall begin with a consideration of his response to human estrangement from nature.

4

Cosmic Freedom

Right from his emergence in prehistoric times, humans found themselves defenseless and insecure before the hostile forces of nature, vulnerable to heat and cold, rain and storms, illness, death, and decay. Their history till now has been one of the collective strivings to conquer nature, whether external or internal to each and to wrest from it whatever they needed for warding off evils and perpetuating themselves.

The birth of science and technology opened new possibilities for humans to realize freedom from nature, though at the same time it fashioned new fetters for them. The conquest and humanization of nature remain very much a task to be completed. Still, compared with us, those who lived in the prescientific age were much more at the mercy of hostile nature. It was at such an age that Jesus lived. As is to be expected, the approach of his contemporaries to natural evils was more mythic-religious than rational or scientific. As we shall see presently, Jesus himself probably shared the same approach.

Humans in Bondage to Satan

Jesus, as portrayed in the Gospels, was a man finely attuned to the world of humans and things. He did not look at nature from the standpoint of one standing outside it and confronting it as an object. Rather he had a sense of kinship with the tangible and the visible. These flowed into him, into the innermost recesses of his being, as though by some mysterious symbiosis, but only to come out in the form of words, which too had the quality of things - the taste, smell, and colour of the objects around him.

He was particularly sensitive to the beautiful, to form and harmony. "Consider how the lilies grow in the fields; they do not work, they do not spin; and yet, I tell you, even Solomon in all his splendor was not attired like one of these" (Matt. 6:28-29). His very sensitivity to the beautiful heightened his awareness of whatever was ugly, of whatever was out of harmony with the well-being of humans. He knew by a sort of empathy the sufferings his fellow humans endured at the hands of a hostile nature. He knew about those who work hard and find the load heavy, those who toil the whole night at fishing and yet catch nothing, those who are anxious for food and drink, and those who have to work to earn their keep. He knew about the seed sown on rocky soil, which sprouted quickly but only to wither away, about the darnel that chokes the wheat, and about the moth and rust that spoil hidden treasures. He spoke of the rain, flood, and wind that destroy houses, of storms that rock boats endangering the lives of many.[1]

In his journeyings, through the length and breadth of Palestine, he came face to face with the sufferings caused by illness, decay, and death. Among the people who came to him for help, there were victims of possession, leprosy, fever, paralysis, hemorrhage, blindness, dumbness, lameness, epilepsy, dropsy, deformation, and many other diseases.[2]

What significance did Jesus attach to these evils which oppressed his fellow humans? For an answer, we have to recall the cultural gulf that separates him from us. The frame of reference for his thinking and judging was far different from ours. To us illness, for instance, is a relatively simple phenomenon intelligible in itself based on laws governing the bodily organism and its interaction with equally intelligible factors obtaining in the external universe. To Jesus, on the contrary, illness constituted a highly complex phenomenon with more than one dimension of meaning.

Cosmic evils like the ones enumerated above had for him, first of all, a demonic dimension of meaning. Though belief in demons played only an insignificant role in the religious history of the Hebrews, in course of time, probably under Persian influence, it became widely prevalent among the people. Illnesses of all kinds were attributed to demons. They were held responsible for natural phenomena injurious to humans, like storms and floods. One attributed to them also the power to enter the souls of humans and induce madness, moral blindness, and even disobedience to God.[3] Jesus probably shared this belief of his contemporaries. Luke narrates an incident that is particularly significant in this context. While he was teaching in a synagogue, Jesus saw a woman possessed by a spirit that had crippled her for eighteen years. He healed her by word of mouth and by laying his hands on her. To the president of the synagogue who accused him of violating the Sabbath, he replied, "Is there a single one of you who would not lose his ox or his donkey from the manger and take it out to water on the Sabbath? And here is a woman, a daughter of Abraham, who has been kept prisoner by Satan for eighteen long years: was it wrong for her to be freed from her bonds on the Sabbath?" (Luke 13:10-17). These words clearly show that Jesus viewed illness as caused by Satan. He seems to attribute even natural happenings to the working of demonic forces. When the disciples called for help for fear of their boat capsizing in the storm, he rebuked the wind as if it were a demon. All this proves that in this matter also he was very much a product of his age.

Jesus did not see demons as so many agents of evil working at cross purposes. He saw them as an organized force under the supreme command of their leader, Satan. (Cf. Luke: 10:17-18; Matt. 10:25.) That is why he could speak of the kingdom of Satan as opposed to the kingdom of God.

This brings us to the religious dimension in Jesus' understanding of cosmic bondage. In his view, illness and other physical evils imply a condition of alienation from God. He tells the paralytic: "My son, your sins are forgiven. . . stand up, take your bed and go home" (Mark

2:5-11). Here liberation from sin coincides with liberation from illness. However, it is doubtful whether he ascribed illness and natural calamities to personal sin as such. For, in the Gospel according to Luke, we hear him say that if the tower fell and killed eighteen people at Siloam it was not because they were more guilty than others (Luke 13:1-5). It is, therefore, more likely that when he attributes natural evils to sin, he has in mind not so much personal sin as cosmic sin, that is, the condition of the man out of harmony with the will of God.

Between God and Satan stood humans, defenseless and helpless, a mere shadow of what they ought to be. How far the sick and the possessed were from humans as God originally willed! Familiar with the Pentateuch as he was, Jesus knew for sure that God created each human in his image and likeness "to rule the fish in the sea, the birds of heaven, the cattle, all wild animals on earth, and all reptiles that crawl upon the earth" (Gen. 1:26). He also knew about the divine command given to humans that they should "fill the earth and subdue it" (Gen. 1:28). What he saw around him instead were humans reduced to the condition of slaves, slaves to illnesses of varied kinds and at the mercy of demonic powers. He saw them diminished in being and knowing, crippled in spirit and body. He was particularly sensitive to this human dimension of the problem.

Illness, possession, and similar evils constituted a human problem also in another sense. Those afflicted with them were looked upon as objects of the divine wrath, which they justly merited through their misdeeds. Besides, were they not mere playthings, if not abodes, of demons? They had thus become physically, morally, and ritually impure, defiling anyone who came into contact with them. This was particularly true of lepers, who as early as in the time of Leviticus had to cry 'Unclean, unclean', and live apart outside the camp (Lev. 13:45-46). Besides, the sick and the possessed were barred from entering the temple of Jerusalem. They were in every sense rejected by the community of humans.

Setting the Oppressed Free

The response of Jesus to humans' cosmic bondage may be summed up in the words of Peter as recorded in the Acts of the Apostles: "God anointed him with the Holy Spirit and with power. He went about doing good and healing all who were oppressed by the devil, for God was with him" (Acts 10:38). His prophetic 'no' took the form of miracles.

The Gospels record several healings and exorcisms, three raisings of the dead, and seven nature miracles. Under nature miracles come walking on water, cursing the fig tree, finding the coin in the fish's mouth, Peter's miraculous catch, the stilling of the storm, the feeding in the wilderness, and the changing of water into wine.[4]

Are all these miracles historically true? For an answer, we have to keep in mind the cultural environment in which Jesus lived. The people of his age were gifted with vivid and creative imagination, which was a fertile ground for legends and myths. They tended to enhance the greatness of their heroes by attributing to them all sorts of superhuman deeds. This the early Christian community did also to Jesus whom they believed to be the saviour of the world. The Gospel accounts of the miracles, therefore, are not to be taken as newspaper reports. What happened, in reality, became overlaid with legends and myths. However, it would be wrong to dismiss all the miracle stories in the Gospels as mere products of creative phantasy. There is no doubt that Jesus performed some miracles of healing and exorcism, though it is impossible to determine which among them are genuine. Much less certain are we whether the so-called nature miracles contain any historical nucleus.[5]

Jesus attached great importance to his works of healing and exorcising. He did not view them as peripheral to his mission. On the contrary, he went to the extent of summing up his entire mission in terms of them. To the Pharisees who came to warn him against Herod's plan to kill him, he said, "Listen: today and tomorrow I shall be casting out devils and working cures; on the third day I reach my goal" (Luke

13:31-32). It is clear from this that Jesus saw the working of miracles as an integral part of his mission, from which no earthly power could deter him. The same overriding concern expressed itself in the mission he entrusted to his disciples. He charged them not only to preach the good news but also to heal and to cast out devils. He gave them the power to tread underfoot snakes and scorpions and all the forces of the enemy (Mark 3:14-16, Matt. 10:7-8). And he rejoiced exceedingly when they came back to report their successes.

Why did he attach much importance to miracles? Because he saw in them so many instances of God's victory over the kingdom of Satan. When the disciples returned after their mission to tell him that even the devils submitted to them, he replied, "I watched how Satan fell, like lightning, out of the sky" (Luke 10:18). He saw in the cures and exorcisms he performed the inbreaking of the reign of God in the world. "If it is by the finger of God that I drive out the devils, then be sure the kingdom of God has already come upon you" (Luke 11:20).

It is important to note in this context that Jesus does not put himself in the center of things. He does not claim the miracles to be manifestations of his power. He attributes them to 'the finger of God', i.e. to the power of God. Neither does he demand faith in him as a prerequisite for working miracles. In most instances, he tells the beneficiaries, "Your faith has cured you" (Matt. 9:29; Mark 5:34; Luke 17:19). The implicit meaning is: God has responded to your faith and has healed you. He even explicitly mentions God as the object of faith, "Have faith in God" (Mark 11:20-22). Jesus himself comes into the picture only as the one in and through whom divine power is at work. In the words of Luke, "the power of the Lord was with him to heal the sick" (5:17). Miracles are therefore primarily God's response to humans' faith. So too they are a sign of divine forgiveness. "My son, your sins are forgiven" (Mark 2:5). All this shows that for Jesus the miracles constituted God's victory not only over Satan and his kingdom but also over humans' unbelief and un-repentance.

Does this mean that he regarded the victims of sickness and possession as no more than mere means, guinea pigs, used by God to manifest his power over Satan? Far from it. For the victory of God over Satan is man's freedom from the forces of evil. The result is each human reborn from the condition of a slave to that of a son, restored to inner harmony and at peace with oneself. In sum, it is a human rendered whole, no longer fragmented, no longer a shadow of what he/she ought to be: "Your faith has made you whole."

The wholeness of humans, the fruit of the miracles, is also social. Miracles are the manifestation of God's redeeming power, of his liberating love. But how did his power and love reveal itself? Through the man, Jesus of Nazareth. To put it differently, it was in meeting him that the sick and the possessed experienced the power and the love of God. Through him, the divine became a social reality. Where humans reached out to help their fellow humans, God was born. It is from this angle that we should see the tenderness and warmth with which Jesus reacted to the infirm and the oppressed. He told the mad man of Gerasa, "Go home to your folk and tell them what the Lord in his mercy has done for you" (Mark 5:19). When he saw the widow of Nain accompanying the body of her only son to the grave 'his heart went out to her' (Luke 7:13). He was moved with compassion when he saw the large crowd on the lakeside without having anything to eat (Mark 8:2). His surrender to the Father overflowed into surrender to his brethren in need.

We have seen that illness and other maladies carried with them social ostracism. Miracles reversed the process. The sick and the possessed were reintegrated into society. Jesus saw to it that the social stigma was removed also legally. That is why he told the healed leper, "Go and show yourself to the priest and make the offering laid down by Moses for your cleansing; that will certify the cure" (Mark 1:43-44).

God's reign as mediated by Jesus makes humans free from all alien forces and free for wholeness, personal as well as social. The wholeness is, of course, only germinal and anticipatory and will come to full bloom only in the New Heaven and the New Earth.

The Mission to Heal and to Humanize

We have seen that Jesus attached great importance to the work of healing and exorcizing and that he wanted his disciples to do the same. But living as we are, two thousand years after him, we cannot fully identify ourselves either with his understanding of cosmic bondage or with his response to it. The challenge of illness and other natural calamities presents itself differently to us than it did to him. Hence the need to distinguish what is historically conditioned from what is perennially valid in his word and deed.

Jesus like any human of his time believed in the existence of devils as personal beings endowed with intelligence and will. This was but natural in those days when men did not know that illnesses and other evils had their natural causes, intelligible in themselves and capable of being mastered through human resources. And what they did not know and could not master they naturally attributed to the working of supernatural forces. This we cannot do today, thanks to the power science and technology have placed at our disposal to discover and subdue the forces of nature. We cannot consequently share the belief in demons.

This does not imply that Jesus did not work any miracle. It only means that he was mistaken about the causes of the various maladies he had to deal with. That he healed them by a mere word or gesture cannot be doubted. But how to explain this fact? Is it not contrary to the laws of nature?

First of all, we must rid ourselves of the false notion that miracles are contrary to the laws of nature. They are effected essentially by the laws of nature, although realized exceptionally. Viewed from this angle, humans are essentially workers of miracles. By their very nature, they bring order and harmony into the universe around them. In the measure in which one is human, one fashions order out of disorder, cosmos out of chaos. One assembles scattered blocks of stones, pieces them together, and we have the miracle of a mansion. One gathers together the hues and colors strewn around him/her, forms them into a pattern, and we have the miracle of painting. One takes old words, breathes new meaning into them, strings them into a garland of thought and feeling, and we have the miracle of a poem. One assembles pieces of metal and wood, molds them into a whole, couples them with the currents of the air and energy, and we have the miracle of an airplane.

The greater the incandescence of the human spirit the greater is its capacity to mould the powers of the cosmos to house its dreams and visions. And what extraordinary miracles may we expect from a human whose spirit was taken hold of by the spirit of God so that the two formed but one flame? What wonders of healing may not one, in whom the ultimate ground of all deigned to manifest itself uniquely, do? Now Jesus was such a human. Wherever he went, the power went out of him and healed all who were attuned to the divine, all who had faith. His miracles are therefore instances where nature conformed most to its ultimate law, which is human rooted in God. In them, nature was at its most natural because it was at its most human.

Jesus was so taken hold of by the power of God that he could work miracles. We cannot rule out the possibility that even today God so takes hold of the spirit of a human that he becomes capable of healing the souls and bodies of fellow humans by a mere word or gesture. However, such cases can only be exceptional. The exceptional is but a concentrated, intense manifestation of the universal power that every human has in virtue of the original divine command to subdue the earth. This command we fulfill today when we conquer the hostile forces of nature with the help of science and technology.

The fulfillment of this task, by its very nature, devolves primarily on the community and only secondarily on individuals. For only the pooled resources of society as a whole are capable of meeting the magnitude of the challenge posed by natural evils. The working of miracles has, therefore, become not only a scientific but also an economic and political problem. The command Jesus gave his disciples to work cures and drive out devils thus becomes for us a command to organize our collective resources for the conquest of nature.

But to conquer nature is to humanize it. A human is never fully oneself, fully at home in the world, so long as nature is fully the other. One attains to freedom only in the measure in which he/she refashions nature in his/her image. One becomes free only in the measure in which one becomes natural, and nature becomes human. Cosmic freedom is the humanization of nature. The liberation of humans from nature is, therefore, at the same time the liberation of nature from its nonhuman existence. If so, the New Humanity can come into being only in the New Heaven and the New Earth.

But humans' struggle with nature and its forces will lead to authentic freedom, only if it has for its aim the well-being of the 'whole human' and all humans. The whole human is one considered in all one's dimensions, as body and soul, intelligence and will, action and passion, centred upon oneself and centred upon others. Any conquest of nature aimed exclusively at producing material goods to satisfy physical needs can make one only a prisoner of one's own needs. To conquer nature for the benefit of the whole human is to produce not only the useful but also the beautiful. Only when the aesthetic becomes its main criterion will production contribute to the wholeness of humans. For the aesthetic is a privileged point where the human merges into the divine, where the wholeness of man reflects the wholeness of God.

We said that freedom from cosmic bondage must be won for the whole man and all humans. A deeper reflection will show that this distinction is a false one. For the whole human is all humans. Everyone - in one's being, thinking, and loving - includes all humans. He/she must bear the burden of all. The conquest of cosmic forces must, therefore, benefit all humans. Hence the perennial relevance of Jesus' compassion for the multitude and the centrality of love in his teaching. Love as responsibility for one another and the community must be the beginning and the end, the motive and the outcome, of all struggle for cosmic freedom.

Where this is not the case, every effort at subduing nature serves to fashion ever-new fetters for humans. Where the well-being of all is not the determinant form, the fruits of collective research and labour become so many instruments in the hands of the privileged few to inflict hunger, illness, and death on the underprivileged many, as is happening in India. By utilizing natural resources primarily for the production of conspicuous consumption goods, the economic system condemns millions to a subhuman existence which in turn results in illness and premature death. Consider also the danger to life posed by the unhealthy conditions of work in factories, by the proliferation of slums, and by atmospheric pollution. These evils can be obviated only if love finds structural expression in the system of production, distribution, and consumption.

Yet one more condition has to be fulfilled for human's struggle with nature to lead to genuine freedom. Such a struggle has to be guided by the same spirit of God that made it possible for Jesus to work miracles. In other words, it has to be in response to the God who is to come and is already 'becoming' in history. A human should never lose sight of the horizon of the absolute future that beckons him/her from beyond the beyond. This absolute horizon is not something that limits his possibilities. It is rather the unconditioned condition for the very possibility of transcending all limits. To ignore its call is to run the risk of being imprisoned in one or other of one's historically conditioned creations. It is equivalent to the denial of the transcendence of humans.

Liberation from cosmic evils, especially from decay and death, is a task that mankind has to accomplish in dialogue with the Lord of history. That this task will be accomplished is a matter of hope. But what of the millions of men and women who came before us only to succumb to the inexorable law of death? What of us who shall not live to see the day when mankind will have brought illness and death under control? To this question, we shall return later, in Chapter 9, on existential liberation.

5

The Poor Shall Possess the Earth

Humans free themselves from the bondage of nature by harnessing its wealth and wresting from it the means whereby they may satisfy their needs. However, in satisfying their basic needs, such as food, clothing, housing, and medicine, they develop ever new and ever more complex needs, which, in turn, can be satisfied only by still newer forms of struggle with the environment. This process is essentially a social one. Individuals work with and for the community. Where, however, one section of the community has, by some means or other, appropriated the means of production, the rest are condemned to poverty and misery. Thus, in the very struggle to win freedom from cosmic forces, humans become the slaves of unjust economic systems.

The Poor of Israel

Economic exploitation and its concomitants, poverty, and inequality, have existed in one form or another in all countries ever since the birth of organized social life. And the Palestine of Jesus' time was no exception.[1] There also a wide gulf existed between the rich and the poor. Under the very rich we may mention, first of all, the royal aristocracy of Herod, the imperial aristocracy of the Sadducees who also had their headquarters in the Holy City, the big absentee landlords who owned large areas of landed property in the countryside, and, finally, the big traders and merchants. There was also a middle class made up of retail traders, and craftsmen owning their premises.

The bulk of the population belonged to the poorer classes. One such class consisted of the small peasants who cultivated the property of the absentee landlords. They were victims of multiple exploitations, for they were obliged to pay taxes to Rome to the tune of twenty-five percent of the total yield, and tithes to the temple that amounted to twenty-two percent of the remainder. There was also an additional tithe collected to help those among the poor who could not help themselves. Poorer than the small peasants were the wage laborers who were paid one denarius per day, which was scarcely enough for their day-to-day subsistence. Many of them were underemployed or even unemployed. Jesus makes a reference to them in the parable of the workers in the vineyard (Matt. 20:1-7). The small peasants and the workers were at the mercy of the moneylenders. If insolvent, they had no other way out except to sell themselves as slaves to their creditors. The institution of slavery existed in Palestine in the time of Jesus, and there is evidence for it in the Gospels themselves.[2] Slaves, however, did not play any significant role in the rural economy, most of them being employed in Jerusalem as domestic servants.

The poor lived in small houses with only one door. Their food consisted of wheat or barley bread and dried fish. They had only one set of clothes each, a tunic and a cloak. Want, insecurity and misery weighed heavily on their shoulders. How did Jesus respond to their situation? What message had he for the poor and the exploited of his day?

Blessed Are the Poor
The Gospels make it abundantly clear that he considered his mission as principally directed to the poor. "The spirit of the Lord is upon me because he has anointed me; he has sent me to announce the good news to the poor" (Luke 4:18). Before proceeding to ascertain the burden of the 'good news' let us examine what he understood by the term poor. Did he mean the materially poor or the poor in spirit, i.e., the pious and the humble? The words, cited above, in which he describes his mission, are a free quotation from the prophet Isaiah, Ch. 61, where the 'poor' is equated with 'the broken-hearted', 'the captive', 'those in prison',

'those who mourn', and 'the heavy of heart'. This is in itself sufficient indication that the poor stood for people placed in certain objective conditions of misery. This conclusion finds further support in the fact that the Hebrew word for 'poor', anawim, literally meant 'bent'. If so, when Isaiah spoke of the poor he had in mind a class of people who were bent under the weight of exploitation and had no one to defend their cause. This meaning accords well with the social conditions in those days when the rich and the powerful flagrantly violated the rights of the poor.

However, during the subsequent Babylonian exile, the word 'poor' took on the additional meaning of 'the pious and the humble', denoting those who looked to God alone for liberation from sorrow and misery. This is understandable enough, since the exiled Jews had lost all their property, and all distinctions between the rich and the poor had vanished. In their total degradation and helplessness, they could count on none but God. However, the word 'poor' continued to retain its original reference to a distinct class of people. During the time of Jesus, too, the term had these two dimensions of meaning. We may therefore safely assume that when he spoke of announcing the good news to the poor, he had in mind not only those who cast their hopes on God alone but also the exploited classes, who were materially poor.[3]

The fusion of the two meanings - one economic and the other religious - in the same term 'poor' probably has its social basis in the fact that the materially poor of those days were also the ones who humbly looked to God alone for liberation. The poorer classes had no reason to expect any improvement in their condition either from the generosity of the rich or from the initiative of the rulers. Nor could they envisage the possibility of overthrowing the social system through organized revolt. It was therefore natural that they expected God to intervene and redress the evil. By and large, the same attitude is found even today among the unorganized poor in the villages of India who rely on God or fate to usher in better days.

Let us now come to the more important question: What was the good news Jesus brought to the poor? It was the imminent coming of the reign of God, 'the year of the Lord's favor' (Luke 4:19). Paraphrased, his message would mean,

> "The Lord has listened to your cries and lamentations. The time is ripe. The promises made to your fathers are going to be fulfilled. God is soon to come, nay, he is already knocking at your door. He is coming to shatter your fetters and set you free, to satisfy your hunger, to confer on you, the dispossessed, the possession of the earth, and to lead you into the New Heaven and the New Earth"[4]

In other words, Jesus announced to the poor and the exploited that God would soon come to vindicate their cause. Nourished as they had been on the Old Testament, his hearers could not have failed to grasp what he meant. They knew that God was 'the avenger of blood' who never forgets the cry of the poor (Ps. 9:12), that he lifts the poor man clear of his troubles (Ps. 107:4), that he richly blesses the destitute and satisfies the needy with bread (Ps. 132:15), that he puts the land to rights and shares out afresh its desolate fields (Isa. 49:8), and that he rescues the poor from those who do them wrong (Jer. 20:13). They knew too that their God is no respecter of persons and is not to be bribed, and that he secures justice for widows and orphans (Deut. 10:18). They had listened to his words spoken of old to their forebears, "For crime, after the crime of Israel, I will grant them no reprieve, because they sell the innocent for silver and the destitute for a pair of shoes. They grind the heads of the poor into the earth and thrust the humble out of their way" (Amos 2:6-7). They could not have forgotten his words spoken through the prophet Malachi, "I will appear before you in court, prompt to testify against sorcerers, adulterers, and perjurers, against those who wrong the hired laborers, the widow, and the orphan, who thrust the alien aside and have no fear of me" (Mai. 3:5).

Now that God, Jesus told the poor of his day, was soon to come to set right the wrongs they suffered and to usher in a new order of things. Did history prove him right? It didn't. Two thousand years have passed since he brought good news. Still the poor are very much with us. Exploitation and injustice continue to be rampant. The earth is soaked with the blood of the innocent and the downtrodden. If so, the only conclusion that would impose itself is that Jesus was mistaken in his belief that the reign of God was to break out soon. He erred as many a prophet before he did.

Or, perhaps, we are not fair to him when we say that he was mistaken. We see an error when a statement does not conform to reality. But every statement has to be understood against the background of the mental world of the speaker. Now, Jesus' mental world was that of the prophet. As such, he lived in his own time just as a worker lives in his, a lover in his. Time was not for him, as it is for many of us, a long line of which the end is an eternity. In his eyes, any moment in time was a window opened into that which is beyond time, into eternity understood as the fullness of being. In other words, in his prophetic consciousness, the eternal impinged on the temporal, the future on the present. The ultimate future and the immediate present coalesced to form but one image. What in reality would require ages for maturation was therefore experienced by him as imminent future, like the present, as presenting itself to his senses. We have therefore no right to judge him by our understanding of time. We are closer to the truth when we say that his announcement of the Kingdom was prophetically true, though not historically verified as we understand the term today.

And the prophetic truth which he proclaimed and which is valid for all times may be formulated as follows: 1. God is the absolute, unconditional No to every evil in every form, to everything that destroys the human. 2. As one who rejects evil, his coming is always imminent, at every moment irrupting into our lives challenging us to decision. 3. The decision he demands is that we make our own the unconditional No that he is. This last point provides the clue to the riddle why the poor are still with us today. The God of Jesus is a suffering God who cannot fully become what he already is without our lending him a helping hand. Hence the persistent appeals Jesus made to all to decide there and then for God and his kingdom (Matt. 22:1-4; Luke 16:1-13).

He called upon them to meet the God who came to meet them and to work with him. But they did fail to respond, just as we have. If, therefore, injustice and oppression continue it is because we have not allowed the divine No to reverberate through our word and deed. It is because we have failed to avenge the blood of the innocent.

From an Economy of Having to an Economy of Giving

As one taken hold of by God, Jesus could not but be the vindicator of the poor. This role he could play all the more effectively because he knew the misery and degradation of the poor from the standpoint of one who belonged to their social condition. Both by circumstances of birth and by choice he was among the poor. He was born into a poor family. This we know from the fact that his mother, Mary, at the time of her purification had to make use of the concession granted to the poor of offering two turtle doves instead of one dove and a lamb (Luke 2:24). His life was of such privation that he could say of himself, "Foxes have their holes, the birds their roosts, but the Son of Man has nowhere to lay his head" (Matt.8:20). On one occasion, when, in the course of a controversy with the lawyers and the Pharisees, he needed a coin to illustrate a point, he had to ask for one from the bystanders, which shows that he did not carry any money with him (Luke 20:24). He lived on charity and had to depend on the help provided by the well-to-do women who accompanied him in his travels (Luke 8:1-3). He looked at poverty with the eyes of the poor. How true was his observation that two copper coins which the poor widow put into the temple treasury meant all she had to live on (Mark 12:41-44). He understood too what trouble a woman takes to find her lost silver piece, and how much she rejoices on finding it again (Luke 15:8-10).

As one among the poor, he must surely have seen the injustices of the prevailing economic system, which allowed a privileged few to grow richer and richer at the expense of the many poor. At the root of such a system lay man's aggression against one's neighbor. The rich have their hands dripping with the blood of the poor and the exploited. Besides, they set up riches as the supreme object of worship and thereby cease to be worshippers of the true God. "No servant can be the slave of two masters; for either he will hate the first and love the second, or he will be devoted to the first and think nothing of the second. You cannot serve God and money" (Matt. 6:24). That is why Jesus said, "How hard it will be for the wealthy to enter the kingdom of God! It is easier for a camel to pass through the eye of a needle than for a rich man to enter the kingdom of God" (Mark 10:23-25). It is an illusion for the rich to think that they can belong to the kingdom while remaining within the economic system that made them rich. This is, in fact, the meaning of the story of the rich young man who came to Jesus with the question, "Good Teacher, what must I do to inherit eternal life?" (Mark 10:17). On being told that he should observe all the commandments, his answer was, "But Master, I have kept all these since I was a boy." This shows that he was one who strictly observed the Law but within the system of private ownership. Jesus, however, demanded something more, "One thing you lack: go, sell everything you have, and give to the poor, and you will have riches in heaven; and come, follow me." Paradoxically, what the man lacked had something to do with what he had in plenty, namely, riches. How could he inherit eternal life so long as he clung to an economic system which violently deprived the many of their inheritance of the earth? To become a member of the community of the future he had to sell what he had and give to the poor. In other words, he had to break with the economy of private property and embrace an economy of giving. This he was not prepared to do. Hence his departure with a sad face.

The Poor Shall Possess the Earth

Contrasted with him, the disciples of Jesus were prepared to rupture the bonds of private property. Simon and Andrew "left their nets and followed him" (Mark 1:18). The sons of Zebedee went off to follow him "leaving their father Zebedee in the boat with the hired men" (Mark 1:20). Similarly, Levi, the tax-collector, relinquished his lucrative job and followed Jesus empty-handed. The other disciples did the same, as is clear from Peter's claim, "We here have left everything to become your followers" (Mark 1:28). What they did at the outset of their discipleship was to determine also their subsequent mission to preach the good news, work cures, and drive out demons. They were instructed not to rely on private property in the form of bread, bag, money, or even an extra tunic, but to live from hospitality; i.e., from an economy of giving (Mark 6:7-13). When he was faced with a large famished crowd, Jesus rejected the disciples' suggestion that they buy provisions from the villages nearby. Instead, he asked them to give what they had, being sure that what was given in love would multiply and meet the needs of all (Mark 6:34-44). That he also taught his disciples to devalue the money economy seems to be implied in his comment on the widow's mite: "I tell you this, this poor widow has given more than any others; for those others who have given had more than enough, but she, with less than enough, has given all that she had to live on" (Mark 12:43-44). Here too we meet with a paradox. She who gave the least gave the most. What mattered in the eyes of Jesus was not the exchange value of what she put in (which was but little) but its use-value (which was much, being all that she had to live on).

It follows from our analysis that the life and message of Jesus were in principle disruptive of the prevailing economic system. However, for him, criticism of the existing conditions was but a prerequisite for marching ahead to a new order of things. Consequently the demand, "Follow me." And the guiding principle of the new social order to which his followers were to commit themselves is well expressed in his saying, "Take note of what you hear; the measure you give is the measure you will receive, with something more besides." (Mark 4:24). The 'something more besides' which he promised represents the fullness of the age to come, a fullness which is to be understood also in the material sense. In an economic order in which each gives what one has, each also receives the whole of what the community has. Here lies the secret of the superabundance that will characterize the community of the future. In order to express the plenty that will mark the new age, Jesus uses many and varied symbols: the seed buried in the ground which produces first the blade, then the ear, the full grain in the ear (Mark 4:28); the mustard seed that becomes the greatest of all shrubs (Mark 4:32); the seed that fell into the good soil and grew up yielding thirtyfold and sixtyfold and a hundredfold (Mark4:1-9); and the few loaves which, multiplied, satisfied all (Mark 6:42 and 8:8). The disciples who left everything to follow him receive the promise of plenty in terms of material goods and social fellowship. "I tell you this: there is no one who has given up home, brothers or sisters, mother, father or children, or land, for my sake and for the Gospel, who will not receive in this age a hundred times as much — houses, brothers and sisters, mothers and children, and land — and persecution besides; and in the age to come eternal life"(Mark 10:29-30). It is disputed whether or not this phrase 'and in the age to come eternal life' is part of the authentic saying of Jesus. Even if it were, it could not have meant a spiritual world above this world of ours, because such a concept was alien to the Hebrew mode of thinking. The essential thing to remember is that the fullness of the age to come is at once continuous and discontinuous with the present age: continuous because it is our earth (land, houses) and our society (mothers, brothers, sisters) filled with an abiding love; discontinuous, because it is the definitive superseding of all alienation.

The earliest community of believers understood very well the call of their master to relinquish the economy of private property and commit themselves to an economy of giving which multiplies the given and satisfies the needs of all. Their practice is, in fact, the best commentary on that future that Jesus envisioned.

> "The whole body of believers was united in heart and soul. Not a man of them claimed any of his possessions as his own, but everything was held in common, while the apostles bore witness with great power to the resurrection of the Lord Jesus. They were all held in high esteem; for they had never a needy person among them, because all who had property in land or houses sold it, brought the proceeds of the sale, and laid the money at the feet of the apostles; it was then distributed to any who stood in need" (Acts 4:32-35).

From each according to his ability, to each according to his need - such was the economic creed of the earliest community of disciples.

All four Gospels testify to Jesus' profound concern for the poor and his stringent criticism of the rich. This should not, however, be interpreted to mean that in his view the rich are necessarily barred from entering the kingdom of God or that poverty in itself assures entry into it. The rich have access to the New Age provided they are prepared to call in question the conditions that have made them rich and to give up their possessions in response to the call of the Kingdom. The rich young man forfeited his chance to enter the Kingdom when he refused to part with his wealth, whereas Zacchaeus, although rich, met his salvation because he showed himself willing to put an end to his exploitations of the people and give away half his possessions in charity (Luke 19:8-10). The poor also, no less than the rich, have to put the reign of God before everything else. Mere material poverty is no passport for entry into the New Humanity. Just as the rich can make an idol of the riches they already have, so can the poor, the riches they long to have. However, such a warning was not necessary for the poor of Jesus' time, since they, expecting little from their initiative or an initiative on the part of guardians of the status quo, looked to God alone for liberation. It is this openness to the future, not their passive acceptance of their lot, which is to be regarded as of permanent value in their attitude. For how can the poor of any age be fit for an economy of giving if they cling to the relics of the past or the realities of the present? No radical change, personal or social, is possible so long as the enslaved love their fetters. The kingdom of God will belong to the poor only if they are also poor in spirit; i.e., open to the future. The openness in question must manifest itself as a hungering and thirsting for justice, as an organized struggle for liberation, even to the point of inviting repression from the powers that be. "Blessed are those who are persecuted for the cause of justice, for theirs is the kingdom of heaven" (Matt. 5:10).

6

Towards the Total Human

The Despised of the Earth

Humans cannot live on bread alone; they live also on every word uttered by their fellow humans whereby each is a recognized person and accepted as an equal. If some are poor and destitute it is because others have refused to recognize them as brothers/sisters and equals. The wealth of the few is achieved at the cost of the want of many. Only those can amass wealth who choose to reduce their fellow humans to the condition of mere objects which they can manipulate at will. Economic inequality, therefore, carries with it social inequality. Poverty has its concomitant social degradation. The poor are also unloved and unwanted in the society.

This was true also of the poor of Jesus' day. But in their case, poverty bore an additional social stigma, since it was considered a sign of divine punishment, just as wealth was attributed to divine favour. However, poverty did not necessarily imply social degradation; nor did wealth necessarily win popular esteem. For instance, the publicans, though wealthy, were held in contempt, whereas such doctors of the law as happened to be poor were nevertheless esteemed.

There were also other factors based on which large sections of the population were either despised or even rendered social outcasts.[1] One such factor was occupational taboo. Those who engaged in certain professions were deprived of civil and political rights, besides being despised and hated by the people. Such, for instance, were gamblers with dice, usurers, pigeon-trainers, dealers in the produce of the Sabbatical year, herdsmen, tax collectors, and publicans. They were hated for indulging in swindling or resorting to extortion. There were others, such as goldsmiths, flax combers, hand mill cleaners, weavers, barbers, and launderers, who incurred social ignominy for the, to us, curious reason that they had to deal with women in running their trade and, for that reason, were morally suspect. To the socially disreputable belonged also slaves and the racially impure, such as bastards, the fatherless, foundlings, eunuchs, and the illegitimate descendants of proselytes. If even those with only slight racial blemish were the object of orthodox scorn, how much more the gentiles! The latter was considered outside the pale of divine favour.

Though not despised, the womenfolk occupied an inferior position in Jewish society. Their condition finds a fairly accurate description in the saying of Josephus, "A woman is in every respect of less worth than a man."[2]Even in religious matters women were considered inferior to men. In the temple they had access only to the court set apart for them. They were exempted from reciting the Shema morning and evening, because, like slaves, they had no right to dispose of their time. Those belonging to the higher social circles in the cities had to confine themselves within their houses. Men considered it a virtue not to have any social contact with them. A rabbinic proverb ran, "Do not speak much with womankind."[3] In the countryside, however, especially among the poorer classes the womenfolk enjoyed greater freedom.

Far removed from the despised classes and comfortably anchored in their self-righteousness stood the respectable classes - the Pharisees, the scribes, the priests and, generally, the rich. They avoided any contact with the socially underprivileged lest they are defiled. It was into such a society, fragmented by false religion and morality, that Jesus came. How did he react to it? Both his teaching and conduct constituted defiance of the status quo and a declaration of solidarity with the outcasts of society.

The Dream of the Total Human

The despised classes received the good news from Jesus, that the final coming of God will coincide with the 'becoming' of humankind into his people, into a community bound by love, that he will gather together and weld the many fragments of humanity into the Total Human. The birth of the Total Human will result in liberation from all social barriers, and inequality, injustice, and oppression. Naturally, Jesus did not give expression to this hope in conceptual language. Instead, he used symbols and images drawn from the religious heritage of his people.

He speaks of the New Humanity as the flock which he gathers around him and for which he gives his life (Luke 12:32; John 10:14-15). He refers to it as the family of God (Matt. 23:8-9), as the banquet of salvation (Matt. 8:11), as God's plantation (Matt. 13:24 ff.), like a net that a fisherman casts into the sea to gather in fishes of all sorts (Matt. 13:47 ff.), as the temple of God (Mark 14:58), as the assembly of God (Matt. 16:18 ff.), and as the people of the New Covenant (Matt. 26:28). All these symbols stress one thing: What Jesus envisions is the salvation not of the individual in isolation but of the community of humans. The ultimate possibilities of man can be realized only in a people-centered upon God. So too in a community can God become what he already is.

Does this mean that for Jesus what mattered was the collectivity and not the individual? Does this mean that he subordinated the individual to the community as a means to an end? Not at all. For him, the collective was not an abstraction but a communion of persons bound by love. For this very reason, he was also concerned with the final liberation of the individual. Many sayings and parables testify to this. Inclusion in the New Humanity is conditional upon the personal decision of each (Mark 3:31-35). The God of Jesus is like a shepherd who leaves the ninety-nine in the open pasture and goes after the missing one until he has found it (Luke 15:3-6). He is one who cares for the least and the last: "Anything you did for one of my brothers here, however humble, you did for me" (Matt.25:40). Hence Jesus' vision of the Total Human steers clear of both collectivism, which considers the individual merely as a function of the group, and individualism, which subordinates the group to the individual and his/her private salvation.

New Humanity is the definitive supersession of all barriers consisting of exclusive claims and privileges. It is constituted based on neither kinship, nor religion, nor race. Once, while addressing a crowd, the word was brought to him that his mother and brothers were standing outside asking for him. He replied, "Who is my mother? Who are my brothers?" And pointing to those who were sitting around and listening to him, he said, "Here are my mother and my brothers. Whoever does the will of God is my brother, my sister, my mother" (Mark 3:31-35). What is envisioned here is a new community that transcends all bounds set by kinship, one whose sole principle of unity consists in doing the will of God. Neither is the entry into the New Humanity determined by membership in any particular race or religious community. This is borne out by the fact that Jesus proposes a Samaritan as the model of behavior proper to the New Age. The latter is commended simply because he responded to one in need of help. The helper's race or religion was immaterial.

The truth that the New Humanity is open to all irrespective of racial or cultural distinctions comes out clearly in the cleansing of the temple, which is a parable in action. The key to its proper understanding are the words, "Does not the Scripture say, 'My house shall be called a house of prayer for all the nations'? But you have made it a robbers' cave" (Mark 11:17). That the temple was destined for worship by all nations was indicated by the fact that a section of it was set apart for the use of the gentiles. It was precisely there, in the 'court of the gentiles', that Jesus saw trafficking going on. Therefore, by upsetting the tables of moneychangers and the seats of dealers in pigeons, he was doing nothing less than vindicating the rights of the gentiles to offer worship to God. Before God, there is no distinction between Jew or gentile. This idea is expressed much more forcefully in the saying of Jesus that the temple itself will be destroyed to make way for another one not made with human hands (Mark 14:58). The new temple is the new community of men which God will gather around him to offer worship 'in spirit and truth' (John 4:23).

He found faith, which is the condition for belonging to the New Age, also among non-Jews like the Samaritan leper (Luke 17:11-19), the Syrophoenician woman (Mark 7:26-30), and the gentile nobleman. It was of the last-mentioned Jesus said, "I tell you, nowhere, not even in Israel, have I found faith like this" (Luke 7:10). Gentiles were also recipients of the favors of the New Age, as is clear from the miracles worked on their behalf. All-inclusiveness of the reign of God will find its final expression at the summing up of history when "many will come from east and west to feast with Abraham, Isaac, and Jacob in the kingdom of Heaven" (Matt. 8:11).

The Social Practice of Jesus

It is in light of this hope for the New Age that Jesus lived and moved among men. It also determined his attitude towards the outcasts of society. As a prophet and a teacher, he was expected to associate himself exclusively with the respectable classes. In reality, it was, above all, the despised and the disreputable he chose to mingle with. He saw in them the stuff out of which the New Humanity will be formed. For only they, in his view, were open to all the possibilities of humans, and disposed to welcome the initiatives of God. That is why he said to the respectable classes who prided themselves upon being the favored friends of God, "I tell you this: tax-gatherers and prostitutes are entering the kingdom of God ahead of you." In Aramaic, the language Jesus spoke, the statement would have meant, "I tell you this: tax-gatherers and prostitutes will enter the kingdom of God, and not you" (Matt. 21:31).[4] One can well imagine how shocking these words would have been to the orthodox Jews who gloried in their self-righteousness. The offense was carried still further when Jesus invited the outcasts of society to sit at the table with him. "When Jesus was at table in his house, many bad characters - tax-gatherers and others — were seated with him and his disciples; for there were many who followed him. Some doctors of the law who were Pharisees noticed him eating in this bad company, and said to his disciples, 'He eats with tax-gatherers and sinners!' Jesus heard it and said to them, 'It is not the healthy that need a doctor, but the sick; I did not come to invite virtuous people, but sinners' "(Mark 2:15-17). Now eating for the Jews was something more than merely satisfying a bodily need. More importantly, it was a form of social intimacy. When, therefore, Jesus invited social outcasts to sit at the table with him he was offering them, intimate human fellowship. What is more, the fellowship he offered was in the real sense also divine. Among the Jews, common meals had a religious significance. Food and drink shared was a symbol of fellowship with God. By eating and drinking with the socially despised, Jesus showed indeed that God was with them as one who accepted them as they were and came to meet their need. For they were like the sick who needed the services of a doctor and knew that they needed it. True, the respectable people too were objectively in need of God, but in their pride did not recognize it and thereby shut him out from their lives.

No wonder the teachings and practice of the young rabbi from Nazareth profoundly shocked the religious sensibilities of the orthodox Jewry. Hence their mocking description of him as a 'glutton and a drunkard, a friend of publicans and sinners' (Matt. 11:19). By his conduct, he repudiated all the artificial barriers that false religion and morality had set up between humans. What he did was a powerful onslaught on the walls erected by the privileged classes between God and the unfortunate among his children. It challenged the religious arrogance of the orthodox Jews who looked upon God as their monopoly and used him to safeguard their vested interests. Positively, the practice of table-fellowship with social outcasts meant for Jesus partial anticipation of the New Humanity in which all the children of God will gather around to sit at the table with him in total love and self-giving.

The practice of table-fellowship occupied a central position in the life of Jesus. It summed up indeed the whole of his preaching. It was therefore but natural that on the eve of that fateful day when he knew that he was going to be killed, he, as usual, invited such of his friends as were with him to share his meal for the last time. The so-called Last Supper is but the culmination of the innumerable suppers he had had with his disciples and with all those who sincerely sought the face of God. It is in these frequent meals that we have to seek the deeper roots of what subsequently came to be called the Eucharist.[5]

Originally, the Eucharist was a full meal like any family meal in a Jewish home. It was only later that the emphasis shifted from the meal as a whole to two of its elements, namely, the bread and the wine, symbols respectively of the body and blood of Jesus.[6] Naturally, the body and blood in question could only be those of the risen Jesus, who is outside the flux of history. This meant a twofold alienation. First, the symbolism of the meal was impoverished. Second, the prophetic meaning of the Eucharist as the anticipation, in the symbol as well as in reality, of the New Humanity of the end-time was lost sight of. This makes it all the more necessary for us to go back to the table-fellowship of Jesus and from its vantage point recapture the original meaning of the Eucharist.

Reinterpreted in the light of the meals Jesus used to have with social and religious outcasts, the words attributed to Jesus, 'This is my body, this is my blood' may be paraphrased thus: "When you come together in the name of your common hope in the New Humanity without distinction of classes and, in love, share the fruits of your labour, you are truly making your own my faith, my hope, my commitment, and my destiny. Thereby you become in the real sense my flesh and blood, my prolongation in history." It is only when the products of labour like food and drink become the bond between humans, instead of being instruments of exploitation of humans by humans, it is only when the world of things mediates one's love for God and one's fellow humans, that the meaning of Jesus' table-fellowship becomes realized in history. Seen from this perspective, the love-meal Jesus instituted is an invitation to overthrow all structures of inequality and to construct a new social order in which everyone is the keeper of one's brothers and sisters.

The same fundamental option that moved him to seek the company of the marginalized also determined his choice of disciples. These too belonged to the despised classes. He spoke of them as 'the little ones' (Mark 9:42), 'the humble' (Matt. 25:40), 'the simple' as opposed to the wise, and the uneducated, the ignorant, in short, of those for whom, according to prevailing conceptions, salvation was difficult, if not impossible. The historical movement he initiated was, in the main, of the lowest stratum of Jewish society. In no sense of the term was it elitist.

No less revolutionary than Jesus' table-fellowship with publicans and sinners was his rejection of the social taboos surrounding relations between the sexes. Nothing, perhaps, was more shocking for his contemporaries than the freedom with which he associated himself with women, considering the inferior position of women in Jewish society. Though a bachelor, he had close friends among them, as is clear from the story of Martha and Mary (Luke 10:38-42). We find a retinue of women accompanying him wherever he went and supporting him out of their means (Mark 15:40-41; Luke 8:1-3). He allowed a woman of doubtful reputation to wash his feet with her tears and wipe them with her hair (Luke 7:37-38). Contrary to the accepted social norms he freely engaged in conversation with a woman he met casually by a well-side, something that amazed even his disciples (John 4:27). He also worked miracles in their favour (Luke 8:43; 7:11-15). Not only men but also women were to be found among his audience (Luke 11:27).

In accord with his conduct was also his teaching on marriage. He annulled the prevailing custom, which permitted a man to discharge his wife on any silly pretext merely by giving her a bill of divorce, and, thereby, he restored the indissolubility of marriage as originally willed by the Creator (Mark 10:2-9). By enjoining also on the woman the obligation not to initiate proceedings of divorce against her husband, he implicitly affirmed the fundamental equality of man and woman as persons (Mark 10:11-12). The same equality finds expression in his saying, "Whoever does the will of God is my brother, my sister, my mother" (Mark 3:35). Here the value of a person is judged solely by the standard of obedience to the will of God and not by that of the distinction of sexes.

All this means that with Jesus a new spirit entered into history, a spirit that could not be contained within the wineskins of the old social and religious traditions, and was bound to burst them from within. It was a spirit of refusal and acceptance: refusal of every mutilation and fragmentation of human, and acceptance of togetherness in love and mutual concern as authentic human existence. This new social ethos did give history a new orientation by shattering old fetters and creating new bonds between humans. But over time, its destructive-constructive force came to be domesticated, if not smothered, by the same community whose mission it was to keep it alive and active. Now the time has come to release its pristine energies for the construction of a new humanity.

The Cost of Freedom: Political Death

Of all the sufferings of the Jewish people, the most intensely felt was their subjection to Roman domination. Jesus himself could not have been unaware of it, coming as he did from Galilee, whose inhabitants were known for their fanatical zeal for the ancient traditions and their struggle against foreign powers. Conscious of his mission to set free the oppressed, he could not have avoided taking a stand about Rome either. What was that stand? Before attempting an answer let us focus on the historical setting.

The Challenge of Foreign Domination

After their return from the Babylonian exile (586-538 b.c.), the Jews had settled down in their native land, secure in the hope of a long period of peace and prosperity to come. But their hopes never fructified. They were destined to live as a subject people under successive foreign powers - the Persians, the Greeks, the Egyptians, the Syrian Seleucids, the Parthians and, finally, the Romans. Palestine came under Roman power in 63 B.C. when Pompey conquered Jerusalem. The Romans appointed Herod, a half-Jewish Idumean, as the king of the Jews. On his death, in 4 B.C. the kingdom was divided among his sons by Emperor Augustus. Archelaus ruled Judea in the south, while Herod Antipas ruled Galilee. The former was, however, deposed in 6 A.D for reasons of misrule, and his territory passed into the direct charge of the Romans.

But as far as the common humans were concerned, the rule of Herod was as detestable as that of the Romans.

The people had ample reasons to feel resentment against Rome. The Law had forbidden setting up a foreigner to rule over them; Yahweh alone was to be their king (Deut. 17:15). The Roman practice of census, too, met with popular disapproval, since Yahweh had censured David for numbering his subjects (2 Sam 24). Worse still, the Roman procurator, Pilate, had only contempt for the natives and went out of his way to humiliate them. He revoked the order, which his predecessors had passed as a concession to Jewish religious sensibilities, that the Roman army should remove the Emperor's image from its standards whenever it entered the Holy City. He even looted the temple treasury, a deed deemed sacrilegious by every Jew. The reference in Luke 13:2 to the many Galileans who were slaughtered by Pilate while they were offering worship in the temple, is further proof of his ruthless character. No less unwelcome to the people were the economic consequences of Roman rule. The burden of taxation weighed heavily on them and it was further aggravated by the unscrupulous manner in which the tax-gatherers went about their business. In the prevailing circumstances, only those who collaborated with the foreign regime could succeed in getting rich. Did all these grievances lead to a popular revolt?

There was a tradition of popular resistance to foreign domination. When in 168 B.C. the Syrian king, Antiochus Epiphanes, conquered Jerusalem, desecrated the temple, and tried to destroy Jewish religion by introducing Hellenistic cults, the people rose to a human in revolt under the leadership of the Maccabees and threw out the hated aliens. Again in 6 A.D. when the Romans introduced taxation, a certain Judas of Galilee raised a rebellion which, however, was ruthlessly put down by Quirinus, the governor of Syria. Though the revolt was a failure, it gave birth to an extremist movement whose members were called the Zealots. The word zealot meant those who were prepared even to use force in defense of the traditional law, which, as we have seen, forbade rule by foreigners. It is not certain whether Zealotism already existed as a political party in the time of Jesus. Probably it was then no more than an underground movement indulging in sporadic acts of violence.[1] However that may be, we find a representative of this radical wing among the disciples of Jesus.

However, not all Jews were committed to driving out the Romans by force. The religious power structure was dominated by the Sadducees,[2] who formed an aristocracy of about two hundred families. It is from among them that the High Priests were drawn. Unlike the Essenes and the Pharisees, the Sadducees constituted a political party. They made up the hardcore of the Sanhedrin, the High Court of Justice. They enjoyed controlled autonomy in the internal matters of Jewish society. For the rest, they were mere puppets in the hands of Rome. They had everything to gain by following a pacifist policy in political matters. First, there was the perennial lure of power itself, religious as well as political. Besides, in charge of the temple, the priestly ruling class controlled the treasury and, at the time of great festivals, carried on a lucrative business in foreign exchange.

The other dominant group, the Pharisees, too, followed a policy of pacifism vis-a-vis the occupying power. They were professedly religious men and did not concern themselves with politics except when their religious sensibilities were outraged. When in 6 B.C. Herod put up a golden eagle over the main entrance of the temple, they struck it down, for which some among them had to pay the penalty of being burned alive. In normal times, however, they held to the view that God was making use of Rome to chastise Israel for its infidelities and sins.

No to Political Messianism

Any consideration of Jesus' political attitudes has to start with the undeniable fact that he was put to death by crucifixion by the then Roman procurator, Pontius Pilate. Crucifixion was a Roman penalty, which implies that the authorities conducted a formal trial and found the accused guilty. What then was the accusation? The charge sheet affixed to the cross read, 'Jesus of Nazareth, King of the Jews.' This means that Jesus was accused of leading a rebellion against Rome to install himself as king. This is borne out also by the charge the Jewish leaders brought against him before the Roman tribunal. "We found this man subverting our nation, opposing the payment of taxes to Caesar, and claiming to be Messiah, a king" (Luke 23:2). Was this accusation true? When asked by Pilate, "Are you the king of the Jews?" Jesus gave what sounds like an evasive answer, "The words are yours" (Mark 15:2). His reply has been variously interpreted — as affirmative, as negative, or as noncommittal. One thing is certain. He could not have admitted to being king of the Jews in the sense of a political Messiah. To grasp this we have to interpret Jesus' words in the context of his life and teaching as a whole.

Right at the beginning of his public career the Spirit of God invaded him and drove him into the desert, there to be tempted by Satan. What the Gospels describe as three distinct temptations are but variations of one temptation, namely, to follow the way of the political messianism.[3] "Again, the devil took him to a very high mountain, and showed him all the kingdoms of the world and the glory of them; and he said to him: All these I will give you if you will fall and worship me." (Matt. 4:8-10). What Satan held up before Jesus was the Zealot ideal of an Israel ruling over all the kingdoms of the world. But that ideal was against the original revelation from God which forbade Israel to have anyone but God to rule over them. Hence Jesus' reply, "Begone, Satan! for it is written: You shall worship the Lord your God and he only shall you serve." (Matt. 4:10). It is against this background that we should understand his other saying, "For what does it profit a man, to gain the whole world and forfeit his life?" (Mark 8:36). What use gaining universal political power if thereby human is denied the possibility of leading a rich and full life?

In the desert, Jesus definitively opted against political messianism. And Satan retreated for the time being, but only to reappear and confront him with the same temptation at various points in his life. He did so first through the people, who by and large shared the Zealot hopes. There are indications in the Gospels that the crowd, on seeing the marvels he worked, began to nurse the hope that he would come out into the open and proclaim himself the political leader they were eagerly awaiting. This explains their persistent efforts to pursue him wherever he went. Equally persistently he withdrew from them. We find him seeking clandestinity in private homes (Mark 1:29; 3:1; 3:19; 7:24), in desert places (Mark 1:35; 6:31), by the seaside (Mark 2:13; 3:7; 4:1), and in boats (Mark 4:35; 5:21; 6:45; 8:10,13). The Gospel according to John explicitly states that when, after the miraculous feeding of the multitude, Jesus realized that the people wanted to seize him and proclaim him a king, he "withdrew again to the hills by himself" (John 6:14-15). The contrast between the nationalist hopes of the people and the role he assigned to himself may be seen also in the narrative of his entry into Jerusalem. The crowd acclaimed him with the words, "Hosanna! Blessed is he who comes in the name of the Lord! Blessed is the kingdom of our father David that is coming! Hosanna in the highest!" (Mark 11: 9-10). This shows that they expected him to restore the kingdom of David. This conclusion imposes itself all the more if 'Hosanna in the highest' meant, as a recent interpreter has tried to show, 'Save us from the Romans'.[5] That any such plan was foreign to the mind of Jesus follows from the fact that he chose for his means of transportation a colt rather than a horse, the beast of war par excellence.

Yet on another occasion did Satan raise his head, this time in the person of Peter. When, at Caesarea Philippi, Jesus asked his disciples what they thought of him, Peter enthusiastically replied, "You are the Messiah." But what he meant by that term was a political Messiah who would rule over the nations. This is clear from the sequel of the story. For, when Jesus went on to say that his destiny was to go to Jerusalem, there to face death at the hands of his enemies, Peter took him by the arm and began to rebuke him saying, "Heaven forbid!... No, Lord, this shall never happen to you." At this, he got the stunning reply, "Away with you, Satan. You think as men think, not as God thinks" (Mark 8:27-33). Nor were the thoughts of the other disciples any less the thoughts of men, as may be seen from their quarrel as to who should be greatest in the kingdom of God (Mark 9:33-34), from the request of the sons of Zebedee to be allowed to sit one on his right and the other on his left when he came in glory (Mark 10:37), and from the fact that one of the disciples betrayed him, and another resorted to violence and struck off the ear of the High Priest's servant.

Seen in the light of his resolute opposition to political messianism, the agony in the Garden of Olives assumes special significance. There was an ideological rift between himself, on the one hand, and the disciples and the crowd, on the other. It looks as though it took on, on the eve of his death, the form of a chasm in his soul between what he willed (the thoughts of men) and what God willed (the thoughts of God): "Abba, Father, all things are possible to thee; remove this cup from me; yet not what I will, but what thou wilt" (Mark 14:36).[6] The agony ends with his final acceptance of the thoughts and purposes of God. With that decisive victory won, he surrendered himself to his enemies.

His teaching too was in accord with his repudiation of the Zealot ideal of a restored theocracy. We do not find in it overtones of Jewish nationalism, as would have been the case if he were committed to political messianism. Besides, he did what no Zealot would ever have dreamt of doing: he foretold the destruction of the temple, the very center, and hearth of the Jewish religion (Mark 13:2). Relevant in this context is also his teaching on nonviolence. Jesus required of his disciples that, if anyone should slap them on their right cheek, they should turn and offer him their left as well. Such a person could never have been a follower of the Zealots, who indulged in violence (Matt. 5:39).

The Cost of Freedom: Death on the Cross

It follows from our discussion thus far that Jesus' response before Pilate could not have meant an admission of his being the messianic king of the Jews. Does this mean that he was indifferent to the political slavery of his people or that he was a political conformist? On the contrary. His very commitment to the Kingdom, as a community of freedom, brought him into conflict with the political power not only of Rome but also of the Sanhedrin in Jerusalem and of Herod in Galilee.

Herod, whose territory was the main scene of Jesus' activity, had John the Baptizer beheaded for criticizing his incestuous relationship with his brother's wife (Mark 6:14-29). By censuring the immoral conduct of the king, John implicitly questioned the divine legitimization of his authority to rule. If so, Herod had equal reason to get rid of Jesus as well, for he too preached the indissolubility of marriage, all the more so since he believed the latter to be John himself risen from the dead. Luke, in fact, explicitly states that some Pharisees approached Jesus to persuade him to quit Galilee because Herod was seeking to kill him (Luke 13:31). That Jesus himself was aware of the threat may be seen from his reply to them, "Go and tell that fox: Behold, I cast out demons and perform cures today and tomorrow, and the third day I finish my course." (Luke 13:32).

Jesus' teaching and conduct were subversive also of the religious-political power of the Sanhedrin. First, his radical interpretation of the Law, his rejection of the distinction between the sacred and the profane, his reaffirmation of the primacy of love over the cult, and his prediction of the destruction of the temple, undermined the religious authority of the High Priesthood. Second, the universal character of the New Humanity that he proclaimed contradicted the nationalist particularism of the Jewish authorities. Third, the ruling clique had a vested interest in maintaining the status quo, since they ruled by the favour of Rome. And it was just the status quo of their use of religious-political power to exploit the people that Jesus challenged when he threw out the vendors and the money-changers from the temple. Hence their question, "By what authority are you acting like this?"(Mark 11:28). In all likelihood, the cleansing of the temple was the immediate provocation that led to Jesus' arrest and trial before the Sanhedrin.

Now we come to the crucial question: Did Jesus oppose Roman imperialism in Palestine? Much as he rejected the reformist, nationalist aspirations of the Zealots, he certainly shared their opposition to foreign domination. Very much to the point is the well-known saying of his, "Render to Caesar the things that are Caesar's, and to God the things that are God's" (Mark 12:17).[7] At first blush, his reply sounds like a piece of advice to abide by the Roman laws of taxation. But we must remember that it was to trap him in words that the Pharisees and the followers of Herod came up with the question of whether it was lawful to pay taxes to Rome. If he said yes, he would thereby have declared himself a friend of the Romans and an enemy of the people. If, on the contrary, he said no, he could have been produced before the Roman authorities on the charge of sedition. His answer, therefore, had necessarily to be guarded, which makes it equally necessary for us to read between the lines. To arrive at the true meaning we have to keep in mind the creation story in Genesis according to which man alone was made in God's image, and, further, the Jewish belief that Israel was forbidden by God to make images of anything in heaven or on earth (Deut. 5:8). To use coins bearing the image of Caesar was therefore contrary to the will of God. Hence 'Render to Caesar the things that are Caesar's' could as well have meant: "Have nothing to do with this coin or with the economic and political power it represents. Return it to Caesar whose image it bears. But you, unlike this coin, bear the image of God and, as such, belong to him. To him alone, therefore, shall you be subject, to no one else, not even to Caesar." Naturally, this meaning could have been grasped only by those 'who had ears to hear', i.e. by those whose hearts were not hardened by the worship of idols.

A more explicit and unambiguous rejection of foreign domination is contained in the words, "You know that in the world the recognized rulers lord it over their subjects and make them feel the weight of authority. That is not the way with you; among you, whoever wants to be great must be your servant, and whoever wants to be first must be the willing slave of all" (Mark 10:42-45). Here the subversiveness of Jesus' teaching extends beyond the Jewish and the Roman power structures to all states that use their authority to grind the heads of people in the mud.

In yet another sense, did Jesus pose a threat to Roman imperialism. The Romans needed the support of the Sanhedrin to maintain their rule in Palestine, which the latter was all too willing to provide. And it was just this support that Jesus threatened to weaken, if not to destroy when he used his prophetic authority to cleanse the temple and preached a message that shook the religious foundations of the priestly ruling class. Such being the case, it was in the interests of Pilate as well as to get rid of the prophet from Galilee.

This brings us to the crucial truth often forgotten by the followers of Jesus. Traditional teaching has instilled in them the idea that Jesus' death is in itself endowed with value as a sacrifice offered to God as if it had no relation to his teaching and practice. The truth is that his life was prematurely and brutally brought to an end by the collusion of the religious and political powers of his day who found in his life and teaching a threat to their survival. Death was the price he had to pay for his merciless criticism of religious formalism and bigotry, for his condemnation of the religious authorities who sought to cleverly combine the service of God with the service of Mammon, for his fellowship with the outcasts of society, for his commitment to a New Humanity open to all who hunger and thirst for justice, in one word, for his having sought, first and above all things, the kingdom of God and its justice. And he opted to pay the price, knowing full well what it would cost him in terms of human suffering. In his honesty unto death, we have the highest expression of the radiance of the human and the divine in a human, the supreme revelation of what it means to be human.

It is in the light of Jesus' unconditional commitment to the kingdom of God that we must define the essence of discipleship under him. Discipleship consists, above all, in total self-dedication to the creation of a new human community, in which love will replace violence, service will replace the brute exercise of power, in which no barrier will separate human from human, in which the first will be the least of today, namely, the wretched and the dispossessed of the earth. Such commitment will necessarily call for preparedness to lay down one's life, wherever those who wield political power, act as agents of oppression. The disciple of Jesus is, more than anyone else, a political animal condemned to death. He/she cannot be greater than his/her Master.

8

Meeting God in Human Fullness

Every domain of life, whether economic, social, or political, has a depth-dimension, a dimension of transcendence, where the human impinges on the Divine, where our proximate concerns merge into the ultimate concern. In the decisions and deeds that go to make up everyday experience, the depth-dimension is only implicitly perceived, as something that inspires us from within or beckons us from beyond, as a presence or an absence. What is thus existentially experienced becomes articulate in the form of symbols, verbal or actional. Thus formulas of faith, as well as rites, rubrics, norms, and institutions, come into being. It is this articulate expression of the depth-dimension of individual and collective life that we traditionally call religion.

Just as economic, social, and political life can become alienated, so too religion can deteriorate and become untrue to its essence. As an expression of man's transcendence, religion, more than anything else, ought to stand for his/her freedom from everything that imprisons him/her within narrow walls. But where it has ceased to draw nourishment from the original encounter with the Absolute, it loses its meaning and becomes mere deadwood. Instead of helping humans to transcend themselves and march ahead, it chains them to a dead past or a decaying present.

This is what had befallen Jewish religion in the time of Jesus. It had deviated from its original purity and had even become an obstacle to the realization of the divine purpose in history. The overgrowth of religious beliefs and practices weighed heavily on the common humans, crippling what was genuinely human-divine in them. Jesus reacted to the situation in the same manner as did the prophets. He set out to free his people from false religion. This he did by criticizing the religious status quo and by revealing what true religion should mean.

Mercy, Not Sacrifice

Jesus told his contemporaries that cult, divorced from the existential encounter with God, has no meaning. And for humans, an encounter with God is possible only when they encounter their neighbors in self-giving love. Human love is the privileged locus where God unveils his presence. Therefore any cult, not born of brotherly love, is an aberration and an exercise in futility. This is the essence of his saying, "If, when you are bringing your gift to the altar, you suddenly remember your brother has a grievance against you, leave your gift where it is before the altar. First, go and make your peace with your brother and only then come back and offer your gift" (Matt. 5:23-24). Peace with humans is an essential condition for the cult to be meaningful as a symbolic expression of peace with God.

Similarly, Jesus rejected those practices of the cult which have no impact on life. "Not everyone who calls me 'Lord, Lord' will enter the kingdom of Heaven, but only those who do the will of my heavenly Father" (Matt. 7:21). Not the number of prayers and supplications offered, but effective surrender to the demands of God assures membership in the New Humanity. The proliferation of cultic practices can easily become a substitute for meeting the challenges of life. Jesus, therefore, advised his disciples to cut out verbosity in prayer, "In your prayer do not go babbling on like the heathen, who imagine that the more they say the more likely they are to be heard. Do not imitate them. Your Father knows what your needs are before you ask him" (Matt. 6:7-8).

Jesus went a step further and proclaimed the primacy of love over the cult. This comes out clearly in his conversation with the lawyer as reported by Mark. To the lawyer's question as to which was the greatest commandment of all, Jesus replied, "Love the Lord your God with all your heart, with all your soul, and your entire mind, and with all your strength." The lawyer then said to him, "Well said, Master, you are right in saying that God is one and beside him, there is no other. And to love him with all your heart . . . and to love your neighbor as yourself - that is far more than any burnt offerings or sacrifices." The Evangelist concludes the story with these words, "When Jesus saw how sensibly he answered, he said to him: You are not far from the kingdom of God." (Mark 12:28-34) To recognize the primacy of love over sacrifices and burnt offerings is in itself to draw near to the kingdom of God. How much more living it out! Jesus used the same principle of the centrality of love to justify his befriending the outcasts of society, even at the risk of violating the rules of cultic purity. He told his accusers, "It is not the healthy that need a doctor, but the sick. Go and learn what that text means: I require mercy, not sacrifice." (Matt. 9:10-13)

To understand the full significance of the reversal of values Jesus affected by affirming the primacy of love over cult, it is necessary to study his attitude to the Jewish law. For many of the prevailing laws had themselves to do with the practice of cult. Besides, his criticism of law will give us a deeper insight into the nature of the love whose primacy over cult he affirmed.

Humans Were Not Made for the Sabbath

A human's existential encounter with God normally translates itself into a system of norms. Thus every religion develops its complex of laws. The Ten Commandments represent the crystallization into law of the religious experience of the Hebrews. In course of time, around the nucleus of the commandments, there sprang up other laws, prescriptions, and taboos, which subsequently found written expression in the first five books of the Bible. The written law underwent further elaboration when, after the exile, the lawyers set out to apply it to the concrete situations of everyday life. Thus an oral tradition was formed which eventually gained normative value comparable to that of the written law itself. According to the scribal calculation, the commandments and prohibitions of the written law already numbered no less than 613. With each of them again giving rise to many oral traditions, Judaism had degenerated into a religion of legalism and casuistry. To what ridiculous extent casuistry went can be gauged from the nature of the controversies the lawyers used to indulge in. To cite but two examples, it was hotly discussed whether it was a sin to eat an egg laid on the Sabbath and whether wearing an artificial tooth amounted to a violation of the law that forbade carrying burdens on the Sabbath.[1]

By falling into the legalism of this type Judaism had betrayed its true essence. The stress was no longer on what man was but on what he did or did not do. Besides, since laws, however, elaborate, could not cover the whole of individual and social life, the areas left out fell outside the pale of morality, as though they had no depth dimension and were God-less. Finally, the proliferation of laws made impossible demands on the common people, who could not reconcile strict observance with the requirements of day-to-day life.

Himself a teacher, Jesus had to take a stand about the interpretation of the law. His fundamental attitude comes into bold relief in the following incident, "One Sabbath he was going through the cornfields: and his disciples, as they went, began to pluck ears of corn. The Pharisees said to him: Why are they doing what is forbidden on the Sabbath? He answered: 'Have you never read what David did when he and his men were hungry and had nothing to eat? He went into the House of God, in the year of Abiathar the High Priest, and ate the sacred bread, though no one but a priest is allowed to eat it, and even gave it to his men. He also said to them: The Sabbath was made for the sake of man and not man for the Sabbath." (Mark 2:23-27) For Jesus, the sole purpose of the law was the good of humans. The law was but a means, and not an end in itself. Where it prevented the satisfaction of a basic need such as hunger, it ceased to have any binding power. David, therefore, did the right thing when he defied the accepted taboos regarding the eating of consecrated loaves and shared them with his companions. If so, his disciples, too, did nothing wrong in violating the Sabbath to satisfy their hunger.

It is significant that Jesus does not relate the observance of the Sabbath to the glory and honor of God. The Sabbath was set apart - which is what 'sacred' means - for divine worship. Therefore one would have expected him to say, "The Sabbath is for the honor of God, who alone is Lord over it." The reason for his failure to do so can only be that in his eyes the honor of God is the fullness of man. It is in human's face that the glory of God shines forth. This tallies also with his identification of human's love for his/her kind with the love for God. Where human is loved God is loved. Similarly human honored is God glorified. There is for Jesus no dichotomy between humanism and religion.

If one's good is sufficient justification for the violation of the Sabbath, how much more the good of others! To those who criticized him for healing a man with a withered arm on a Sabbath day, he said, "Is it permitted to do good or to do evil on the Sabbath, to save life or to kill?" (Mark 3:4). The meaning is clear: If the Sabbath is for the good of humans, an act of goodness like healing can only be in keeping with the original intention of the law. Any law that forbids doing good to others is by that very fact null and void. More so, if it sanctions evil. Hence Jesus' violent attack on the institution of corban based on the legal provision that if someone had a grudge against his aged parents, he had only to make a fictitious dedication of his wealth to God to be freed of any obligation to support them. Referring to this practice Jesus said, "Thus by your tradition, handed down among you, you make the commandment of God null and void" (Mark 7:9-13).

The same protest against the law that kills the spirit may be discerned in his criticism of the prevailing rules of ritual purity, especially those concerning the washing of hands before and after meals. Originally only priests were bound by the rules regarding the washing of hands, and that too only when they ate the tithe or the priestly offering. Subsequently, the Pharisees also took over the practice. Possibly they expected the common people to follow suit. Neither Jesus nor his disciples had any scruples in disregarding these rules. When the latter was accused by the Pharisees of eating with defiled hands, he defended them saying, "Isaiah was right when he prophesied about you hypocrites in these words, "These people pay me lip-service, but their heart is far from me: their worship of me is in vain, for they teach as doctrines the commandments of men. You neglect the commandment of God to maintain the tradition of men" (Mark 7:6-8). The rules of purity are manmade. And those who hold them up as God-given end up by frustrating the original intention and purpose of God himself. In the beginning, God created everything and found it good. Then came humans on the scene, ruling certain things pure, and others impure. What is worse, the very persons who classified things into pure and impure failed to look into the evil that bred in their hearts, vitiating everything they said or did. In their concern for external cleanliness they neglected the cleanliness of the heart; i.e. sincerity and truthfulness. Thus they fell into inauthentic existence. Jesus, therefore, invited his critics to turn their gaze from mere externals to the center of their being and see there the matrix of all evil: "Nothing that goes into a man from outside can defile him; no, it is the things that come out of him that defile a man" (Mark 7:15). It is from the 'heart' - which in biblical usage means the center of personhood where thinking, feeling, and loving converge and have their common root - that evil proceeds. In other words, it is the fundamental attitude of the humans that renders things meaningful or meaningless, good or bad, pure or impure. It is the humans who confer meaning and value on the world around them; not the other way around. Jesus thus affirmed the supreme dignity of humans as the creator of meaning and value.

Understood in this sense, Jesus' teaching on ritual purity is a charter of freedom for the human spirit. He declared null and void all irrational taboos based on ignorance and superstition. From now on, humans can move freely in the world unafraid of being defiled by it. They can approach with inner freedom sex, eating, drinking, love, and friendship. They can without moral inhibitions seek the company of all, irrespective of caste, color, class, or community. The whole world of things, persons, and deeds become capable of mediating truth, beauty, and goodness. The universe is rendered transparent, without unchaste demons inhabiting every nook and corner.

Jesus directed his criticism not only against the oral tradition but also against the written law, which no Jew dared to do until his day. His radical stand on ritual purity is itself a criticism of the rules laid down in Leviticus (11:1-15:33) and Deuteronomy. He radicalized the written law by extending its demands beyond observable actions to the domain of thoughts and desires, to that intimate sphere of existence beyond the pale of social control where humans are alone with themselves. "You have learned that our forefathers were told, 'Do not commit murder; anyone who commits murder must be brought to justice.' But what I tell you is this: Anyone who nurses anger against his brother must be brought to judgment" (Matt. 5:21-22). Again, "You have learned that they were told, 'Do not commit adultery'. But what I tell you is this: If a man looks on a woman with a lustful eye, he has already committed adultery with her in his heart" (Matt. 5:27-28). What Jesus envisages here is a new type of humans, who in the very depths of their being are responsive to the demands of God, who have no inner recesses where they may take refuge from the God who pursues him.

Jesus went even to the extent of abrogating specific precepts of the written law. He forbade swearing, which the law permitted. "You are not to swear at all . . . Plain 'Yes' or 'No' is all you need to say; anything beyond that comes from the devil" (Matt. 5:33-37; Exod. 20:7). Swearing implies that words uttered in ordinary conversation do not have that claim to truth which statements made under oath have. Jesus, on the contrary, demanded that every word uttered be true and binding solely in virtue of its having been uttered by humans. Not anything outside them, but the integrity of their whole life should be the guarantee of truthfulness. Here also the call is to authentic existence, in which one speaks what one is. Equally forthright was his rejection of the law of retaliation. "You have learned that they were told, 'Eye for eye, tooth for tooth.' But what I tell you is this: Do not set yourself against the man who wrongs you. If someone slaps you on the right cheek, turn and offer him your left" (Matt. 38-42; Exod. 21:24). Evil cannot be conquered with evil. It should be met not in the weakness of anger but the strength of love. The tide of evil can be driven back only by releasing the creative energies of love locked in human hearts.

We have already seen how Jesus repealed the Mosaic law of divorce and reaffirmed the indissolubility of marriage (Mark 10:1-11). He likewise repudiated the Old Testament notion of divine vengeance on the enemies of Israel. This may be deduced from the fact that in quoting the Scriptures he leaves out those verses containing the idea of vengeance.[2] Such omissions take on their full meaning when seen against the background of his teaching on the universality of love characteristic of the reign of God. "You have learned that they were told, 'Love your neighbor, hate your enemy.' But what I tell you is this: Love your enemies and pray for your persecutors; only so can you be children of your heavenly Father, who makes his sun rise on good and bad alike, and sends the rain on the honest and the dishonest. . . . There must be no limit to your goodness, as your heavenly Father's goodness knows no bounds" (Matt. 5:43-48). By asking his hearers to love also their enemies, i.e. non-Israelites, he broke the narrow shell of nationalism within which Judaism had imprisoned itself. Here, as elsewhere, his vision transcends all bounds and reaches out to the Total Man.

But, did not Jesus sanction the law in its entirety when he said, "Do not suppose that I have come to abolish the Law and the prophets; I did not come to abolish, but to complete" (Matt. 5:17)? The saying means no more than that he considered it his mission to bring the

Old Testament revelation to its completion. This he did precisely by stressing the original purpose of the law, which was the realization of love. He fulfilled the law by transcending it. One may still press the objection by pointing out the subsequent saying in Matthew, "If any man, therefore, sets aside even the least of the Law's demands and teaches others to do the same, he will have the lowest place in the kingdom of Heaven, whereas anyone who keeps the Law, and teaches others so, will stand high in the kingdom of Heaven" (Matt. 5:19). It is now generally recognized that the statement as it stands could not have come from Jesus himself since it is at variance with the fundamental thrust of his teaching and practice. Its origin is to be attributed to the Evangelist himself, who in this context has toned down the radicalism of Jesus to meet the missionary needs of the Palestinian Christian community.[3] The same tendency to domesticate Jesus for reasons of expediency is also to be found elsewhere in the Gospels, as also in the history of the Christian churches.

Woe to the Religious Elite

If Judaism had become a religion that oppressed the spirit of man, it was mainly due to the teaching and practice of its religious leaders: the Pharisees, the doctors of the law, and the priests. The Pharisees considered themselves the true Israel 'set apart' from the common folk. In contrast to the masses, they scrupulously observed the rules regarding the payment of tithes, ritual purity, and the practice of prayer and fasting. But in spite of, or even because of, their strict observance of the law, they were far from God. For they sacrificed the inward to the outward, reality to shadows, the central to the peripheral. Jesus lashed out at this hypocrisy of theirs, "You pay tithes of mint and dill and cummin; but you have overlooked the weightier demands of the Law, justice, mercy, and good faith. . . Blind guides! You strain off a midge, yet gulp down a camel!... You clean the outside of the cup and dish, which you have filled inside by robbery and self-indulgence! Blind Pharisee! Clean the inside of the cup first; then the outside will be clean also . . . You are like tombs covered with whitewash; they look well from outside, but inside they are full of dead men's bones and all kinds of filth. So it is with you: outside you look like honest men, but inside you are brim-full of hypocrisy and crime. . . You snakes, you vipers' brood, how can you escape being condemned to hell?" (Matt. 23:23-33).

In equally incisive language did he criticize the doctors of the law, who were professional theologians officially ordained and invested with the right to act as teachers and judges. They were authorized to make binding decisions in religious and civil matters. But they used their learning and authority to impose insupportable burdens on men and to exploit them in various ways. It was of them that Jesus said, "They make up heavy packs and pile them on men's shoulders, but will not raise a finger to lift the load themselves" (Matt. 23:4). They use religion as a means to maintain and enhance their standing in society. They like to have places of honor at feasts and the chief seats in synagogues, to be greeted respectfully in the street, and to be addressed as 'rabbi' (Matt. 23:7). Hypocrites, "they say one thing and do another" (Matt. 23:3). Hence the rebuke, "You shut the door of the kingdom of Heaven in humans' faces; you do not enter yourselves, and when others are entering, you stop them" (Matt. 23:13).

Jesus criticized also the official priesthood, the supreme guardian of the religious power structure. However, the target of his attack was not the lower ranks of priests spread all over the country but the priestly aristocracy in Jerusalem. His crucial confrontation with the religious authorities occurred on the occasion of the cleansing of the temple we commented on in an earlier chapter. His charges against them fall under three categories: First, they failed to safeguard the sanctity of the temple by allowing the pilgrims to use its court as a thoroughfare for carrying goods. Second, by misusing 'the court of the gentiles' they violated the latter's right to worship in the temple. Third, by organizing commerce and money exchange in the temple precincts, they exploited it to fill their coffers.

This critique of religion is at the same time the inauguration of a new form of religion that has its focal point in human's encounter with the living God who acts in history. In other words, Jesus shifted the axis of religion from the realm of cult and law to that depth-dimension of personal-social life.

The Secular Jesus

Jesus lived what he taught. The center of his life lay not in the cult but man's history with God. By Hebrew law, he was a layman, not a priest, priesthood being the hereditary right of the members of the tribe of Aaron and Levi. He was born of a tribe 'no member of which has ever had anything to do with the altar' (Heb. 7:13). He did not claim to be a priest. Nor was he acclaimed as one by the common folk, by his disciples, or by his opponents. The Gospels do not represent him as one who lived by, for, and around the altar. We do not see him offering sacrifices or organizing public worship. Not the altar but the world was the center of his life.

It is in the heart of the world that he met his God - at weddings, at festal meals, by the lake-side where fishermen cast and hauled their nets, by wayside wells where the womenfolk came to fetch water, at gatherings of people in the company of outcasts, in the fellowship of his disciples, in the togetherness of friendship, and the innocence of children. The mustard seed growing into a mighty tree, the yeast leavening a huge mass of dough, the fishes hauled ashore, the fig-tree putting forth its early shoots, the hen gathering her young under the wings, the earth yielding a hundredfold, all these mediated to him the presence of God. It was in and through the myriad facets of the life of his people that he communed with the God of his fathers.

His final meeting with God, his death, was no less a secular event. It was not in the temple of Jerusalem, the center of Jewish cult, that he met his end. His was not even 'a happy death' assisted by priests chanting supplications for the 'departing soul'. He was killed outside the 'Holy'

City on the 'profane' hill of Calvary. He died the utterly secular death of a political criminal. But was not his death at least a sacrifice? Not if by sacrifice we understand the offering of gifts symbolizing human's self-surrender to God. For him, death was not a symbol, it was reality itself, the reality of a life lived out in self-giving to God in his fellow humans. If his blood was poured out 'for many', so is the blood of any human poured out in the service of others.

9

Existential Liberation

Up to now, we have been critically examining the response of Jesus to the cosmic, social, political and religious bondage of his people. Now it remains for us to see how he reacted to what we termed at the beginning of this book as the bondage within. We shall leave out of consideration the problem of psychic determinism originating in the subconscious and the unconscious since it could not have been perceived as such by Jesus or by his contemporaries. In this chapter, we shall focus our attention only on three fundamental issues: ignorance about the meaning of life, the ambivalence and vulnerability of freedom, and the experience of life as *being-unto-death.*

Admittedly, Jesus could not have posed these questions in the same terms in which we frame them. We of the twentieth century have a more articulate awareness of our existence as subjects than people of earlier ages. The conquest of nature through science and technology has sharpened our awareness that we are not mere playthings in the hands of blind cosmic forces but real subjects of history. Besides, the capitalist system in which we live, with its dominant ethos of private interest and competition, tends to reduce each one to an island, thus forcing one to look at the nakedness of one's subjectivity. Finally, researches in psychology have brought to light the existence of the subconscious and the unconscious in humans and their influence on conscious decision and behavior. For these reasons the problems of subjectivity have assumed new dimensions of meaning that they did not have for our forebears.

In the earlier stages of their history, the Israelites led a tribal life. What mattered then was the group, not the individual. The consciousness of the individual was subsumed under that of the collectivity. It was only later, at the time of the monarchy, that the individual as such emerged. With that, the problem of individual destiny began increasingly to occupy Hebrew minds.[1] Still, the individual as a subject had not completely come into his own. It is probable that even at the time of Jesus his emergence was an ongoing process. It is therefore but natural that in his time, the problems of subjectivity were not acutely felt or sharply focused. This being the case, it would be futile to look for a clear formulation or discussion of them in the Gospels. Such problems were existentially experienced rather than consciously and explicitly articulated. Probably, even that existential experience was only inchoative and germinal when compared with our own. The following reflections are, therefore, nothing more than an attempt to draw out what is implicitly contained in the message of Jesus.

Discovery of Ultimate Meaning

Nowhere in the Synoptic Gospels does Jesus pose the problem of the meaning of life in abstract, philosophical terms. In the Bible, the notion of meaning, when applied to human existence, tends to coincide with that of the good. A person is good if he is as he ought to be. The entire message of Jesus may be characterized as a call addressed to humans to become what they ought to be, in other words, to pass from inauthentic to authentic existence. The call is made not only to individuals but also to the community as a whole. Communal life is meaningful in the measure in which it approximates to what God intended it to be. And what God intends as the final outcome of the historical process is the realization of his reign, the maturation, and plenitude of the New Humanity. The communion of all with one another and with God is the horizon of ultimate meaning. That humans, individual and community, will meet God, and in meeting him, achieve the fullness of meaning is an essential feature of the message of Jesus. "How blessed are those whose hearts are pure; they shall see God." It is in seeing the face of God that humans will see their true visages and discover their true identities. It is from God that they will receive their true names. The name each human gives oneself is a false name or at least an inadequate one. Truer is the name others give him/her. Truest of all is the name one receives from God. For God to name is to create. And the name whereby God will call each human will express one's true essence as a member of one's household: "How blessed are the peacemakers; God shall call them his sons."

It would, however, be wrong to think that man will meet God apart from, or over the heads of, his fellow humans. It is in the radiance of the myriad human faces that surround one that each human will discover the face of God as well as one's true visage. It is the millions who call one 'brother' or 'sister' that constitute one as a son/daughter of God. God is not outside the human community. He is the depth-dimension of the love that binds the many into the one.

For the individual as well as for the community the final revelation of meaning is a matter of hope. A human is ever a pilgrim in search of him who renders everything meaningful. This does not mean that life is like passing through a tunnel whose end alone brings us to the realm of light. Absolute meaning reveals itself to us, though only inchoatively, in the here and now of everyday life. It is experienced not only as an absence but also as a presence. And there are privileged moments when the Presence is so intense that it grips us at the very roots of our being and radically reorients us from within.

To take hold of this Presence or, rather, to be taken hold of by it, a human has to remain inwardly open to it. This inward openness is an essential element of the faith that Jesus demanded from his hearers. The meaning remains hidden from all those who shut themselves up within the shell of their self-sufficiency. That is why Jesus could speak of God's 'hiding these things (that is, the things concerning the birth of the

New Humanity in the heart of the old) from the learned and the wise, and revealing them to the simple' (Luke 10:21). The same idea seems to underlie the following saying, "To you the secret of the kingdom of God has been given; but to those who are outside, everything comes by way of parables, so that (as Scripture says) they may look and look, but see nothing; they may hear and hear, but understand nothing; otherwise they might turn to God and be forgiven" (Mark 4:11-12). Joachim Jeremias has shown that what we have here is a detached saying which has nothing to do with parable proper. The term parable here stands for the original Aramaic word, matla, meaning 'riddle'. According to him, the original would be, "God has disclosed the mystery of his reign to you, but to those outside, everything happens in riddles . . . unless they return and God forgives them."[2] It is significant that turning to - which is what conversion means - is indicated as a prerequisite for understanding the hidden purposes of God. Some truths can be known only by the pure of heart, by those who are prepared for unconditional surrender and the risk of total love. Ultimate meaning unveils itself only to those who in faith and love remain open to its presence.

To encounter meaning is to arrive at a moment of decision. And where the ultimate meaning is in question, the decision has to be radical, affecting life in its entirety. It requires putting on a new mind and a new heart. The call of absolute meaning assumes priority over all other concerns and requires the relativization of all other values. "The kingdom of Heaven is like treasure lying buried in a field. The man who found it, buried it again; and for sheer joy went and sold everything he had, and bought that field" (Matt. 13:44-46). More, he who has encountered the ultimate meaning and has made a radical option in favor of it has to remain faithful to it, cost what it may. "No one who sets his hand to the plough and then keeps looking back is fit for the kingdom of God" (Luke 9:62).

The decision required by an encounter with meaning has to be translated into practice - personal and social. The meaning perceived has to be endowed with a body; it must find structural expression in the customs, laws, and institutions of society. The practice aims to bring individuals and society closer to their ultimate horizon of meaning. To do so is to create new meanings. And to create new meanings is to encounter the ultimate meaning at a deeper level. The appropriation of meaning is a spiral movement from the encounter to praxis and from praxis to deeper and richer modes of encounter, and so on indefinitely. It is on purpose that we qualify the process as indefinite, for neither encounter nor praxis will exhaust the possibilities of ultimate meaning. Even with the realization of the New Humanity, the Absolute will remain not only a presence but also an absence.

Jesus not only taught but also uniquely embodied in his person the meaning of life. His teaching was not something added on to his life. It was the radiance of his life itself. To encounter him is to be in the presence of someone whose word and deed somehow reveal the meaning of all human existence. In his openness to the Absolute, in his unconditional loyalty to the reign of God, in his resolute opposition to evil in every form, in his single-mindedness, in his stubborn refusal to compromise, in his undaunted courage in facing the consequences of his commitment, in his encompassing sympathy for the poor and the outcast — in all this we have a concrete manifestation of what it means to lead an authentic life.

Reintegration of Freedom

A human is the only being on earth that is always more than what it is. Every other being has set limits, definite boundaries. They change and grow within certain foreordained limits. A human, on the contrary, is always reaching out beyond oneself into the infinite. One lives and moves within an absolute horizon that confronts him/her with unconditional demands. At every step, one is faced with an 'ought'. One cannot ignore this 'ought' without denying oneself. The 'ought' implies that one can act in accordance with it. Freedom consists precisely in the spontaneity with which a human grows into what he/she ought to be. It consists less in the possibility of choosing between good and evil than in the self-unfolding of the spirit unto the good and the true.

Freedom is the spontaneous doing of what one ought to do, the joyous pursuit of the good and the true, and hence it is more an ideal to be striven after than a quality humans already possess. If in actual life one often does what one ought to do, it is not without struggle and suffering. The pursuit of good is accompanied by tension, conflict, anxiety, and doubt. One is often torn between the urge to do good and the temptation to do evil, as though in the innermost recess of one's soul there is a rupture and a division. In consequence, one is prey to internal instability and insecurity. One finds oneself vulnerable at the center of one's selfhood. One faces the constant threat of falling away from the pursuit of the good. One realizes that one is condemned to the frightening possibility of using one's freedom to hate rather than to love, to inflict death rather than to bestow life, to demolish rather than to build up. In short, freedom itself appears to one as a burden and bondage. It is this crucial problem that St. Paul had in mind when he wrote,

> "I discover this principle, then: that when I want to do the right, only the wrong is within my reach. In my inmost self, I delight in the law of God, but I perceive that there is in my bodily members a different law, fighting against the law that my reason approves and making me a prisoner under the law that is in my members, the law of sin. Miserable creature that I am, who is there to rescue me out of this body doomed to death?" (Rom. 7:21-24).

The ambivalence and vulnerability of freedom are at the root of sin; i.e., one's failure to do what one knows one ought to do. Repeated sins react to the character of the individual and predispose him to deviate further from the good. In this way, freedom becomes all the more vulnerable. Moreover, sins leave in the doer a sense of guilt, which paralyzes one's spirit and cramps his/her creativity. It is to this complex of vulnerability, sin, and guilt that we refer to when we use the term 'bondage of sin' in this chapter.

The bondage of sin is to a considerable extent historically and culturally conditioned. In any society, the rigorous enforcing of obsolete and inane laws and the proliferation of ever-new ones create a sense of spiritual impotence among the people. In consequence, such laws are honored more in their breach than in their observance. Those who violate them in bad faith become burdened with the sense of guilt. Similarly, economic exploitation and inhuman social conditions force the poor to take to thieving, prostitution, and the like to make a living. Thus structural sin begets personal sins. Conversely, the personal sinfulness of individuals may give birth to structural evils in society in the form of dehumanizing laws, institutions, and customs.

How did Jesus respond to the challenge of liberation from the bondage of sin? His radical criticism of law and cult strikes at the social roots of sin. His teaching on a man's being the master of the Sabbath means that the violation of laws does not constitute a sin where these do not serve the good of humans. The same conclusion may be drawn from his criticism of cult. The primacy of mercy over cult that he proclaimed removes the very source of much useless guilt feeling among believers who fail to observe all the minute observances prescribed by traditional religion. Furthermore, he abolishes every form of obligation in the sense of 'being bound', since he makes love the fundamental principle of all human striving. And where there is love there is no sense of being bound. Or, rather, love is both necessity and freedom in one. To be bound by love is the supreme realization of freedom.

However, Jesus was concerned more with the roots of the bondage of sin in the hearts of humans than with its social basis. And the roots of human can be healed only if one is open to the forgiving love of God. This, in a nutshell, was his answer to the problem of human frailty, sin, and guilt. To grasp it meaningfully it might help to reflect on a human analogy.

It is a matter of common experience that love is a force that heals and integrates humans. One who is not loved feels inwardly insecure and vulnerable when faced with the innumerable demands that the world makes on him/her. One lacks that vital milieu in which alone one can be truly spontaneous and free. But the day one receives genuine love from a human, one undergoes a profound internal change. One finds one's moorings, feels secure and rooted in the center of one's being, in the center of all being. The wide range of possibilities and options, which used to confuse and bewilder one, become from now onward subordinated to one's new-found love. His/her life takes on direction and meaning. What is more, before the person one loves, one regains spontaneity. The experience of love dissolves all that inhibits and constricts him/her. Even one's failures and defects cease to be a burden to him/her. One knows that one is accepted as one is with all his/her shortcomings. In short, the invasion of love from without brings about a reintegration of one's personality and frees one from his/her internal shackles. All this is true in its way also of a person's relation to society. The love of the community shown through recognition, acceptance, and forgiveness heals and reintegrates its members from within. This is the basis of our hope that a truly socialist society in which the person is recognized as the supreme value will have a therapeutic effect on its members and will help release their creative energies.

Now, if the limited, and in itself ambivalent, love of our fellow humans can help heal and reintegrate us from within, how much more can divine love!

Jesus brought the good news that the forgiving love of God is always there for man to take hold of. Divine forgiveness is available to all those, only to those, who are poor, i.e., those who recognize their need for it. The first beatitude must be understood in the exclusive sense to mean, "Only the poor have the blessings of God." Mark says so explicitly, "I came to invite not virtuous people, but sinners" (Mark 2:17). Similarly, the saying, "I tell you this: Tax-gatherers and prostitutes are entering the kingdom of God ahead of you", means: "Publicans and prostitutes will enter the kingdom of God, and not you."[3] The supreme generosity of divine forgiveness comes into bold relief in the parable of the prodigal son. The father of the family does not wait for the son to come and fall at his feet asking for pardon. On the contrary, while the son 'was still a long way off, his father saw him, and his heart went out to him. He ran to meet him, flung his arms around him, and kissed him' (Luke 15:20).

Jesus describes the forgiveness of God as a creative, saving force that touches a human in the depth of one's being, where one is alone with oneself, and refashions one from within. He expresses this idea in the language of symbols. Forgiveness is compared to the remission of debt where the debtor is freed from bondage to the moneylender (Matt. 18:27). It is likened to bringing home a lamb that had strayed away and got entangled in a mesh of briars and thorns (Luke 15:5). Here too the idea of liberation is stressed along with that of the offer of security. The son who erred is welcomed back, clothed in the best robes, offered ring and shoes - all of which are gestures whereby the father recognizes him as a free man. Forgiveness brings about also the reconciliation of the sinner with the community. The prodigal son is received back into the family to enjoy once again the freedom that belongs to him as a son. From now on he is like one risen from the dead.

The power of forgiveness to remold human from within is brought out still more clearly in the story of the adulterous woman who wetted Jesus' feet with her tears, wiped them with her hair, and anointed them with myrrh. To the Pharisee, his host, who was scandalized at this, Jesus said, "I tell you, her great love proves that her many sins have been forgiven; where little has been forgiven, little love is shown" (Luke 7:47). It is not said that her sins were forgiven, because she loved much. Just the opposite is what is meant: She loved much because she was forgiven much. In other words, it was the experience of divine forgiveness that made her capable of loving much. That experience touched the core of her being and released the powers of loving that were atrophied. If love is what is most human in humans, then we may say that forgiveness humanized her. Love is also that act that is supremely free. If so, we may equally say that forgiveness, by activating her capacity to love, brought her inner freedom. It saved her from internal disequilibrium and vulnerability. Elsewhere in the miracle stories, the re-creative effects of divine forgiveness are represented as overflowing into the body and rendering it whole.

What is remarkable about the teaching of Jesus is that he views divine forgiveness as something that man can mediate to his fellow humans. It was the gracious presence and words of Jesus, the man from Nazareth, that communicated the forgiving love of God to the woman of ill fame. Similarly, when he told the paralytic, "Your sins are forgiven", he was not claiming to be the ultimate source of forgiveness. (The use of the passive is a device the Hebrews resorted to lest they profane the name of God.) What he meant to convey was: "God has forgiven you your sins." Jesus was not more than the vehicle that conveyed to the sick man the forgiveness of God. Any human may become the instrument of divine forgiveness, as is clear from the prayer Jesus taught his disciples, "Forgive us the wrong we have done, as we have forgiven those who have wronged us" (Matt. 6:12). What we have here is not a petition that God may forgive us in the same manner as we forgive others or because we forgive others, but a declaration of our willingness to pass on to others the forgiveness we have received. The petition may, therefore, be paraphrased thus: "Grant your forgiveness to us who are ready to mediate it to our fellow humans." Where one forgives one's neighbor we have a revelation of the forgiveness of God. It is in the measure in which one experiences the liberating forgiveness of God that one becomes capable of liberating others from internal insecurity, sin, and guilt.

However, a human is not a mere passive recipient of divine mercy. The reverse of divine forgiveness is repentance on the part of humans. The offer of forgiveness is accompanied by the call to repent. Repentance demands the restructuring of one's whole life, a coming back to one's senses (Luke 15:17), a recognition of one's guilt, and a preparedness to be reconciled to others and give up one's evil ways (Luke 19:8-9; Matt. 5:23-24; Mark 10:17-31). If repentance and divine forgiveness produce identical effects, does not the one render the other superfluous? The problem resolves itself when we realize that the relation between the two is analogical. It is divine forgiveness that disposes a human to repentance. Conversely, it is repentance that makes one inwardly attuned to receive the forgiveness of God, which heals and restructures one at one's roots.

Love Is Stronger than Death

What is the use of winning freedom from ignorance and sin, if such freedom as is won is doomed to succumb to the necessity of death? It is small consolation to suggest that mankind as such will continue to exist even if individuals die and disappear from the scene. Are individuals mere tools that some blind destiny makes use of to achieve its inscrutable ends only to discard them once they have served their purpose? Are they mere stepping-stones to help humanity climb higher and higher until it reaches the New Heaven and the New Earth? Let us see what light the message of Jesus sheds on the problem of individual survival.

It is necessary to see things from a historical perspective. The early Hebrews did not believe in any real survival after death. They saw the dead confined to a desolate region called Sheol and endowed with some sort of shadowy existence. It is only in the postexilic writings that we find traces of belief in an afterlife and resurrection, which, in all probability, the Jews took over from the Persians or the Egyptians. In the time of Jesus, it was the Pharisees who believed in the resurrection. The Sadducees, on the contrary, rejected such a belief as alien to the original revelation contained in the Pentateuch.

It is beyond doubt that Jesus shared the Pharisaic belief in the resurrection of the dead. To discredit belief in the resurrection, the Sadducees posed him the following question: If the dead rise from the dead, whose wife will a woman be in the life to come, who while on earth was wife to seven brothers consecutively, all of whom died without leaving any children? Jesus replied: "You are mistaken, and surely this is the reason: you do not know either the scriptures or the power of God. When they rise from the dead, men and women do not marry; they are like angels in heaven. But about the resurrection of the dead, have you never read in the Book of Moses, in the story of the burning bush, how God spoke to him and said, 'I am the God of Abraham, the God of Isaac, and the God of Jacob'? God is not God of the dead but the living" (Mark 12:18-26). If God declares himself as being in the present the God of the patriarchs, the latter could not have just succumbed to death forever. The argument of Jesus may not be convincing, but his mind is clear enough. Elsewhere in his reply to the disciples of John the Baptist, he includes the resurrection of the dead in the blessings of the New Age: "Go and tell John what you have seen and heard: how the blind recover their sight; the lame walk, the lepers are made clean, the deaf hear, the dead are raised to life, the poor are hearing the good news" (Luke 7:22-23).

Belief in some form of survival after death is presupposed also in the teaching of Jesus on righteousness and its reward. A human's conduct here and now is of decisive significance for one's absolute future. "Be careful not to make a show of your religion before men; if you do, no reward awaits you in your Father's house in heaven. . . Do not store up for yourselves treasures on earth, where it grows rusty and moth-eaten, and thieves break in to steal it. Store up treasure in heaven, where there is no moth and no rust to spoil it, no thieves to break in and steal" (Matt. 6:1, 19-20). Note that the reward promised will be realized not in the present alienated existence but 'in heaven', in other words, in the New Humanity.

What is it that entitles a human to membership in the New Humanity that is not subject to death? Here we meet with an astounding paradox in the teaching of Jesus, namely, that he promises reward only to those who do not seek any reward. "But you must love your enemies and do good, and lend without expecting any return, and you will have a rich reward" (Luke 6:35). Not self-interest but self-giving is what assures survival after death. Those who live for their selfish ends will forfeit the true life. "Whoever seeks to save his life will lose it; and whoever loses it will save it, and live" (Luke 17:32-33). Now, to give without expecting a return is the essence of love. If so, there is a strict correlation between love and the true life that does not succumb to death.

Underlying his teaching is a conception of history as made up of two opposing currents - one leading to decay and death; the other, to life that endures forever. The current of life is in the final analysis God as self-giving love, living and working in history. He is at work giving himself to humans and gathering them into a community of love. A man has the frightful option to identify oneself either with the current of death or with that of life. One opts for death when one makes one's fragile self the center of all and reduces one's fellow humans to a position of means to one's ends. This, in the language of Jesus, is what is meant by 'seeking to save one's life'. Those, on the contrary, who, like God, give themselves to others in service insert themselves in the current of life that carries them forward into the absolute future that lies beyond death. Belief in the resurrection expresses the hope that God accepts the life of those who surrender themselves to him by living for their fellow humans. Therefore, it is also a challenge addressed to humans to affirm the forces of life, such as love, friendship, cooperation, and the solidarity of all, and to fight the forces of death—illness, poverty, egoism, hatred, injustice, inequality, and oppression. Only those will rise to new life who help their fellow humans break the fetters that chain them to powers that kill both body and soul.

At this point, a word of caution is in order. Survival after death as taught by Jesus is not to be confused with the immortality of the soul. This latter concept was smuggled into Christianity from Greek philosophy. In contrast to the Greeks, the Hebrews did not conceive of man as a soul imprisoned in a body. For them, a man was a unity, an animated body rather than an enfleshed spirit. The soul was nothing but the inwardness of the body, and the body nothing but the outwardness of the soul.[5] They could not, therefore, have conceived the existence of the soul without the body. In their eyes, any survival was bound to have a bodily dimension. It is along the same lines that Jesus, too, must have conceived the destiny of many after death. It is equally probable that he could not have thought of the resurrection of the individual apart from the community of men. For Hebrew thinking, the body, not the soul, was the principle of human solidarity.[6] The body was also the basis of continuity with the material universe. Presuming that Jesus shared the Hebrew mode of thinking, we may conclude that he too thought of individual survival as intimately bound up with that of the community and the material world. But how are we to concretely envisage individual survival after death? To this question, Jesus does not give any answer. Possibly he did not know the answer. Or he would answer as he did the Sadducees, "You do not know the power of God."

10

Jesus and the Oppressed of Today

In the life and message of Jesus, we witness the emergence of a new force in history for the liberation of man, a force at once human and divine, subversive and constructive. For those who have encountered him, he represents the most powerful and authentic expression hitherto of human striving for the fullness of being. He is a brother to all who believe in the fraternity of humans, a friend to all who look forward to the dawn of the age of freedom. As a quester after freedom, Jesus can be a source of light and inspiration to the millions in India who are groaning under the weight of organized oppression. In this concluding chapter, we shall try to show how his message can become a creative force for the liberation of the Indian masses. We shall deal only marginally with the problem of existential liberation, not because it is unimportant but because it has all along received sufficient attention, whereas liberation from the social system and the system of values has been sadly neglected.

The question regarding the relevance of Jesus for social liberation today could be raised from two different standpoints. First, from the standpoint of one who is not a disciple of Jesus but has a certain appreciation of his person and message, and is open to the conviction that he may have something relevant to say. Thus a Hindu, a Muslim, or even a Marxist may study the Gospels and derive from them inspiration and guidance for radical commitment. Second, from the standpoint of a disciple who has encountered Jesus and identified himself/herself with his faith, commitment, and destiny. A disciple is personally involved with one's master and, therefore, cannot view his teaching in a spirit of detached objectivity. It is in the spirit of personal loyalty that we are approaching the problem.

The Jesus-Community

No disciple of Jesus is an island. He/she is related to other disciples in time and space. The roots of one's discipleship go back to the past, to the simple Galilean fishermen whom Jesus called to be with him, i.e.to share his vision and commitment, and to the millions of others who have laid down their lives for his cause. A disciple of Jesus is also in communion with his/her counterparts all over the world. He/she is thus inserted into an invisible fellowship of humans, one in their oneness with Jesus. Let us call this fellowship the Jesus-community. It is in solidarity with this community that we are raising the problem regarding the relevance of Jesus for human liberation. The answer too depends, to a great extent, on the self-understanding of the same Community. For it is primarily through this fellowship of his disciples that Jesus of yesterday can become present to the oppressed of today. A few reflections, therefore, on the nature of the Community may be found useful.

What distinguishes the Jesus-community from all other religious communities is its being centered upon Jesus through sharing his faith and hope. Now, the object of Jesus' faith and hope was the God ahead who is to come to sum up everything. Every fiber of his being, all the energies of his soul and body are strained to that ultimate future. Hence to be centered upon him means for the disciples to be drawn into a current that carries them beyond him to God. Their destiny as disciples is to march with him to the unknown ahead. They are essentially a community of pilgrims.

But the God of Jesus is one who is at work in the world fashioning New Humanity by giving himself to all, irrespective of caste, creed, community, race, region, or culture. Of this universal community, the fellowship of disciples is only a fragment. Hence the paradox: What distinguishes the Jesus-community is its belief in the New Humanity, which does not admit of any distinction. A disciple of Jesus has, therefore, to accept as brothers and sisters all those to whom God reveals himself in whatever way he chooses. He/she must further recognize that those outside the Community may have encountered God at a deeper level than those within. If so, the Community is not a sect opposed to other sects; nor does it represent a religion opposed to other religions.

All this represents a departure from past Christian attitudes. There was a time when Christians believed that those who did not share their faith were barred from the road to salvation and therefore went all-out to convert them. Eventually, when the theology of conversion became discredited, they began to think of their mission in terms of developing the underdeveloped, an approach based on the, to them, comforting assumption that they were developed while others were not. In recent times, the concept of development having gone out of vogue, they have started chanting the slogan of liberating the unliberated. All through these developments, one thing remained constant, namely the conviction that they were the 'haves' and the rest the 'have-nots'. The Community has to disown this arrogant, self-righteous understanding of its mission in history. They must recognize, and rejoice in, the fact that those outside are being saved, developed, and liberated to the degree to which they respond to the challenge of God in history. Their mission consists not so much in work for the liberation of others as in seeking liberation with others. They have as much to learn from others as others have to learn from them. The only thing they have and others do not, is their personal encounter with Jesus as mediating the presence of God. It follows from this that their presence and action in the world has always to be ecumenical in the sense of *being-with-all* and *working-with-all.*

For the Community, to be centered upon Jesus is to follow the way he showed. He did not seek to establish the reign of God using economic, social, and political power. He refused to turn stones into bread, just as he shunned the path of political messianism. His attitude to secular power is particularly relevant today, living as we do in a society that is becoming progressively secularized. Secularization means the vindication of society because of its relative autonomy vis-a-vis faith and organized religion and, as such, points to the coming-of-age of humanity. It must be welcomed as an instance of the self-liberation of humans in history. The Community, therefore, has no right to claim any special competence in secular matters in virtue of its religious faith. Nor is it empowered by its faith to exercise any secular authority over fellow citizens. As regards, for instance, the organization of production or the structuring of political power, it has no exclusive source of knowledge. In these matters, it has to depend as much on reason as any other group of citizens. By recognizing this, it will have a clearer understanding of the limits within which it has to work for the construction of a better world, and therefore also of the need for dialogue and collaboration with others.

These preliminary reflections on the nature of the Community must be understood as applicable to all that we are going to say on its liberating role in India. One more word of caution: The reader should not conclude from our discussion thus far that commitment to liberation is something added on to the nature of the Community viewed as already constituted in itself. The Community is what it does. It has to fashion its nature in the very process of commitment. It is, therefore, less an institution than a 'project' in the root sense of the word. It is always in the process of becoming what it is, what it ought to be.

Keeping Hope Alive

The mission of the Jesus-community is the same as that of Jesus, namely, to set the oppressed free. To fulfill this mission it must first of all quicken and sustain man's hope in New Humanity as the ultimate point of arrival of all struggle for liberation.

Hope is not just one virtue among others, like chastity or patience, which one may fail to practice and yet live. It is the very climate of the human spirit, the air it breathes to live. To lose hope is to die, is to lapse into nonbeing. This holds of the individual as well as of society. When, for instance, someone takes up a profession, he is making an act of hope that he will be able to cope with the task. When a boy and a girl decide to marry, they do so in the hope that they will be true to each other and be able to meet the demands of life together. Similarly, when people opt for a new model of society they do so in the hope that they will be able to create and maintain it. All those who undertake to teach the young, or reforming the deviant, harbor the hope that their efforts will bear fruit in the future. Where hope has withered away, individuals end their lives, families disintegrate, political systems collapse, and the educational system comes to a standstill. If so, hope is a constituent of all secular life, whether individual or collective. Of this secular hope, religious hope is the depth-dimension. The latter comes to the foreground when, for example, the professional, the politician, or the educationist is willing to sacrifice everything else for the sake of his or her respective hope. What renders everything else relative can only belong to the dimension of the absolute.

If hope is the mainspring of history, any crisis affecting it bodes ill for the future of humanity. There are in fact symptoms of such a crisis in India: the widespread cynicism of the intellectuals, the deep sense of frustration found among the exploited masses, their servile, almost fatalistic submission to exploitation, the loss of idealism among the youth, and the dearth of committed leadership at all levels. The underlying vacuum of hope has to be filled if India is to march forward to a more just and humane society.

Who will fill this vacuum? Hinduism has still to exploit the wealth of its tradition to develop a vision of history fully in harmony with the self-understanding of contemporary humans. Marxism, with its hope in a classless society, did fill the vacuum up to a point, especially in the early stages of its presence in India. Unfortunately, it has in the meantime come to terms with the power politics of a caste and class society. As a result, the concept of classless society itself is fast degenerating into a sort of opium for the masses. Christians too have sinned against their hope by substituting for the New Heaven and the New Earth either the salvation of souls or the power and prestige of their respective churches.

Hence the relevance, more than ever, of Jesus' hope in the New Humanity as the absolute future of man. The oppressed masses will find in that hope a powerful motivation for radical action. Besides, by living within the horizon of their absolute future they will feel inwardly free from the tyranny of the past with its obsolete laws, institutions, and customs, and from an uncritical clinging to the present. It will foster that detachment which is so necessary for permanent revolution. Where it is lacking the revolutionaries of today will end up as the conservatives of tomorrow.

Hope in the New Humanity should not be regarded as alien to the people of India. It is implicit in the very longing of the oppressed masses for better days ahead. Even their hopelessness today presupposes that hope. Nor does the Jesuan hope stand in irreconcilable opposition to the original Marxian vision of the classless society, the latter being but a secular version of the former. The very dialectical thinking that helped Marx project the goal of a classless society also underlies the thought and language of Jesus, if not of the entire Bible. For what is the reign of God but the negation (the final supersession) of the negation of man (consisting of illness, death, inequality, domination, and sin)? In saying this we are not overlooking the basic difference that for Jesus the negation of negation is the work of humans in dialogue with God, whereas for Marx it is to be achieved solely through collective human effort. But do not Marxists affirm in the act of unconditional commitment what they deny in theory? The scope of this chapter forbids our enlarging upon this theme. Suffice it to remember that the hope in the New Humanity is in accord with the implicit aspiration of the masses and with the fundamental thrust of the Marxian vision. It is this convergence of hopes that provides the basis for common effort for the liberation of the masses.

The ultimate hope is not a product of creative phantasy but a life-force sustaining individual and collective life. Therefore it cannot be instilled in the masses solely through writing, preaching, or propaganda. Of course, art, literature, and the mass media can to some extent be used to instill that hope. But the more powerful generators of hope are to be sought at the level of social practice. What is the use of trying to communicate hope in a classless society to people who have little hope of earning enough bread for the morrow or of breaking loose from the clutches of the moneylender? Hope grows only where chains are broken, barriers overcome, and walls pulled down. It dies out where man is not able to overthrow the oppressive structures of the present. There is, therefore, no more effective way for the Community to create and foster collective hope in the New Humanity than to participate in the day-to-day struggles of the people. Such participation is necessary also to legitimize and validate its hope. For how can it proclaim the New Humanity as the fulfillment of history if it chooses to live outside the main current of history? How can it bear witness to the New Age as the fruit of theandric dialogue if it refuses to have a dialogue with the God manifesting himself in the life of the people? How can it hold up the Total Human as the final goal of liberation if it shuns holding hands with the fragments of humanity around?

But is not the Jesuan vision of the New Humanity incapable of inspiring the humans of today, considering that it is conceived as the end of history, and therefore also as the end of all creativity, quest, friendship, and love? True, traditional Christianity has popularized the notion of 'the end of the world'. The term is wrong if taken in the literal sense; right if taken in the dialectical sense. The New Age is not the end of history in the sense in which we speak of the end of colonialism in India. What ends history cannot, at the same time, fulfill it. The New Age is, therefore, the end only of history as we know it, of the history of man's alienation. In a very true sense, it is equally the dawn of the authentic history of humans, of history, still, of quest, growth, friendship, love, and creativity.

Towards a Penultimate Model

The ultimate horizon of hope will always remain an asymptotic concept, i.e. one that can never adequately express the reality it signifies. It belongs to the order of legitimate myth. The perception of the depth-dimension of any reality can be expressed, if at all, only in symbols and myths. The mythical character of the ultimate hope is at once a strength and a weakness: a strength because only myths symbolizing the ineffable can elicit commitment unto death. They alone can galvanize humans into concerted action, appealing, as they do, to the conscious as well as the subconscious, to the rational as well as the emotional. None will lay down his life for an abstract system of philosophy or dry economic formula. That is why every revolution hitherto has projected its array of myths. The mythical character of the ultimate hope is also a weakness and a limitation. For the mythical cannot provide concrete guidelines for action here and now. To become an operative concept it has to crystallize into a workable project, which is what we mean by the penultimate model.

How this model has to be formulated can be none other than how the ultimate hope itself emerges in human consciousness. The latter, we have seen, is not just an empty dream or phantasy. It takes shape in consciousness through a spontaneous negation of the evils of today. In formulating the penultimate model, we are but making explicit the path of negation taken by the human spirit in projecting the ultimate hope. Negation here is to be understood dialectically as implying also an affirmation of whatever is true and good in the existing conditions. Also, it has to be based on a scientific analysis of the prevailing social system and its ideology.

Any model, however scientifically constructed, will necessarily be provisional. It will need constant revision in the light of subsequent experience. The model thus revised will become the basis for further action, which in turn will demand a further revision of the model, thus indefinitely. Though provisional at any given stage, it may call for an unconditional commitment until it once again proves itself to be inadequate.

The construction of such a model is, understandably, an ecumenical and interdisciplinary task. The Community alone is not competent to formulate it. It can, however, bring the Jesuan vision of man and his destiny to bear upon the desired model so that it is in harmony with the integral good of humans. To give but one example, it cannot derive from the message of Jesus any concrete program for the reorganization of the bureaucracy. It can, however, demand that the bureaucracy is so structured as to promote the responsibility and the initiative of all citizens and criticize any model that is not likely to fulfill this condition. With these formal considerations in mind, let us now approach the problem of determining the content of a new model of society for the people of India. Prescribing a detailed model being out of the question, we shall confine ourselves to indicating the main structural principles that should guide its formulation, principles derived from our introductory analysis of Indian society.

CONTINUITY WITH THE PAST

Centuries of foreign domination and colonialism have made us materially and mentally slaves. Our economy is still, to a considerable extent, geared to the benefit of foreign capitalism or Soviet socialism. We are likewise subjected to a steady and powerful cultural invasion from the West to which we all too easily succumb. Even the refuse of Western civilization finds an honored place on our altars. We are progressively being reduced to a nation of cultural bastards. The colonial mentality has taken such deep root in the country that we can envision our future only in terms of imported models, whether American, Soviet, or Chinese. Now the time has come to reverse this trend by rediscovering our soul and establishing continuity with the past. This is not a defense of chauvinism or a plea for revivalism, but an appeal to construct a model incorporating the genuine values of our tradition. Only a society with deep roots in the past can promote true creativity.

PRODUCTION FOR THE PEOPLE

As regards the national economy, the existing disparities in wealth and income can be abolished only through need-based production and equitable distribution. By need-based production, we mean a system of production that gives priority to meeting the essential needs of the masses rather than to promoting conspicuous consumption on the part of the rich. Equitable distribution means apportioning income according to the service one renders to society (not according to discriminatory norms such as the superiority of intellectual over manual work) and, insofar as resources permit, also according to the objective needs of people, so that those who, for no fault of their own, are unable to contribute their share of work—children, the sick, the cripples, the aged, and the unemployed—will have enough to have a decent life.

SOCIALIZATION

It would, however, be wrong to think of human welfare solely in terms of production and consumption. As long as people have no control over the economy, a society with a high degree of consumption can be more dehumanizing than another that can provide only the bare necessities of life. Hence the need to stress the principle of socialization. Socialization does not consist in the equal distribution of the means of production, which, even if feasible, would mean not the abolition but the universalization of private property with its ethos of private interest and competition. Neither is it to be equated with nationalization which, instead of abolishing wage labor, reduces every citizen to the position of an employee of the state. True socialization demands that society as a whole at the various levels of its organization determines the ownership and the use of the productive forces. In a fully socialized society, there will no longer be private property understood as the absolute right to use and to misuse. All property will be either personal or communitarian: the former being owned by individuals but used by the will of the community as a whole; the latter being property owned and used by the community, whether it be of the village, the panchayat, the district, or the state.

SOLIDARITY

In a truly socialist society, there cannot be any dichotomy between economy and politics, between the community of producers and the community of citizens. In such a society, political decisions will also be a productive force; and the producers, active participants in political decisions. With this reservation in mind, let us consider the main principles that should determine the political structure.

One such principle is that of solidarity. The political community must be organized in such a way that the free development of all will be the condition for the free development of each. No individual or group should be allowed to use society as a whole as a means for furthering their ends. No one should be able to march ahead to a higher level of economic well-being or of culture without at the same time carrying along with him his weaker brothers and sisters. This means striking at the very roots of laissez-faire and individualism. However, the solidarity aimed at should not be that of a feudal society based on personal loyalty and dependence or of caste and joint-family, whose members were not real centers of decision. Nor should it be equated with that of dictatorship, which reduces the citizens to the level of mere things. What we should strive to achieve is the solidarity of persons as centers of decision and creators of their destiny. Our aim should be a form of human togetherness deriving from each one's concern and responsibility for all. Hence our initial formulation of the principle of solidarity must be read also in the reverse order to mean a society in which the free development of each will be the condition for the free development of all.

SUBSIDIARITY AND PLURALISM

To promote the free development of each we should, in constructing a model, adhere to the principle of subsidiarity. Subsidiarity requires that what any lower unit of society can accomplish should not normally be undertaken by a higher unit. For instance, what is within the competence of the individual should not be taken over by the family or the village community. Similarly, what the latter can do should not be done by the district or the state. Subsidiarity, therefore, implies the decentralization of power and decision making. The function of the state in the new order of things must not be to rule by dictates from above but to promote and coordinate initiatives from below, i.e.from the community of persons.

If subsidiarity is necessary to prevent over-centralization and dictatorship, respect for pluralism is necessary to prevent solidarity through rigid uniformity. India is a vast country with many religions, races, and regional cultures, each having its distinctive genius. Socialism does not require the leveling down of all these differences. It is not barrack communism. The different cultures and subcultures must be allowed to grow and bear fruit. Similarly, the uniqueness of each as a source of creativity must be cherished and fostered. So too, associations and fraternities representing diverse talents and interests must be encouraged so long as they do not hamper the common good.

A penultimate model in accord with the principles we have enunciated demands a new type of human, with a new consciousness, vision, and sense of values. What should the content of that new consciousness be? What should be the nature of law, morality, philosophy, and religion in the new society? What should be their function vis-a-vis economic and political life? These and similar questions, though crucial, cannot be gone into here. One thing, however, needs to be said: In the new social order, there should be no place for class consciousness based on class exploitation. Nor should there be any law, morality, philosophy, or religion emanating from the privileged classes and calculated to safeguard their interests. All forms of consciousness will have to draw nourishment from society as a whole and reflect its struggles and hopes.

Prophetic Protest

From our discussion so far, one might be tempted to conclude that Jesus-community is concerned more with the future than with the present, especially if one is used to think of the future and the present in terms of either-or. The future, whether proximate or ultimate, is not to be seen as a rival to the present. We have seen that it is in the present that the ultimate hope is encountered. It is equally the consideration of the present that enables us to construct a model for the future. In either case, we are thrown back on the present. The present was also the central concern of Jesus. What distinguished him from the prophets that went before was his message that the reign of God was already germinating in the present. It was he who, for the first time, invited his contemporaries to turn away from the excessive preoccupation with the future or the past and listen to the call of the present, of the present that summed up the past and was pregnant with the future. He demands the same attitude from his Community today.

READING THE SIGNS OF THE TIMES

If the New Humanity is silently growing in our present history, it is important for us to learn to recognize its presence. For how else could we take a stand about it? That is why Jesus enjoined his listeners to read the signs of the times. The signs are not just any event or situation but only those that carry significance for the ultimate future of humans. To discern them, one has to ask whether the event or situation in question contributes to the fullness of humans or not. Seen in this light, whatever embodies or fosters freedom, love, equality, cooperation, and solidarity are positive signs of the times; and whatever does not are negative signs. In many cases such discernment is easy enough; in others, truth is far different from what appears on the surface. For instance, putting up exclusive hostels for the benefit of Harijan boys and girls may seem a positive step in the direction of helping the underprivileged. But a little reflection is enough to show that such hostels will only perpetuate caste inequality. Where social processes or political movements are concerned, it is necessary to supplement or even correct mere impressionistic evaluations with social analysis.

The type of social analysis required for the correct reading of the signs of the times must fulfill certain conditions. It must, first of all, be structural, i.e. aimed at unveiling the dehumanizing character of the social system as a whole, not merely its superficial inadequacies. It is not enough, for example, to ascertain the depth and extent of poverty in India. What is needed is to lay bare its structural causes and show how they are detrimental to the true development of humans. The analysis must also be global, covering not only the laws and institutions of society but also the domain of ideology and human subjectivity. Thirdly, it must be futurological, by which we mean that it should bring out the long-term consequences for a human of the social facts under study. Finally, it must be scientific, as regards not only the tools of analysis but also the data it makes use of. The Community must take into consideration the result of the analysis conducted along these lines before making sociopolitical options. In other words, it must combine the prophetic and the scientific in one single commitment.

FOSTERING THE ENERGIES OF THE NEW AGE

The Community reads the signs of the times to act upon them. And its action will have to be twofold: fostering the energies of the New Age to come (the positive signs of the times) and fighting the forces of dehumanization (the negative signs). Its role in society is to be a two-edged sword that cuts to heal as well as to destroy. Its mission resembles that of the prophet Jeremiah, who was sent by Yahweh 'to pull down and to uproot, to destroy and to demolish, to build and to plant' (Jer. 1:10).

The positive social trends in India that need nurturing are many: the substitution of feudal loyalty with loyalty to goal-oriented associations and political parties: the organization of the working class; the politicization of the masses; the process of secularization; the progressive interdependence, in practice and consciousness, of the different castes, classes, races, and regions; the erosion of feudal ideas and values; the spread of a genuinely critical attitude to religion; the revolt of the youth against bourgeois morality; the transition from elitist to people's literature and art. These trends are, admittedly, riddled with ambiguity and internal weaknesses. Still, they are to be welcomed as representing the gropings of the people of India towards the horizon of the New Humanity.

Of all the humanizing forces the most significant are the socio-political movements of protest against prevailing conditions. The political parties inspired by the teachings of Marx and his followers have been in the vanguard of the people's struggle against feudal and capitalist forms of exploitation. They have to their credit the organization of the urban and rural proletariat in many parts of India. Very recently the Sarvodaya, which believes in a synthesis of Marxism and Gandhism, has come forward as the champion of the oppressed, especially in Bihar. Even in the more conservative Congress, there are critical individuals and groups sincerely committed to the eradication of social injustice and inequality. Finally, there is the wordless protest written large on the faces of the exploited millions whose collective resentment can, given the right kind of leadership, break out into open revolt.

NOT PEACE BUT THE SWORD

The disciples of Jesus cannot but make their own every form of legitimate protest in the country. They should feel a certain spontaneous affinity with all who denounce the oppression of man by man since they cherish the memory of Jesus, who had to pay the price of death for his option to protest. To refuse to join in the protest against injustice is to disown the God of the poor whom he proclaimed and join the ranks of his enemies, who make a living by killing the souls and bodies of men; it is a form of practical atheism.

Unfortunately, the socio-political movements of protest in India suffer from many limitations. They are often based on an inadequate or even false analysis of society and, therefore, are incapable of delivering the goods. Their leaders are also victims of dogmatism and ideological fixation. There is not enough self-criticism and independent thinking among them. Besides, the forces of protest neutralize one another, for their leaders indulge in mutual hatred and suspicion. For these reasons, the Community cannot fully identify itself with any of the existing radical movements. Neither can it ignore them; for despite their present limitations they alone have a record of service to the people. Such being the case, the most it can do is to offer them critical collaboration on issues where there is sufficient consensus. Meanwhile, it must also strive to provide a common platform where radicals of differing convictions can meet and sort out their differences.

However, neither critical collaboration nor efforts to reconcile warring radical factions seem to be adequate to meet today's challenge. The existing leftist movements resemble ancient decaying trees that are no longer capable of putting forth fresh shoots. There is little hope that they can be rejuvenated either through critical collaboration from without or through participation from within. Therefore, the most urgent need today is the creation of a new socio-political movement of liberation with a clearer perception of goals, a more adequate methodology of action, a truly committed leadership, and with a broader base among the masses. The cynicism of the common humans in the more politically conscious States of India regarding all existing political parties is clear proof that the time is ripe for such a venture. Nothing less than a new movement for liberation can mobilize the revolutionary potential contained in the silent protest of the masses.

The Community has to protest not only against the existing social system but also against the failure of its leaders to protest when protest was their bounden duty. What protest the latter made till recently was highly selective regarding its target. They fumed with moral indignation when their minority rights were tampered with; but showed little concern when the rights of the underprivileged, who form the majority, were brutally violated. They protested vehemently against those who called in question the traditional sexual morality but callously closed their eyes to the inhumanity of a social system that forces thousands of innocent girls to take to prostitution to make a living. They roared in anger against those who defended the legitimacy of artificial contraception but chose to be silent in the face of an economy that condemned millions of children to illness and premature death. In their zeal for the unborn, they forgot about those others who had the misfortune to be born. True, in recent times they have come out with radical pronouncements on social justice. But, these were not seriously meant became abundantly clear when they disowned and victimized the few who tried to put the teaching of their leaders into practice.

Freedom Through Revolution

The protest must be translated into action for the radical restructuring of society and the fundamental revision of its ideology. The transformation aimed at must also be rapid. Resigning ourselves to a gradual transition to a more just society will amount to condemning generations of men, women, and children to subhuman existence. The rapidity of change is, up to a point, conditional upon certain objective factors, such as the extent of corporate production, the progress of mass media, and the degree of organization of the masses. But much more decisive are the subjective factors related to the conscious intervention and free decision of humans. The objective need for change must also become a subjective, felt need. The intensity with which the members of a society experience the contradiction between the prevailing system and their emergent self-understanding will largely determine the speed of change. And when people commit themselves to bring about radical and rapid change through conscious and planned intervention they are opting for social revolution as distinguished from social evolution.

But revolution should not be understood merely in the narrow sense of overthrowing the social system. Its goal is, in the final analysis, the creation of a new human; and, since what distinguishes human from animals and the world of things is consciousness, it is, at the same time, the creation of a new consciousness, consisting in a new sensitiveness, a new sense of values, and a new vision of the world. A merely structural revolution will prove itself self-defeating where there has not been a corresponding revolution of consciousness. For new structures, however perfect, are liable to be exploited by individuals and groups to serve their selfish ends.

If the goal of revolution is the creation not only of a new social system but also of a new consciousness, it is evident that the process of revolution itself must be such as to give birth to that consciousness. In other words, there must be a continuity between the consciousness of the future and the consciousness of the men of today who create the future. How could a people, ruled by private interest and lust for power, usher in a society in which each person will see in the good of all his good? How can those moved by envy, hatred, and revengefulness create an order in which man's greatest need will be his fellow humans? How can selfishness beget concern for others, hatred beget love, competition begets cooperation? Hence the need to stress the importance of developing the right type of revolutionary consciousness.

If revolutionary consciousness is itself a process of growing into the consciousness of the new human, it is clear that it cannot be viewed merely as a means for overthrowing structures. What is the very source of human creativity cannot be made subservient to any of its functions or creations. Humans are greater than the structures they bring into existence. The growth of revolutionary consciousness is therefore not only a step towards the structural revolution but also a realization, however partial, of the revolution itself. The radicals who forget this are likely to fall victim to discouragement and frustration when they see the goal of structural revolution receding into a distant future. If as a result of their action, some more people have become critical of the status quo and concerned about the fate of their weaker brothers and sisters, they can rest assured that they have already sown the seeds of total revolution.

What should be the content of revolutionary consciousness? In answer, we can provide here only a few general observations. The consciousness in question must, first of all, be critical; i.e.it must include an awareness not only of the fact but also of the extent and the mechanisms of exploitation and dehumanization. Secondly, it must be practical, in the sense of being oriented to — and, wherever possible, born of — concrete involvement in the struggle for liberation. Thirdly, it must be humane, i.e.instinct with gentleness, kindness and an encompassing concern and compassion for all. Fourthly, it must be communitarian, by which we mean that the consciousness of the many must fuse into one collective subversive force, which, naturally, is not possible without the organization of the exploited. Fifthly, it must be prospective, having for its goal the construction of a new model of society. Finally, it must have the character of the unconditional and the ultimate, lest revolutionists, having put their hands to the plow, look back or, what is worse, betray the cause of revolution for lesser values.

Revolutionary consciousness and revolutionary practice are dialectically interrelated. They condition and draw nourishment from each other. No revolutionary action is initiated without there being people conscious of the evils of the status quo and the need for a new social order. The quality of action, too, depends on the quality of consciousness. The reverse is also true. It is through actual involvement in subversive action that the revolutionary elite and the masses gain a deeper understanding of the structures of exploitation and of the type of society they want to construct. However, it is not enough to regard the relation between consciousness and practice merely as one of mutual conditioning. For it might create the false impression that active participation in the struggle is an essential prerequisite for any, even provisional, revolutionary consciousness. It is closely bound up with freedom from existential bondage. Religious teachers, educators, doctors, psychiatrists, and social workers have evolved their methods to help individuals solve the problem of psychic determinism, meaninglessness, sin, and death. Their methods continue to be relevant so long as efforts are made at the same time to create the social conditions necessary for an adequate solution to the problem.

In our discussion thus far we have laid more stress on revolutionary consciousness than on revolutionary practice for two important reasons: First, the creation of revolutionary consciousness does not get the attention it deserves in radical circles today. The stress is unduly on revolutionary practice, and there is not enough criticism of the type of consciousness that inspires it. We have already noted elsewhere the fact of Communists fighting capitalism in the name of the values of capitalism. The second important reason has to do with the mission of the Jesus-community itself. The Community is not a political party though it has a stake in the political life of the people. Essentially a prophetic movement, its primary concern is the self-transcendence of man into the New Humanity which, though realized through economic and political programs, can never be identified with any of them. And what enables a human to transcend oneself in response to God, who calls one from beyond, is one's consciousness—one's vision, faith, and hope. As already pointed out, it is in virtue of one's consciousness that one disengages oneself, though only in a provisional manner, from the present and projects oneself into the future even before one is actively involved either in pulling down the present or constructing the future. If even a provisional revolutionary consciousness is an authentic form of man's self-transcendence in dialogue with God, how much more so is mature revolutionary consciousness. That is why the Community should lay particular stress on consciousness as the potential for revolution. This does not imply that it should devalue praxis. It should devalue only uncritical praxis, which hampers rather than promotes the growth of the New Humanity.

Love or Violence?
By the faith and hope it shares with Jesus, the Community is in conscience bound to work for the liberation of the downtrodden masses of India through a total revolution. But does not revolution necessarily involve the use of violence, which goes counter to the teachings of Jesus?

Violence may be understood in two different senses. It may mean the use of force to effect the mutilation and destruction of persons. It is exercised directly when, for instance, the police or the army kill people; indirectly by those who maintain a system legalism and cultism, its hypocritical combining of verbal radicalism with practical conservatism, its spirituality of resignation, its ethics of stoic prudence, and its servile acceptance of imported theologies and ideologies. All this shows that they are today placed in a situation similar to that of Jesus, who had to liberate himself from tradition-bound Judaism to be radically honest to God and his kingdom. For them too, as for Jesus, the price of radical honesty will be death. But then, it is necessary for some to lay down their lives that others 'may have life, and may have it in all its fullness' (John 10:10).

PART - 2
ESSAYS

The Eucharist and the Quest of India for a New Vision of History

The crisis that India is facing today is essentially spiritual and religious. Its roots lie in the conflict between the traditional world-outlook and the requirements of action in this age of technology and industrialization. In her effort to solve this crisis, India is instituting an anguishing reappraisal of the views, she has inherited from the past on the historical destiny of man. Let us enter into the spirit of this search and see how far the message of the Eucharist contains an answer to the problems which India is grappling with.

Without Beginning or End
The traditional Hindu view of history has been formed after the pattern of cosmic processes. In nature, everything seems to follow a certain cyclic rhythm of emergence, disappearance, and re-emergence. The sun rises in the morning, sets in the evening, but only to rise again the following dawn. Plants spring up from the womb of the earth, grow, and then decay, thus returning to where they came from until they sprout once again from the soil. The seasons too follow a pattern of birth, death, and rebirth. The Indian mind has always thought of man as part of the cosmos and therefore, subject to the law of cyclic return. History is "a

perpetual creation, perpetual preservation, perpetual destruction", as we read in the *Vishnu Purana* (I, 7). The world emanates from *Brahman* into which it is reabsorbed at the end of every Kalpa and where it remains in a state of pure potency until it emanates again, thus initiating a new cycle. The world periods (*kalpas*) and the subsequent periods of repose form consecutively the days and the nights of *Brahman*.[1] This process of creation and dissolution is without beginning and end. History is eternal as is *Brahman*, which is its source. Besides being cyclic and eternal, history contains also a principle of inevitable deterioration. The world periods are divided into *Mahayugas* and each *Mahayuga* is further divided into four *yugas: Kritayuga, Tretayuga, Dvaparayuga*, and *Kaliyuga*, each deteriorating successively. The *Kritayuga* is the period of perfection both physical and moral. At the other end, we have *Kaliyuga*, the age of universal misery, evil, and untruth. The present human race has been living in the *Kaliyuga* for the last 5063 years and will have to live through another 420,000 years before it can see the end of this age of ever-increasing decadence. The cyclic, eternal, and deteriorating nature of history has serious implications for man's attitude towards life. To these, we shall turn our attention now.

The Vision of the Past

For each man, the awareness of his individual history takes primarily the form of the memory of the past. Man recalls the events, deeds, and values of his past years. More, he forms his own attitude towards the past inasmuch as he evaluates it and passes judgement on it. He rejects what was imperfect and immature in the past while accepting what was true, good, and of perennial value. "When I was a child, my speech, my outlook, and my thoughts were all childish. When I grew up, I had finished with childish things" (1Cor. 13:11). Such a view of the past is a source of creative inspiration for the future. The same is true also of human communities. Each community has its own collective memory and its own attitude towards the ages gone by. And where this attitude is correct, past events and values are brought before the tribunal of the present, either to be accepted or rejected in the light of objectively valid standards. To return now to the Indian scene, the concept of time and history explained earlier contains in principle an ambivalence. It may lead one either to indifference or to the cult of the past: to indifference because the unending creation and destruction of the universe make the achievements of the past devoid of any real meaning since nothing matures in the past to bear fruit in the present; to the cult of the past, since belief in the principle of deterioration implies the acceptance of a golden age. In reality, however, it is the latter attitude that has characterized the Indian mind even to the present day. There is much truth in the oft-repeated saying that India is a country where nothing is forgotten. The existence of a scrupulously faithful oral tradition, the tenacity with which millions of people even today cling to age-old customs and practices, and the tendency to attach more value to the past than is due: all this points to a certain nostalgia for the past. But one should also bear in mind that such an uncritical affirmation of the past is not a properly historical attitude. It is looked upon by many educated Hindus today - and rightly so - as characteristic of a people that has not yet come of age. Maturity demands that one opposes oneself to the past and transcends it, without, however, sacrificing the genuine values realized in it.

The traditional Hindu view of the past is slowly losing ground under the impact of western culture and philosophy. Not a few Indians have gone to the other extreme and veered round to a total rejection of the past. There are also many among the intelligentsia who are striving towards a more balanced approach which would help them preserve the abiding values in the cultural and spiritual heritage of India and reject what is provisional in it. Still, a third group tries to remain faithful to the time-honoured social and ritual practices, though it is totally divorced from the faith that animated them.

If India has failed to develop a valid view of the past and acquire an authentic memory, the proximate reason for it seems to be that she considers man as but part of the cosmos and therefore conditioned by the forces governing it. This leads us to the crucial question regarding the ultimate reason why the Indian mind has been unable to free itself from the cosmos and assert its transcendence. The following analogy might give us the key to a solution. A child remains in blissful identity with the cosmic milieu in which it finds itself until it is addressed by a 'thou', be it father or mother. On that day, it becomes conscious of being 'other' than the universe, of being its own centre, of being a person. With that, it becomes also the bearer of a memory. What is true of individuals is true as well of peoples and nations. A community needs to be spoken to, for it to become aware of its unique destiny. Hence, it must enter into a dialogue with other cultures and civilizations. But to awaken fully to its distinct and specific mission, it must hear the voice of the living God, the Lord of history. Only in the light of such a mission do the events of the past become meaningful and memorable. A community begins to have true memory only when it knows that its past is gathered into the heart of the Eternal. Now the people of India, all along her history, have never come to a universal awareness that God has spoken to them and entrusted them with a mission, notwithstanding the fact that individual saints and seers have realized the need, perhaps even recognized the fact, of such a revelation.[2] Consequently, India has little sense of a mission in history. Hence also her past is buried in eternal solitude. The India of today, that is in search of a new vision of the past will, therefore, succeed in her effort only if she accepts her mission from above, from him who in former times spoke to our forefathers in fragmentary and varied fashion and "in this, the final age has spoken to us in the Son ..." (Hb. 1:1).

For the Hebrews, the memory of the past was closely bound up with the recollection of God's election, of his promises made through the prophets, of his successive interventions in human history especially in leading them away from servitude in Egypt to the promised land. The memory of the deeds of Yahweh formed the very warp and woof of their national consciousness. The same is true also of the Christian's vision of the past, but with this capital difference that, for him, the object of memory is not merely the dealings of Yahweh in the Old Testament but also, and above all, the radical fulfillment of his promises in the incarnation, death, and resurrection of his only begotten Son. The Eucharist as the memorial of Christ, of his paschal mystery, sums up for the Christian the whole of sacred history. Everything in the past, right from the creation of the world, converges to the Eucharist and through it becomes present and meaningful to us. The alliance between Yahweh and his people culminates and finds fulfillment in his new alliance with the Church sealed in the blood of the Lamb. "This cup is the new covenant sealed by my blood" (1Cor. 11:25). But the Eucharist is the virtual fulfillment not only of sacred history but also of all profane history. It is in view of the Risen Christ, present under the symbolism of bread and wine, that God chose the people of India and, mysteriously, guided their destiny down the ages. He is the point of confluence of all the currents of genuine religious thought and life that have sprung up from the soil of India. Hence, only he can reveal to Indians the meaning of their past and thereby endow them with a true memory. The light of the Risen Christ refracted backward in time, will light up the panorama of India's past and bring to the open the purposes hidden in her tortured history.

The Future and the Beyond

The past is only a springboard to the future. The future holds the promise of growth and maturation. It has in store the opportunities man needs to unfold and realize his potentialities to the maximum. But man looks, also, beyond the future, beyond history, to a state where he will be in eternal possession of the values realized in the course of his existence on earth. This hope is enshrined in the heart of individuals and peoples who have a genuine sense of history. But, the cyclic view of time has among many other factors prevented the birth in India of a vision of the future which does justice to the true aspirations of man. In a repetitive pattern of world cycles, there is no scope for real progress and maturation. The values of the present are not carried over into the future since they are doomed to destruction in an eventual pralaya. All that man creates, therefore, is stamped with the sign of death. The new creation that follows the night of *Brahman* is not any the richer for the achievements of the past. Further, the end of each world period being nothing more than a mere return to the beginning, nothing new, nothing original, ever appears in history. Such a view of the future is apt to beget a sense of the futility of all human endeavour. Moreover, the belief that history has no definitive end, takes all seriousness out of human existence. This is still accentuated by the accepted ideas regarding the transmigration of souls. The result is that life is denuded of its uniqueness and the sense of tragedy. There is, however, a current of thought in traditional Hinduism which strikes one as the severest judgement passed by Indians themselves on the cyclic view of history, namely, the belief in the possibility of redemption from the wheel of *samsara.* The most profound longing of the Indian soul has always been to find salvation from the law of birth and rebirth. What else does this signify if not that Indians have never been able to reconcile themselves to the cyclic view of history? Unfortunately, the various ways of liberation (*mukti*) give hope of escape from the fetters of *samsara* only to the individual. The community as such is condemned to the everlasting misery of repeated existences.

The sense of frustration that the classical Hindu view of history tends to create has led contemporary thinkers to explain the future of mankind in terms of progress and fulfillment. For Radhakrishnan, history is the cosmos in travail to bring forth the world's yet 'unborn soul'. Likewise, both Aurobindo and Tagore propound an evolutionary view of history. It is also significant that these thinkers are concerned more with the future destiny of the community than with that of the individual. This points to a deeper realization of the relationship between a person and society. The evolutionary vision of history is not confined to isolated thinkers. Vast sections of the intelligentsia are, consciously or subconsciously, rallying to a view of the future, which admits of some sort of progress. No wonder that Marxism has a tremendous appeal for the educated young men and women of India. It gives them a sense of purpose and a weapon to revolutionize society.

That the Marxist view of history appeals to the intelligentsia is significant also from the Christian point of view. For Marxism at its best is but an inverted form of the Judeo-Christian world-outlook. Hence, we may rightly infer that the perspectives which Christianity opens in respect of the future of man will have an equal, if not greater, appeal for present-day India. For the Christian, mankind's future is not handed over to blind cosmic forces. His outlook is shaped by the memory of an event that gave human history a new centre and a new orientation, namely, the incarnation of the Word. The Word became flesh and pitched his tent with men. He inserted himself into the flux of history, identified himself with the very stuff and texture of the universe. In doing so, he took history into his own heart and gave it his own destiny. With the universe planted in himself, he marched through the desert of his passion and death and reached the new Promised Land, the presence of the Father. Thus he brought history to its virtual fulfillment. But the Christ who rose from the dead is still present in history in order to integrate himself into the universe of men and things, and to integrate the universe into himself, in order to make the universe more and more Christian, and himself more and more universal. From now on, something mysterious, something at once divine and human, is growing under the veil of history - the body of Christ, the Church. And it is principally through the Eucharist, through the gift of his glorified body, that Jesus Christ builds up the Church. The Eucharist, therefore, reveals to us the prospect of a history that is maturing, not indeed through any blind necessity, but through the interplay of the twofold initiative of man and Christ.

But the Eucharist is more than the instrument of progress and maturation in history; it contains also the pledge that history will reach final consummation at the end of time. Like Christ, mankind too will undergo the baptism of death and thereby enter into glory. The figure of this world will pass away to make way for a new heaven and a new earth (Rev. 21:1). This perishable being will be clothed with the imperishable, and what is mortal will be clothed with immortality (1Cor. 15:35). Then the redeemed will stand before him who says: "I am the Alpha and the Omega, the first and the last, the beginning and the end" (Rev. 22:13). It is for such a vision of the future that contemporary India seems to be groping. We should, however, bear in mind that this very groping has been conditioned and made possible by the fact that the Indian mind has been influenced by the Christian ideas contained in the philosophy and culture of the West. May we not go a step further and say that the very crisis India is going through is in the nature of a response to the mysterious call of the Risen Christ who governs all history? India is searching for Christ because she has already found him.

The Challenge of the Present

The past is no more; the future is yet to be. The present alone is given to man to redeem the past and fashion the future. It is in the present that man is called upon to fulfill the task of creating history. Let us now enquire what is the attitude of India to the decisive 'now' of history. For one who believes in the cyclic pattern of time, the 'now' pales into insignificance. It is emptied of its unique, critical, and irreplaceable character. The awareness of this is made all the more poignant by the fact that for each man his individual life is but one in an endless chain of existences. Moreover, since no past value is assumed by the present, and no present value will find a home in the future, man is condemned to live in the isolated present, in the oppressive solitude of the 'now'. Such a 'now' contains no invitation to man except to flee from it.

There are also other factors in Indian thought which go counter to the demands of commitment to the task of the present. The chief among them is the idea of man current in traditional Hinduism. Creative response to the call of the present is possible only if man has a sense of freedom. But philosophical speculation in India has always tended to belittle the relative autonomy of man and his capacity to determine and shape his own destiny. Man is born with the evil of *Karma*, which determines his concrete mode of existence. His joys and sorrows are the inevitable fruits of the deeds of his past lives. Any revolt against his actual conditions of life is doomed to failure. Enmeshed in *Karma*, he can exercise his freedom only in trying to flee from the world, not in creating history. Furthermore, the reality itself of man and history seems to be called in question. The Indian mind has a native tendency to identify the real with the One, the Immutable, the Eternal, and the Absolute. The concrete individual who works, plans, and suffers, belongs to the realm of the unreal, to the domain of universal ignorance (*avidya*). He has no true being, no consistency in himself. The conclusion, therefore, forces itself upon us that, in her age-long search for truth, India has not been able to gain a view of man as a person, as an incarnate spirit capable of free and responsible action. Consequently, also she has no fully developed sense of society, which is born of interpersonal dialogue. The community, as the subject and the agent of history, does not figure in the philosophical and religious thought of India. For these and other reasons, the Indian attitude to history has always been one of indifference and not of commitment. In this respect, the intellectual climate of contemporary India is less sombre and depressing. The evolutionary view of history which is in vogue among the intelligentsia restores value to the decisive present. Besides, belief in rebirth is slowly but surely dying out, thus paving the way for a better appreciation of the uniqueness of each individual life. There is also a conscious effort to reaffirm the freedom of man. "History is not a meaningless repetition but a creative process, determined by the free act of individuals" (Radhakrishnan). Gandhiji formulated the same thought in the following words, "We are the makers of our own destiny. We can mend or mar the present and on that will depend the future". Such statements imply a reinterpretation, perhaps even a rejection, of the doctrine of *Karma*, and a rediscovery of the true dimensions of man. Moreover, a keener awareness of the reality and value of history is noticeable among the leaders of contemporary thought in India.

Radhakrishnan openly admits that he has so reinterpreted the doctrine of Maya "as to save the world and give it real meaning". In short, India is looking for a new humanism that would provide spiritual motivation for responsible participation in the task of building a new economic and social order. Is not this quest in the last reckoning the quest of India for the 'new man' in Christ?

A salient feature of the Christian view of history - or of any authentic view of history for that matter - is the reciprocal immanence of the three moments of time, the past, the present, and the future. The past contains germinally the present and the future; the future redeems the past and the present; the present, the moment of decision, has within it the promises of the past and the fulfillment of the future. As the bearer of the past and the matrix of the future, the present confronts man with its call for action. Nowhere do we find this better realized than in the mystery of the Eucharist. The sacrament of the Eucharist, as the memorial of the death and resurrection of Christ, makes the past, present to us. Likewise, it makes present to us the final consummation of history beyond history, since to partake of the body of the Lord is to have already now a taste of eternal life. The present becomes, thus, both commemorative and prophetic. In it, Jesus Christ looks man in his face and demands his surrender to the divine plan of redemption. Hence, the most important thing for man, as he stands before the altar, is his decision of the moment, either for or against Christ. To opt for him is to be gathered into sacred history; to reject him is to fall out of it into eternal solitude. The critical 'now' of history is thus endowed with supreme meaning.

In making himself present to man in the Eucharist and in demanding his active response in the successive 'nows' of human existence, Christ affirms his freedom, or better, invites him to recognize and fulfill his freedom. For, it is in deciding for Christ that man gains his full stature as an autonomous being. But Christ affirms the reality not only of man's freedom but also of man's history. To opt for Christ is not to flee from the world. He, it is through whom and for whom the whole universe has been created, and it is in him that all things are held together (Col. 1:16-17). In becoming a member of the family of man, he rooted history in himself. The incarnation is God's affirmation of the value of history. It has its mystical continuation in the Eucharist since the Risen Christ incorporates himself further into the history of mankind through the gift of his body and blood to redeem it from within. Therefore, for the Christian, who shares in the life and the spirit of Christ, commitment to this world and its tasks becomes a sacred duty.

The message of the Eucharist can, on the one hand, wean traditional Hinduism away from its exaggerated other-worldliness, and, on the other, give to the India of today a new humanism capable of inspiring creative action in the 'now' of history. But we must hasten to add that Christianity also stands to gain from dialogue with the culture of India. In translating his 'yes' to the world into action, the Christian may run the risk of forgetting that he is but a pilgrim here on earth, that his final repose is only on the eternal shores. He may try to construct an abiding city here below, disregarding the great Beyond. Have not Christians in the West, perhaps, laid undue stress on their this-worldly commitments, and thus become guilty of a certain secularism? Such a tendency does not take into account all the dimensions of the Christian view of history. The Word of God not only became flesh but also died and rose from the dead. The universe too will have to share the kenosis of his death before it can "be freed from the shackles of mortality and enter upon the liberty and splendour of the children of God" (Rm. 8:21). The final meaning of history is to be sought beyond history. Now the religious and spiritual heritage of India, with its profound sense of the primacy of the eternal over the temporal, of the immutable over the changeable, of the spiritual over the material, could, when brought into the service of the Church, lead Christians to a better and fuller realization of the transcendent destiny of all history as implied by the paschal mystery. May we not further hope that the Christian message of history, when reflected through the prism of the Indian mind, will project a glorious spectrum with a splendour and harmony all its own? That would be India's homage to Christ, the Sun of the Orient.

(*India and the Eucharist*, Lumen Institute, Ernakulam, 1964; Written in the context of the 38th International Eucharist Congress in Bombay in 1964; *Ingathering*, Chapter 1)

12

Christian Participation in Social Work

Philosophical Perspective

Man is existence, freedom, the capacity to transcend himself, to be what he is not, and not to be what he is. He transcends himself through work, through the re-fashioning of 'nature', understood as that which is originally given, be it the material universe or his native human potential:

> "For when a man works he not only alters things and society, he develops himself as well. He learns much, he cultivates his resources, he goes outside of himself and beyond himself."[1]

Work, therefore, is the concrete form in which man humanizes himself through the humanization of nature. The humanization of nature means the creation of a wide spectrum of values ranging from the material to the spiritual, depending on whether man's activity is directed primarily to the transformation of brute nature or to the reshaping of his original human potential. Thus, through work, man produces material values like food, clothing, housing, roads, and so forth; aesthetic and artistic values like cleanliness, order, harmony, art, literature, and so forth; social values embodied in institutions like family, State, trade unions, and so forth; intellectual values like knowledge, literacy, technical know-how, and so forth; ethical values like justice, equality, freedom, fellowship, service, and so forth. It is through the realization of these objective values that man affirms himself as a subject, as the creator, of his destiny.

Man is essentially a social animal; hence his work too has a social dimension. The satisfaction of his needs, which are becoming increasingly complex, demands collaboration with other men. Similarly, the product of work is meant to serve the needs of the community and takes on the nature of a gift to his fellowmen. The concrete values, he realizes through work, can become the embodiment of his concern for his neighbor, the expression of his fellowship with other men. Since man, his work, and his product have a social dimension, all work is in a sense social work. All humanization is carried on by society for the benefit of society. However, the term 'social work' has a narrower connotation meaning a particular form of the humanizing activity of man by which he renders service to those who are incapable of self-maintenance or self-advancement because of defective human eqAuipment, social maladjustment, or unjust social conditions. What defines social work in this narrow sense is not any intrinsic difference in the work done or in the values realized but the fact that it is aimed at the uplift of the underprivileged section of the community. Hence all that we said about the humanizing and social dimension of work in general applies also to social work. We aim to discover the theological significance of social work in the narrower sense and to define the modalities of Christian participation in it in a broader framework of a general theology of work.

The Christian Meaning of Social Work

Through the humanization of nature, man creates the objective world of culture which forms, so to speak, his cosmic-social extension, the prolongation of his mind, his heart, and his hands. The more complex, the more universal this world of culture, the more radical is the change that is brought about in the consciousness and the aspirations of man. With the expansion of human consciousness, with the increasing refinement of his needs, new cultural forms and patterns emerge. Thus, work sets in motion a dialectical movement that is the mainspring of history, of human evolution. In the ultimate analysis, this whole process is mankind's concrete response to the creative call of God, to the divine mandate that man should conquer and subdue the earth:

> "For when, by the work of his hands or the aid of technology, man develops the earth so that it can bear fruit and become a dwelling worthy of the whole human family, and when he consciously takes part in the life of social groups, he carries out the design of God."[2]

Through his work, man continues the work of creation and brings its hidden virtualities to progressive unfolding and fruition. With man, creative evolution becomes an ethical task. Now the question arises: What is the ultimate meaning of man's work and the world of his creation? Are they tending to a fulfillment that is merely terrestrial, this side of history, or are we to look for their final fulfillment beyond history? What is the significance of man's creativity concerning the mystery of Christ? What is the relation between man's terrestrial expectations and the hope implanted in the heart of mankind by the Redeemer?

Creation is in view of the redemption. The continuity between creation and redemption finds expression in the words of the Apostle Paul: "In many and various ways God spoke of old to our fathers by the prophets; but in these last days he has spoken to us by a Son, whom he appointed the heir of all things, through whom also he created the world." (Heb 1:1) The Word that became flesh and dwelt among us is also the Word through whom all things were made and without whom was not anything that was made (see Jn.1:3,14). The universe of men and things is progressively brought into existence for Christ (Col. 1:16) that He may reconcile all things to the Father, "making peace by the blood of his cross" (Col 1:20). Hence man's response to the creative call of God is inwardly oriented to His redemptive initiative. Man is called upon to create himself so that he may offer himself along with his creation to Him who gives Himself in redeeming love through Jesus Christ.[3] Creation and redemption form but two moments in the one dialogue between Cod and mankind. This inner orientation of all human creativity to redemption finds its fulfillment in the insertion of the Word into human history through the Incarnation. The Word of God, in becoming man, assumed human existence in its cosmic, social, creative-historical dimension. He planted Himself in the heart of humanity and planted humanity in His heart. Having thus assumed human existence in its totality, He led it through the kenosis of death to the presence of the Father. He thus represents that privileged point of theandric density in the human evolutionary phylum which has already reached its final fulfillment beyond history and, as such, carries the promise of fulfillment for mankind, its work, and its earthly achievements:

> "This means that the entire temporal dimension and the unabridged reality we call profane can be assumed into God-related life, given that in the Son the eternal has presented itself personally within temporal and terrestrial realities."[4]

This Christian orientation, inscribed in the heart of history, forms henceforth the divine milieu enveloping all human activity and all earthly achievements. Thanks to this redeeming presence of Christ in history, work and its product can become the vehicle of divinizing love between men, and between man and Cod. The world of man's creation becomes the stuff, the material, out of which the new heaven and the new earth will take shape in the moment of the final transfiguration.[5] Hence it would be true to say that,

> "Everything that man produces, in any order, that has real and communicable value, constitutes a soil of enlargement of his own being, an extension and an improvement of his organism, a vast collective body built up by the succession of human generations and no less summoned to resurrection than each of our individual organisms."[6]

The whole of creation, therefore, is waiting with eager longing, groaning in travail, for the revealing of the sons of God (Rom 8:19-22).

This does not mean, however, that the continuation of creation through work coincides with the growth of the Kingdom, that the construction of the earthly city is identical with the construction of the heavenly one. The continuity between creation and redemption reveals also an element of discontinuity. For between redemption in principle and redemption in act stands the autonomy of man, the ambiguity inherent in his freedom affecting what he is, what he does, and what he produces. Man can create either in a spirit of worshipful submission to God or in a spirit of false autonomy vis a vis his Maker. What he produces can become either the embodiment of his surrender in love to God and his fellowmen or the instrument of hatred towards both. Thus The values which man realizes through work can lead to slavery as well as to freedom.[7] The consequences of this human ambivalence are assuming frightening proportions today when "the magnified power of humanity threatens to destroy the race itself."[8] Earthly progress must therefore be carefully distinguished from the growth of Christ's kingdom.[9] Culture and civilization in themselves constitute nothing more than the condition for the possibility of the emergence of universal love; they cannot by themselves produce universal love. Their own eschatological fulfillment depends on the birth of a universal brotherhood in Christ, which is a gift from above:

> "Grace is grace, and profane history is not the source of salvation. Evangelization is of a different order from that of civilization. To feed men is not in itself saving them, though my own salvation obliges me to feed them. To promote culture is not the same as converting men to faith".[10]

However, there is one element in human progress that points unmistakably to the victory of the risen Christ over human ambivalence and sin and as such coincides with the growth of the Kingdom on earth, namely, that of love, fellowship, and selfless service. In the measure in which human activity expresses and promotes love for one another, it already points lo the presence of the Kingdom operative in history. For in the redeemed world in which we live, any act of true love and service, any authentic manifestation of man's concern for his neighbor, is already supernatural and is a gift from the God of love. The growth of the Kingdom is, in the final analysis, the unfolding of a universal love. This love can and should express itself through all earthly activities of man.

However, there is one activity which can express fraternal love more vividly than any other, and that is social work as it is directed to the welfare and advancement of the most backward and underprivileged of God's children. But, where true love is lacking, social work can become a means for achieving selfish ends, for promoting vested interests, or for gaining political advantages. Like all works of man, social work is also ambivalent and needs redemption.

The Church and Social Work

The Church is the People of God that has become the Body of Christ. As a people, united in the same faith, hope, and love, she "has a saving and an eschatological purpose which can be fully attained only in the future world."[11] Her mission is "to proclaim and spread among all peoples the kingdom of Christ and God and to be on earth the initial budding forth of the Kingdom."[12] She is called into being to be an instrument for the reconciliation of all things in Christ, to be an effective sign of the union of all men among themselves and of all men with God. Social work, on the other hand, is a form of secular activity and as such has its own immanent laws and finality. Its proper aim is the well being of man here on earth. It is governed by laws derived from the various branches of the profane sciences such as psychology, sociology, economics,medicine, and so forth. Seen from this angle, the activity of the Church and of social work seems to fall into opposing camps. On deeper reflection, however, this tension itself discloses an underlying unity. First of all, the People of God are also members of the earthly city and recipients of the divine mandate to continue the work of creation and to make the world a better home for the family of man. Faith itself impels them to commit themselves to secular activity:

> "The Christian who neglects his temporal duties, neglects his duties towards his neighbor and even God, and jeopardizes his eternal salvation."[13]

Secondly, the properly religious mission itself of the Church has a temporal dimension. For it is this world with its resources and achievements that she has to lead to God. Thus ecclesial and secular activities penetrate each other and tend to coincide in their ultimate finality. The dialectical unity in tension, continuity in discontinuity, which we observed between creation and redemption, between the growth of the Kingdom and the evolution of the secular city, finds its parallel in the relation between the Church and the secular, between ecclesial activity and social work. The task of the Church in the field of social work must be defined within the framework and according to the demands of this dialectical relationship.

Here two wrong approaches are possible. One is to emphasize exclusively the opposition between the Church and secular activity to the point of denying their inter-penetration. For those who think along these lines, the only aim of the Church is the salvation of 'souls', understood often in an ahistorical, conceptualistic sense. They confine the activity of the Church to the strictly sacral: expressions of religion and faith like prayer, sacrifice, sacramental rites, preaching, and so forth. They view the entire field of secular activity and of human progress as of little relevance to the Church, as realities from which, or despite which, man is redeemed. For them social work is nothing more than a means for converting non-believers. They tend to flee from the world as if the redemptive initiative of God has dispensed them from responding to the creative call of the same God. It is these people whom the Council has in mind, when it says:

> "They are mistaken who, knowing that we have here no abiding city but seek one which is to come, think that they may therefore shirk their earthly responsibilities."[14]

Their attitude may be termed angelism or supernaturalism. Contrasted with these, there are others who tend to identify ecclesial and secular activity as if the construction of the earthly city coincides with the growth of the Kingdom. In concrete practice, this leads to two developments both of which are interrelated. The first consists in the Church's trying to dominate the secular city, its structures, and its institutions. This is the road to theocracy, in its various forms and necessarily implies the negation of the rightful autonomy of the secular. The other consists in subordinating the activity of the Church to the temporal advancement of man so that the Church becomes a means to an earthly end, "as though the divine teaching of Jesus Christ and His work itself were simply a recipe to be used to achieve a purely human result."[15] In this way the Church loses her religious identity and is reduced to a secular ideology or a philanthropic society competing with other similar ideologies and associations. Her eschatological hope is replaced by a terrestrial optimism. To be true to her essence and destiny, the Church should, in her concrete practice, steer clear of angelism on the one hand and of theocracy and secularization on the other.

> The Church as such has no purely secular mission:

> "Christ, to be sure, gave His Church no proper mission in the political, economic, or social order."[16]

Her specific task is not to promote culture, to build civilization, or to construct an ideal terrestrial home for the human family. The mission she received from her founder is a religions one.[17] She must "lead men to God so that they may be given over to Him without reserve."[18] But in leading man to God, his ultimate destiny, she leads man to himself, to his true being in its secular, historical setting. Hence from her properly religious mission itself comes a secular function, a light, and an energy which serve to shape the evolution of human society according to the mind of God.[19]

> "Pursuing the saving purpose which is proper to her, the Church not only communicates divine life to men, but in some way casts the reflected light of that life over the entire earth."[20]

She brings to the world the light kindled from the gospel which reveals to man the ultimate meaning of his personal, social, and creative existence and ennobles human values like justice, equality, freedom, and fellowship. By courageously bearing witness to the dignity of the human person and the equality of all men, she inspires her members and all men of good will to devote themselves to the eradication of unjust and sub-human social conditions. The Church brings to the earthly city not only a light but also an energy, a force, which serves to structure and consolidate human community and inwardly orient its evolution to Him who is the Alpha and the Omega. This force "which the Church can inject into the modern society of man consists in that faith and charity put into vital practice, not in any external dominion exercised by merely human means.[21] The People of Cod must become an energizing point for a mankind on pilgrimage from which light and love radiate into human hearts, into temporal structures, institutions, and activities, only to valorize, heal, and reconcile them in Christ Jesus so that the emerging social order will be "founded on truth, built on justice, and animated by love."[22] The Church offers to the world also a new hope based on the Resurrection of the Lord of history, who will come to lead all human history to its fulfillment and to inaugurate the "new heaven and the new earth," "a kingdom of truth and life, of holiness and grace, of justice, love, and peace." It is, therefore, the mission of the Church to be an instrument in the hands of the risen Christ to redeem the secular from within and to lead it to the eschatological fulfilment. But this mission is to be accomplished in different ways by the official Church, and the laity. In the one Church of Christ we may distinguish two different, though not opposed, dialectical aspects: the one, of the Church as a community guided by the Spirit of God, active in the apostolic office of the episcopy throughout the world; the other of the same Church guided by the Spirit of God active in every individual's conscience.[23]

It is in this context that we should further define the respective role of the hierarchy and the laity in the field of temporal activities. Here we must bear in mind that the properly religious function of the hierarchy, which consists in officially bearing witness to Christ and in building up the Christian community, is in itself of capital importance for the Christian ordering of the secular city. For only a community nourished on the word of Cod and the Bread of life can be a true leaven capable of transforming the secular from within. The official Church has also another function more directly related to activities of the temporal order. In the words of Vatican II:

> "As regards activities and institutions in the temporal order, the role of the ecclesiastical hierarchy is to teach and authentically interpret the moral principles to be followed in temporal affairs. Furthermore, it has the right to judge, after careful consideration of all related matters and consultation with experts, whether or not such activities and institutions conform to moral principles. It also has the right to decide what is required for the protection and promotion of values of the supernatural order."[24]

This applies also to social work, as it is but a domain of secular activity. It is not the function of the official Church to go beyond the proclamation of ethical norms and the moral evaluation of social conditions and institutions and translate them into concrete solutions, much less become involved in concrete socio-economic programs.[25] Such involvement coming from the official Church smacks of clerical triumphalism, implying on the one hand an overestimation of the role of the hierarchy in shaping the world and, on the other, an underestimation of its properly religious mission, and in practice leads to the denial of the rightful autonomy of the secular.

To translate the principles proclaimed by the Church into concrete prescriptions and programs is the proper task of the laity, as members at once of the Church and of the earthly city. The laity "by their very vocation" seek the kingdom of God by engaging in temporal affairs and by ordering them according to the plan of Cod."[26] This role they fulfill on their own responsibility and in collaboration with all men of good will.[27] Such activity, on the part of the laity, is truly an activity of the Church:

> "When Christians as such act, the Church acts in them. Their action is an activity of the Church, not, it is true, wholly directed by the Church's hierarchy, but inspired and guided by the spirit of the Church."[28]

And the spirit of the Church is the spirit of love. Hence Christians should have a special predilection for all forms of social work:

"While every exercise of the apostolate should take its origin and power from charity, some works by their very nature can become especially vivid expressions of this charity. Christ the Lord wanted these works to be signs of His messianic mission. ... For this reason, pity for the needy and the sick, and works of charity and mutual aid intended to relieve human needs of every kind, are held in special honor by the Church."[29]

(Paper read at the Jesuit Educational Seminar, May 1968, Bombay; Review for the Religious, Vol. 28, No.4, St. Louis, Missouri, USA, 1969, p. 586-594; *Ingathering*, Chapter 5)

13

Rite Pluralism in Kerala

One of the most significant insights of Vatican II is that the church is, "by her relationship with Christ, both a sacramental sign and an instrument of intimate union with God, and of the unity of all mankind."[1] But the church can be an effective sign of unity only in so far as she realizes unity within herself, in her life and in her structures. Hence the conciliar insight imposes on us the ethical imperative to subject to critical assessment the entire life and structure of the church to eliminate sources of conflict and disunity and to foster those forces which cement the people of God into one community of believers. As for the church in Kerala, one such structure which calls for urgent critical appraisal is the existing rite pluralism. In the following pages we shall give a sociological description of the contemporary situation, pinpoint the major problems and indicate an approach to their solution.

Here a definition of the word 'rite' is in order. The word may be understood in a narrow sense meaning sacred liturgy. In broader sense it includes, besides liturgy, also Spirituality, theology, law, discipline, etc. Thus in conciliar use the word is often employed as a synonym for 'church'. It is in this broader sense that we use the term in this essay.

Socio-cultural Differences between the Latins and the Syrians
According to 1961 census, there are 2.68 million Catholics in the State (40 per cent of the total Catholic population of India) belonging to three

different rites: 1.17 million to the Sryo-Malabar rite, 0.12 million to the Syro-Malankara rite and 0. 85 million to the Latin rite. The Syrians are found concentrated in the midlands of central Kerala. Recent migrations however, have led to the formation of a new Syrian community in north Kerala. The Syrian claim to be the descendants of the original converts of St. Thomas, the Apostle, and trace their origin to the higher castes like Brahmanas and the Nayars.[2] They fall into two racial groups called the Nordists and the Sudists, which have become assimilated in many respects to the caste-structures. They do not live in separate quarters based on caste or religion but intermixed with the surrounding Hindu population.[3] Though open to the indigenous milieu, they have shown a certain isolationism in relations to the West, due partly to historical reasons and partly to the desire to maintain their separate identity.[4]

The Syrians are by and large a land-oriented people, engaged as they are in agriculture either as land-owners or as tenants. Compared with the Latins, they have a stronger economic middle class consisting of landlords, bankers, businessmen, government officials, etc. However, recent years have witnessed a progressive impoverization of the Syrian community due to fragmentation of land, population explosion and unemployment, which has led to large scale internal migration.

Latins are concentrated in the coastal areas. Smaller communities are also found in the midlands of central Kerala. Quite a few are employed as labourers in the plantations of the Western Ghats. As a community, they represent the fruits of early Latin missionary activity dating back to the apostolic labours of St. Francis Xavier. They are mostly converts from the lower castes or sub-castes like Mukuvars, Nadars, Izhavas, etc.[5] However, there is a sizable number of Latins inhabiting the backwater areas between Quilon and Cranganore who were originally Syrians but were later latinized by the Portuguese missionaries.[6] Among the Latins, we find also a small minority of mixed racial origin resulting from marriages between natives and western colonizers like the Dutch, the Portuguese and the British. The sociological structure of the Latin community varies with their geographical situation. In the coastal areas between Quilon and Cape Comorin, they live in exclusively Latin Catholic villages, whereas between Quilon and Cranganore they live in religiously and socially pluralistic villages, though in separate quarters in the vicinity of the church.[7] Among the Latins, we find three different communities called the Seven Hundred, The Five Hundred, and the Three Hundred, a distinction which has been taken into consideration in the erection of dioceses. These communities manifest, though in an attenuated form, certain features which are characteristic of caste, like endogamy, status by birth, social exclusiveness, particularistic loyalty, etc. With the increase in the tempo of social contact and mobility, these distinctions are gradually disappearing. Contrasted with the Syrians, the Latin Christians have been more exposed to Western influence, secular as well as religious.[8]

The Latins form an economically backward community. The vast majority of them are fishermen by profession and are constantly faced with economic insecurity and exploitation by unscrupulous middlemen. This has impelled many among them to seek low paid jobs as clerks, typists, mechanics, etc. There is also the phenomenon of the migration of individuals and families away from the coastal areas to the inlands of the State and other parts of India. There has been, during the last few decades, an exodus of educated Latin Catholics to countries outside India, like Malaya, Ceylon and the Middle East, mostly in search of employment. Today, the Latins seem to show greater initiative and drive than the Syrians in diversifying the occupational structure of their community. Among them an economic, intellectual middle class is just beginning to emerge.

The Nature of Rite Pluralism

In the context of the socio-cultural differences described above, let us now define clearly the ritual differences existing in Kerala. The faithful of the Syro-Malabar rite follow the East Syrian Chaldean liturgy, which was subjected to comprehensive Latinization at the time of Portuguese missionary activity but has since been reinstated in its original form.

Those of the Syro-Malankara rite are adherents of the West Syrian Antiochian liturgy, which was introduced as late as the beginning of the 19th century. Before that they too were following the latinized version of the Chaldean liturgy.[9] Till recently, the Syro-Malabar and the Latin churches used Syriac and Latin respectively as liturgical languages. Both have now changed over to Malayalam, though the policy of vernacularization has not been fully implemented by either. The Antiochian rite had much earlier adopted the vernacular as a liturgical language under Protestant influence.[10] In the period in which the Syrian liturgies existed in their latinized from, they differed from the Latin in certain cultural modes of expression like language, music, gestures and symbols, while much of their structure and even content was greatly assimilated to the latter.[11] Today on the contrary they have only the use of the vernacular in common with the Latins, whereas in everything else they have regained their distinctive identity.

Liturgy not only expresses but also shapes the spirituality of the people. Hence we may ask the question: Have these different liturgies brought about a corresponding differentiation at the level of the spirituality of the Christian community? In other words, could we speak of the existence of a Latin spirituality and a Syrian spirituality in Kerala? For any such differentiation at the popular religious-psychological level, the various rites must have existed each in its separate identity for a considerably long period. Now, this has not been the case in Kerala. As for the Chaldean liturgy (we shall consider the case of the Antiochian rite separately as it has had its peculiar historical development), it is true it exists today in its original form as distinct from the Latin. But, since it was restored only recently, it has not yet been able to leave any abiding mark on the religious life and spirituality of the faithful. If, on the other hand, we take it in its latinized form, then the points of difference with the Latin liturgy were but marginal. Hence it could not have contributed to the emergence of a typically Syrian mode of spirituality. Nor could such a differentiation be induced by the para-liturgical and devotional practices. The most popular, among such practices in Kerala are: Adoration of the Blessed Sacrament, Devotion to the Sacred Heart, the First Friday Devotion, the Rosary, devotions in honour of Our Lady on the Saturdays of the mouth, and novenas in honour of the Blessed Virgin and the saints. Now, these are common to the Latins and the Syrians or, more precisely, are Latin in origin. There is to our knowledge no devotional practice which one may point out as typically Syrian.

However, in applying this to the Syro-Malankara church we should add a qualification. For the Antiochian liturgy has been existing in Kerala in its separate identity for over a century and has been using also the vernacular as liturgical language. It is therefore, no wonder that of all the three liturgies it is the one that has the greatest emotional appeal for the people.

The lack of any significant differentiation is observed also at the level of the Church's mode of thinking and acting. The Syrian churches have not developed any oriental theology. The main body of theology taught in seminaries is occidental. Neither the preaching nor the writings of the Syrians reveal any oriental bias. The same uniformity obtains also in the sphere of pastoral and missionary activity. The differences that do exist belong to the domain of ecclesiastical law, discipline and customs, which, however, are not of much significance for the concrete religious life of the people. We may sum up this section by saying that 'ritual' pluralism exists in Kerala more at the level of certain objective, ecclesiastical structures than at the level of the religious life and spirituality of the people of God.

Neither socio-cultural nor 'ritual' differences between communities need necessarily create conflict situations. And yet such conflicts have become a permanent factor in the life of the church. This needs further investigation.

Inter-ritual Conflicts

To understand the nature of these conflicts, we must analyze their causes. Rite pluralism is itself a source of tension since each rite is held by its adherents as superior to the others. The Syrians take historical pride in the fact that their faith dates back to the evangelization of St. Thomas, the Apostle, and look down upon the Latin church as a later intruder on the scene. We should note also the historical resentment they feel against the latter because of the unjust latinization they were subjected to. Some are unhappy about the various Latin elements which still persist in their church and which they are unable to exorcise from among them.

As for the Latins, they too entertain feelings of superiority with regards to the Syrians whom they claim to have saved from schism and the Nestorian heresy and brought back to the orthodoxy of the Catholic fold. This sense of superiority is reinforced by the tendency to identify the Latin church with the universal church. A still more important source of tension between the Latin and the Syrian churches is the concrete mode of pastoral, missionary and secular activities within the framework of overlapping multiple jurisdiction.[12]

These are motivated by the desire not only to serve the religious and secular needs of the people, but also to maintain and expand the religious and secular power of the respective communities. For instance, the construction of a Syrian church in one locality is viewed by the Latins as creating a religious power vacuum which can be filled only by putting up a Latin church in the same place. Such ecclesiastical power politics is an important factor underlying the proliferation of institutions, like, convents, schools, colleges and hospitals. This has led to an overgrowth of parallel institutions throughout the State, many of which can in no way be justified on the basis either of the objective needs of the people or of the authentic mission of the church. These institutions in their turn breed mutual rivalry, suspicion and discrimination.

Inter-ritual tension is maintained mainly by a small minority of ecclesiastics who wield power and influence far out of proportion to their number. In this lies its weakness. For it has little support at the popular level. The common man is not concerned about the relative superiority of rites or the institutional dominance of his own community.

There is, however, one source of tension which has a sociological basis in the life of the mass of Christians, namely the distinctions based on caste hierarchy. Neither legislation nor social changes have been able to eliminate caste consciousness from the life of the people. Thus the attitudes and patterns of behaviour especially of Christians of the older generation are still conditioned by the ethos proper to caste. Status consciousness based on caste is still a permanent constituent element in the psychic makeup of the Syrian community.[13] This led in the past to the construction of separate churches for converts from the lower castes. The Latins, on the other hand, have a sense of social inferiority strengthened by economic backwardness. Differences in caste have as a concomitant also differences in economic interests, which in their turn call for varied political loyalties. These loyalties, when sanctioned by the official church become another source of tension between the Christian communities.

Tensions born of rite differences and those resulting from social distinctions should not be thought of as taking place as it were in two separate compartments. They condition and reinforce one another. Thus inter-ritual conflicts created by the present mode of pastoral- missionary activity have a consolidating effect on distinctions based on caste or community. These in their turn influence the formulation of ecclesiastical policy. This is proved by the existence in Kerala of parishes and even dioceses organized based on caste or quasi-caste distinctions. Hence it would seem that Christianity, while professing before non-Christians the equality of all men, has contributed to the consolidation of social inequality among Christians themselves!

Rites in Conflict with Culture

The Latin and Syrian rites, besides conflicting with each other, are also in varying degrees in conflict with the culture and the religious genius of the people. These two types of conflicts are also inter-related. For genuine indigenization would eliminate the very reason for the existence of more than one rite. On the other hand, the existence of a plurality of rites stands in the way of indigenization.

Both the Latin and the Syrian liturgies are like exotic plants transplanted on the Indian soil. They have therefore failed to strike deep roots in the life of the masses. This foreignness is striking in the case of the Latin liturgy, which contains many elements derived from the secular culture of the West,[14] and extends to music, gestures, the structure of prayers, etc. This applies also mutatis mutandis to the Syrian liturgies. Both liturgies are out of harmony with the psycho-religious structure of the Indian mind and with its innate urge to find expression in indigenous cultural forms. This created a situation in the past where the faithful could perceive the meaning of the liturgical service only in an indirect manner, namely, through interpretations and explanations given within the framework of preaching and catechesis. For these reasons liturgy could not fulfill its true function as a concrete, realization of dialogue between God and his people. The vernacularization now being effected remedies the situation only in part, as it still leaves intact many cultural elements that are alien to the people.

As in the case of the pluralism of rites, so too here the perpetuation of their alien character is desired only by a minority of conservative laymen and ecclesiastics. The results even of the partial reforms introduced in the recent past show that the people on the whole would welcome the possibility of offering divine worship in a manner suited to their own culture and religious genius.

Problems

The two-dimensional conflict situation that exists today between the Latin and the Syrian rites on the one hand and between the various rites and indigenous culture on the other —constitutes by itself a major problem for the church, which in turn becomes the matrix for other problems affecting spirituality, pastoral action, ecumenism and evangelization.

Spirituality

Liturgy as the concrete form of dialogue between man and God is the primary source of religious experience for the people of God. Where it fails to fulfill this dialogal function adequately, due to its alien character, religious experience is bound to suffer. And without deep religious experience there is no genuine religious creativity either. Now it is an undeniable fact that the Church in Kerala — and the whole of India for that matter — is suffering from a certain chronic religious anemia and infertility. One has only to consider the fact that there is so little original religious literature in India that is not a mere imitation, or translation of works written in the West, that we have so few religious thinkers, creative theologians and mystics in the ranks of the indigenous clergy or the laity, and that there is scarcely any religious current or movement that bears the imprint of the specific genius of the Indian people. Is not this lack of religious vitality and originality attributable largely to the existence of rites as alien superstructures imposed on the people from outside? How could a tree that has not struck roots deep in the soil bear abundant fruit?

The God we enter into dialogue with, in liturgical service is not the God of the philosophers, but the God of Abraham, Isaac and Jacob, the living God who calls men to be his People, his Church, who gathers all into the Kingdom. Consequently, authentic religious experience for a Christian includes as an essential constituent the experience of belonging to the people of God, to the Church. Hence the alien character of the rites in Kerala, in so far as it stands in the way of authentic religious experience, is also an obstacle to the growth of true ecclesial sense and ecclesial experience. The possibility of such experience is further diminished by the existence of social and inter-ritual conflicts between the various Christian communities. Conversely, these conflicts find nourishment in the lack of any true experience of the Church. The Latins and the Syrians may recognize one another as belonging to the one Catholic Church (even this is not verified in the case of many uneducated Catholics), but this recognition has yet to pass from the notional to the existential level.

Pastoral action

Multi-ritualism and the competitive, parallel growth of rite-based Christian communities make effective pastoral action difficult, if not impossible. The material and human resources of the church are uselessly dispersed or even wasted, as is the case when priests are assigned and institutions put up to meet the pastoral needs of small 'ritual' communities which could very well be looked after within the framework of existing institutions belonging to a different rite. Exclusive interest in the faithful of one's own rite also prevents pastors from attending to the spiritual needs of the followers of other rites who happen to live far removed from their own priests. In the prevailing conditions, it is extremely difficult to organize pastoral action based on what Karl Rahner calls 'the social differential principle' to meet the spiritual needs of social and professional groups like those of students, workers, teachers, doctors, etc., which cut across the boundaries of parishes, dioceses, rites and communities. Particularistic loyalties engendered by rite-consciousness also tend to deviate the attention of the official Church from the serious challenges and problems created for the Christian community by socio-cultural changes like industrialization, urbanization and the spread of communism.

Ecumenism

The present situation affects adversely the prospects for ecumenism. How can the Church hope to bring about the unity of all Christians, if her own life is characterized by disunity, rivalry and conflicts? Besides, dialogue with our separated brethren is considered not so much as the task of the whole church as the concern of individual rites, depending on the nature of the Christian denomination in question. For instance, dialogue, with the Jacobite church is considered the special task of the Syro-Malankara rite even in those places where Jacobites find themselves surrounded by Catholics of the Latin or the Chaldean rite. Similarly, the more westernized Protestants for whom it would be easier to enter into dialogue with the Latin Christians often find themselves surrounded by a dominant Syrian Catholic community. Thus, rite pluralism aid the unequal geographical distribution of Christians in Kerala and create innumerable obstacles in the way of organized ecumenical effort. However, in the case of the Syro-Malankara church, it is argued that its continued existence in the present form is necessary for any eventual reunion with Jacobites. This way of thinking is based on the rather doubtful assumption that an indigenous liturgy, for instance, will be less acceptable to the Jacobites than a Syrian liturgy. Besides, even if this assumption were true, one could still question the validity of promoting unity at the cost of sacrificing truth and the good of the whole Church.

Evangelization

Inter-ritual conflicts diminish the credibility of the Church and the sacrament of salvation and the effective sign of unity before non-Christians. A Church that is in contradiction with herself cannot effectively bear witness to Christ who came to reconcile man and the universe to the Father. This is too obvious to need further elaboration. As in the case of pastoral and ecumenical action, here too any planned effort at evangelization is not possible so long as the different rites are pulling in different directions. There is another element in the present situation, which is out of harmony with the missionary presence of the Church, namely, the existence of rites as alien to the culture of the people. The Church not merely has a missionary function but is essentially mission. This should find its concentrated expression in the liturgy which is precisely an event in which the Church realizes herself in her true being.[15] Liturgical service is not only a 'memoria' of the redemptive action of Christ but also a proclamation of 'the death of the Lord until he comes',[16] a proclamation that should be heard and understood also by those who do not believe in Christ. Now, how can the liturgical service be a proclamation intelligible to the 'nations' if it is expressed in foreign cultural modes? Hence the liturgy, as it is celebrated in India today, has little missionary value.

Even a selective enumeration of problems like these shows that the existing situation of rites in Kerala needs urgent and radical reform. What should be the nature of this reform? In the following we shall limit ourselves to the consideration of the necessary structural reform, which, however, has to be accompanied and sustained by renewal of life.

Towards a Solution: An Indigenous Rite for Kerala

The solution we are seeking should fulfill three conditions: (i) It should be such as to eliminate the objective sources of the various problems enumerated above, (ii) should be in keeping with the self-understanding of the Church, realized through Vatican II, and (iii) should be dictated by a right interpretation of the signs of the times. We believe that the only solution that will adequately meet all these conditions is the one that envisages the planned evolution of a single indigenous rite for the whole of Kerala.

That the proposed solution fulfils the first condition is self-evident. The creation of a single rite for all the faithful will do away with the structural causes for conflicts and usher in the conditions favourable for planned pastoral, ecumenical and missionary action. It will enhance the credibility of the Church in the eyes of non-Catholics. In so far as this single rite is indigenous, it will make the Church rooted in the soil, thereby paving the way for deeper religious experience and greater religious creativity. Thus the liturgy will become capable of revealing to outsiders the Church as a sign raised above the nations,[17] as it will be clothed in cultural modes that are intelligible to all.

As for the second condition, the suggested solution incorporates two of the most basic elements in the self-awareness of the Church which have found repeated expression in more than one conciliar document, namely, unity and catholicity. The Council views liturgical reform itself as a means "to nurture whatever can contribute to the unity of all who believe in Christ."[18] Compared with the unity to be realized, ritual pluralism has only a relative value. It is not an end in itself. Hence it can and should be suppressed if it stands in the way of the unity of the people of God. Although rite pluralism need not necessarily lead to disunity, it does so in Kerala as it is inextricably bound up with divisive, socio-cultural-historical factors. If the search for unity justifies the unification of all Catholics under one rite, the realization of 'catholicity' demands that this one rite be indigenous. The Church is not bound to any culture. In her inner being and ultimate goal she remains transcendent. And it is precisely in virtue of her transcendence that she can become fully immanent in various cultures and historical situations. Like the Word that was made flesh, she assumes various cultural forms and thereby "purifies, strengthens, and ennobles them". Thus "does she foster and take to herself, in so far as they are good, the ability, resources, and customs of, each people."[19] Hence the Council recognizes the need even for a radical adaptation of the liturgy, especially in mission lands. [20] What is said of the liturgy should be extended also to other elements of rites.

Here it may be objected that the Council has emphatically stated that in the case of all lawfully acknowledged rites, the Church "wishes to preserve them in the future and to foster them in every way."[21] To this we answer that the Council has in mind those oriental rites which have sprung out of indigenous cultures. To understand the conciliar wish in absolute sense would contradict the more fundamental concern of the same Council to foster the catholicity of the Church.

The legitimacy and the feasibility of creating one indigenous rite for Kerala will become all the more clear when we consider the signs of the times as revealed in the concrete historical process in which the Church is involved. These signs of the times are two-fold: the forces of symbiosis and the forces of convergence. The first concerns the relationship between the Latin and the Syrian communities and the second the relationship between these two communities and the indigenous culture. In the past, when social life was static, the two communities could exist in comparative isolation. This is no more the case today. Industrialization, urbanization and improved communications have brought about greater social contact between people of various castes, classes and religious denominations, and have contributed to increased social mobility, vertical as well as horizontal. Closed social structures like joint-family, caste and village economy are in the process of disintegration and are being replaced by open social groups. Caste distinction is giving way to class distinction. Caught up in the momentum of these far reaching socio-cultural changes, both Latins and Syrians are coming closer to each other. Their distinctive features are thus becoming progressively blurred. To this symbiosis at the social and cultural level corresponds also a coming together of both communities at the religious level brought about by the same social changes and by the inflow of religious literature from outside Kerala and the West. Thus the leveling down that was achieved through Latinization in the past is now being completed through the process of socialization. In coming closer to one another, the Latins and the Syrians are also converging to the contemporary culture of Kerala. This culture is in itself in the process of evolution and has already assimilated many elements of Western secular culture. The Syrians who were comparatively more open to the Hindu milieu but were less so to Western culture are today assimilating Western cultural elements in so far as they have become part of contemporary indigenous culture. On the other hand, those Latins who were comparatively more open to Western culture are today becoming progressively indigenous in their customs and outlook.

The forces of integration and symbiois between the Latin and the Syrian communities demand as their natural term the formation of a single rite for Kerala, while the forces of convergences require that this rite should become enfleshed in the contemporary culture of the people. Hence the creation of one indigenous rite imposes itself as a historical imperative which is also a divine imperative, since historical processes can also be "authentic signs of God's presence and purpose."[22] This imperative is not yet recognized as such by the uneducated masses. However, it forms an element in the pre-critical, inarticulate experience of the majority of educated laymen and priests. It has of late found its articulate expression in the One Rite Movement that has been launched in Kerala and has found support, among wide circles of priests and laymen.

However, the formation of a single indigenous rite for Kerala should not be thought of as a panacea for all the problems of the Church. Structural changes should be accompanied and supported by the renewal of ecclesial life. Else conflicts and tensions will continue to exist under the mantle of one rite, just as they do today between dioceses of the same rites and people of the same diocese. On the other hand, it would be an illusion to think that a renewal of the life of the Church is possible without the reform of structures.

It is beyond the scope of this essay and also beyond our competence to discuss the shape of the proposed indigenous rite.[23] It will have to be determined in the light of research, experimentation and dialogue between the official Church and the laity. Leaving this for the study of experts, we shall conclude by asking another question: Is the unification of all Catholics in Kerala under one indigenous rite something realizable in a not too distant future? There are reasons which would promote a negative answer. The perpetuation of rite pluralism has become, from the economic, social and ecclesiastical point of view, something like a vested interest for its protagonists. Hence a change in the present policy is not possible without a real metanoia, a conversion of the heart, of which there are not yet enough signs. Besides, the Church in Kerala is still in the pre-conciliar, pre-dialogal era. The official Church tends to live in a psychological ghetto not fully aware of what is going on in the world or even in the Church. Open minded laymen and clergy are reduced to being the Church of silence as there is little freedom of expression in practice. Finally, the message of the Council has not yet been assimilated by vast sections of the clergy and the laity. There are even some who consider the Council itself a major disaster to the Church and look back nostalgically to the good old days of ecclesiastical totalitarianism.

While these reasons do not augur well for the future there are others which inspire hope or at least qualified optimism. To begin with, the attempts to perpetuate the status quo or to return to an imagined golden era are doomed to failure as they will widen the already unbridgeable gulf between outmoded and anachronistic ecclesiastical structures and the ever changing life of the people of God. A minority in the Church will not be able to make the currents of history flow backwards. Secondly, despite the attempts to insulate the Church against 'new' ideas, these are flowing in through various channels into the minds and hearts of the laity and the clergy. These ideas are likely to be accepted by more and more people, as they are but articulate expressions of their own inarticulate thoughts and desires. They have already created stirrings of a new life and a certain healthy restlessness in the Church. Could these not be the fruits of the Spirit who renews the face of the earth? It is in this faith that our hope is anchored.

(Vaidikamitram, Vol.2, 1969, p.17-34; *Ingathering*, Chapter 2)

14

In Defence of an Indigenous Rite for Kerala

(A reply to "A Matter of Rite", a leaflet prepared by Fr. C. A. Abraham in collaboration with many others, Kottayam, 1969)

The contents of the leaflet under consideration, belong to three categories: (a) expressions of sorrow, pain, astonishment, fear and even superlative contempt;[1] (b) distortions of my views and wrong assumptions; (c) arguments meant to refute my thesis in favour of an indigenous rite for Kerala[2]. In the first category of statements, I have no comment to make as they belong rather to the realm of emotions and passions than to the domain of reason. Statements belonging to the second and the third categories demand an answer, since they might mislead uncritical readers. In this reply, I shall limit myself to an internal criticism of the leaflet in order to bring to light the contradictions inherent in the arguments set forth in it.

Distortions and Wrong Assumptions

From my use of the first person plural, the author draws the conclusion that in writing the article on rite pluralism, I was acting as the spokesman of a group. It is surprising indeed, that a man like Fr. C. A. Abraham, trained in Oxford as he is, has not heard of the author's 'we'.[3] At the very outset, I want to make it clear that I am not the spokesman of any particular group, not even of my Jesuit confreres among whom there is a healthy pluralism of opinion regarding the rite question in Kerala. Nor am I a spokesman of the One Rite Movement. I maintain the freedom and the right to disagree both with the One Rite Movement and the many-rite school of thought. The genesis of my article has nothing to do with the One Rite Movement. I also reject the insinuation[4] that I am the instrument in the hands of a movement outside Kerala committed to introducing a single indigenous rite in Kerala. It is my considered opinion that the destiny of the Church in Kerala should be shaped by us and not by outside forces.

Fr. Abraham attributes to me the view that the Syrian rites in Kerala should be suppressed.[5] This is a calculated distortion of the truth. What I stand for is "the planned evolution of a single indigenous rite for the whole of Kerala."[6] This would mean not only the search for new ritual forms but also the subsuming of whatever is authentically Indian and Christian in the present set-up. Planned evolution means continuity-in-discontinuity with the past. Since I am not for suppression, the author's reasoning that I should, in logical consistency, also, demand the suppression of the Society of Jesus is equally unfounded. What I have said of the rites in Kerala, is to be applied to Religious Congregations as well. They too are in need of planned evolution towards more indigenous forms, relevant to contemporary India. Else they are doomed to eventual extinction. This is true not only of the Jesuits but also of other Religious Congregations like the C.M.I. and even of secular priests. The real motive behind the author's repeated unkind references to the Jesuits[7] seems to be to present them as the enemy number one of the Syrians in Kerala, thereby reawaken the ancient antipathy towards the Society of Jesus and in the process win more supporters for the maintenance of the status quo in Kerala.

Another view attributed to me by the author is that rite pluralism is incompatible with the unity of the Church, whereas what I have stated in my article is this:

"Although rite-pluralism need not necessarily lead disunity, it does so in Kerala as it is inextricably bound with divisive socio-cultural-historical factors."[8]

Such distortions betray certain intellectual dishonesty which we do not expect from a mature scholar.

It is this very intellectual dishonesty which makes the author see an anti-Syrian slant[9] in my article which, in reality, is equally critical of the Syrian and Latin rites. Love for the Syrian Churches is not a monopoly of Fr. Abraham. For, after all, before Father Abraham was, I was a Syrian Catholic. So too are the innumerable Syrians, priests, and laymen, who favour one indigenous rite for Kerala.

These instances chosen at random from among many are enough to show how the author cleverly distorts my original affirmations, so that, having made a caricature of them, he may the more easily explode them. But in doing so, he leaves my original statements untouched, un-refuted. His methodology is itself a tacit admission of the validity of my thesis as I have formulated it.

Inter-Ritual Conflicts

Fr. Abraham argues that my affirmation that rite pluralism, as it exists in Kerala, is a cause of conflicts neutralizes and cancels out my subsequent affirmation that the Latins and the Syrians are drawing closer due to the process of socio-cultural symbiosis.[10] A little reflection would have shown him that this contradiction is not in my thinking but in the objective socio-religious situation of the Church in Kerala. This objective situation, interpreted in terms of salvation history, means that, while the working of God through historical and sociological forces is bringing the adherents of the various rites together, a few ecclesiastics and laymen are bent upon tearing these very people apart, allegedly in the name of loyalty to the Church but in truth for the preservation of vested interests. Rite fanaticism is a sin against the 'signs of the times.'

The author goes on to argue that "it would be nearer to the truth to say that conflicts are not caused by the Rites as such but occasionally manifested through them."[11] That the plurality of rites in Kerala is a source of conflicts is an element of the common experience of Christians in Kerala. Even Fr. Abraham indirectly admits it, when he says that if the western missionaries had not established the Latin rite in Kerala (i.e. if there were only one rite here!) there would not be many of the rivalries and tensions now experienced.[12] Besides, the various measures suggested by Vatican II and those others listed by the author[13] to solve the problems created by multiple jurisdictions, presuppose the recognition that the plurality of rites is a source of conflicts in the Church. Even if one were to grant that plurality of rites is only a medium through which various conflicts manifest themselves, still, there is a valid case for one rite for Kerala, since, in that case, sociological conflicts may die out for lack of a proper medium of manifestation. Fr. Abraham fails to appreciate the sociological fact that inter-ritual and sociological conflicts do not operate on parallel lines, that they condition and reinforce each other.[14]

From the fact that conflicts exist even within the same rite, the author draws the conclusion that rite pluralism is not the source of conflicts.[15] The desired conclusion does not follow from the premise. The only conclusion one may legitimately draw is that conflicts may arise even from factors other than ritual, which I have never denied. This is precisely why I have pointed out, in my article, that structural reform must be supported and supplemented by spiritual renewal.[16] On the other hand, the spiritual renewal of the Church is not possible without corresponding reform of structures, since life and structure form a dialectical unity-in-tension. This is why I cannot accept the contention of Fr. Abraham[17] that what is needed is not reform of structures but a greater practice of charity. For charity was preached from the pulpits right from the beginnings of Christianity in India. Still, it has not prevented the emergence of conflict situations in the Church. This shows that even the practice of charity is made difficult without the corresponding reform of structures, just as the practice of equality was not possible without the abolition of caste. Personal sin is closely linked up with the existence of sin as embodied in outmoded socio-religious structures and institutions. To reject the first, while accepting the second, is nothing short of compromising with evil.

Indian-ness of the Syrian Christians

Here, I must point out a basic contradiction that runs through the entire leaflet. On the one hand, the author affirms categorically that Syrian Christianity in Kerala is genuinely Indian, that it was right from the beginning organically integrated into Indian culture.[18] On the other hand, he equally affirms that the Syrian liturgies have still to be Indianized,[19] that the real challenge facing us today is Indianization "in the depth of life and thought."[20] He even concedes that the Syrian liturgies now practiced in Kerala are "most Semitic in Ethos." [21] How can the Syrian Churches in Kerala be called truly and genuinely Indian if their liturgies are most Semitic in ethos, if they still need Indianization in the depth of life and thought?

The author claims that the Eastern Christians in India are Indian because they are part of the Indian heritage which is a synthesis of various cultural strands like the Aryan, the Dravidian, the Muslim, the Christian, etc.[22] I do not dispute his claim that the Syrian Christians in Kerala are Indians. But the assertion that they are bearers of a distinctive culture is true only if by 'culture' is meant religious culture. For, the secular culture of the Syrians, as well as the Latins, is more or less the same as that of the other communities in Kerala. But the existence of the Syrians as bearers of a distinctive religious culture is theologically problematic, as it goes against the transcendence of the Church vis a vis cultures. The Church is not wedded to any culture of her own, but finds expression in the cultures of the milieu where she finds herself. The Church is not universal and truly catholic if she has built her own cultural home distinct from that of the surrounding people. A Church that exists as a cultural unity alongside other cultures is less than the Church of Christ because it is more than the Church of Christ. It is more, since, besides being a Church it is also a culture; it is less, because, being also a culture, it cannot become incarnate in other cultures. Hence the Syrian Churches in Kerala can achieve true catholicity only if they accept to die to and rise from, their own Syrian-ness. This applies to the Latin rite as well.

In his attempt to prove the Indian-ness of the Syrian liturgies in Kerala, Fr. Abraham makes the following assertion:

"After all, the essential structure of the liturgy (which was) handed over to the Apostles by Christ and cannot, therefore, be altered, first took shape in Jerusalem and Antioch. This structure cannot be considered foreign anywhere."[23]

Now this statement may mean either that the essential structure of the liturgy, as willed by Christ, is to be found exclusively in the liturgies that developed in Jerusalem and Antioch or that it is realized also in other liturgies, which developed elsewhere. The first alternative would amount to branding all liturgies other than those of Jerusalem and Antioch as unorthodox, i.e. not true to the essential structure as willed by Christ, a conclusion the author cannot subscribe to as Catholic. If, on the other hand, we opt for the second alternative, it would then follow that the Latin liturgy too contains the essential structure as willed by Christ and therefore is — according to the author's reasoning — as little foreign to India as those of Jerusalem and Antioch. On the other hand, if all the valid liturgies existing in the universal Church, verify the essential structure willed by Christ, in spite of their real difference in form and content, the conclusion imposes itself that the essential structure, willed by Christ, is nothing more than a germinal reality, a primordial nucleus, which eventually took concrete shape in the cultural milieu that obtained in Jerusalem, Antioch and elsewhere. If so, the liturgies of Jerusalem and Antioch, in their concrete historical form and content, represent the embodiment of the essential structure as willed by Christ in the Middle East culture, and therefore are as foreign to India as the Latin liturgy.

Unity in Diversity

Fr. Abraham has tried to justify the continuance of rite pluralism in Kerala, on the basis that such pluralism is in the nature of the universal Church.[24] There is, however, a serious flaw in his argument. Ritual pluralism is justified and is a legitimate expression of the catholicity of the Church only when corresponding to it, there is also cultural pluralism among the believers. This is not the case in Kerala, where there are many rites, although all Christians share one and the same culture. Hence the anomaly that people who speak the same language, possess the same socio-economic laws, customs, and institutions, exhibit the same patterns of thought and behaviour in secular life, enjoy the same type of films, music, and dance, and manifest the same ethos and religiosity are forced to branch off into different groups and betake themselves to different Churches when there is the question of liturgical service. In secular life they are one; in religious-ecclesial life, they form themselves into more or less mutually exclusive groups. Multi-ritualism, therefore, has no cultural basis in the life of the faithful.

Nor can we justify the present multi-ritualism on the basis of the existence in Kerala of different religious communities like Hindus and Muslims. After all, in point of fact, rite pluralism here does not correspond to religious pluralism. In other words, we do not have in Kerala one rite adapted to the Hindus, another to the Muslims. And this is as it should be. For, the Church should adapt herself not so much to the various religious cultures as to the evolving secular culture common to the followers of all religions. This alone will do justice to the logic of the Incarnation of the Logos, which has abolished the radical separation between the sacral and the profane and has thereby in a sense desacralized religion itself. The Incarnate Logos was, before the Law, a layman. He constituted his profane death not in the temple (sacral) but on calvary(profane), the unique cosmic liturgy of all times. He chose a profane element like a family meal to represent sacramentally his sacrificial death. True to this incarnational logic, in trying to express her own nascent self-awareness, the early Church consistently uses terms drawn from the sphere of secular life, like assembly (ecclesia), overseer (bishop), the elder (presbyter), serving at the table (Diakonia), etc., etc. This is the path the Church in Kerala should follow today, in her attempt at adaptation. The scope of this article does not allow us to elaborate on the theological reasoning presupposed here.[25]

The introduction of a single indigenous rite in Kerala will no way violate the principle of the koinonia of the individual Churches.[26] 'Individual Church' is not a ritual or cultural concept as Fr. Abraham seems to think. It is essentially a theological concept which means that the universal Church is in a certain sense fully present wherever the people of God are gathered together around the altar under their pastors. Hence, we may speak of individual Churches existing within the same rite or even within the same diocese.

Fecundity of the Syrian Churches in Kerala
In my article on rite pluralism (Chap. 13) I had indicated the alien character of the rites as an important factor, responsible for the religious-spiritual-theological barrenness of the Indian Church. True to his approach, Fr. Abraham has interpreted this criticism as almost exclusively directed to the Syrian Churches in Kerala and has made an attempt to refute my evaluation. But he does not really meet my arguments. The facts, he points out to prove the vitality of the Syrian Churches, are mainly two: the number of religious and priestly vocations and the proliferation of institutions like schools, colleges, hospitals, etc. [27] These facts are liable to varying interpretations. As for the abundance of vocations, a serious study from the point of view of depth psychology and scientific analysis of the sociological factors like unemployment, poverty, the position of women in homes, etc., which condition the choice of avocations might make us less triumphalistic in our assessment. As for the growth of institutions — educational and otherwise — it could as well be a symptom of the decadence of the Church, the natural outcome of the substitution of her eschatological hope and sacramental mission for a merely this-worldly humanism.[28]

Even if the growth of institutions is taken as an index of the Church's fecundity, one could still question the assumption that they are the fruits precisely of oriental spirituality. Are they not rather manifestations of that western spirituality which, according to the author himself — the Syrians have "in recent times acquired"?[29] Was it not precisely the Latins who gave the lead in this field?

Ironically enough, the author who glories in the fecundity of the Syrian Churches and is critical of dependence on foreign theologians and thinkers[30] is unable to find any scholar in his own community to support his views, and has to fall back on quotations from these very much maligned foreign theologians and thinkers when it comes to buttressing his own arguments!

Return to the Golden Age
Nostalgic longing for a golden age, which never existed, is a phenomenon that emerges whenever a culture or a religion is going through a period of decadence. This cultural-anthropological version of the uterine complex has conditioned much of the thinking embodied in the leaflet in question. Fr. Abraham untiringly harps on the glories and venerable traditions of a Syrian Christianity that existed in some remote past.[31] This uncritical cult of the past, this archeological bias, prevents him from seeing the many positive contributions made by Latin Christianity to the Syrian Churches in Kerala. He seems to be more concerned about bearing witness to this imagined past than to Jesus Christ who is the same yesterday, today and forever.

If Fr. Abraham is committed to a total de-Latinization of the Syrian Churches and to an unconditional return to the pre-Diampur days, then he will have to commit himself to the elimination, from these Churches, of the following Latin elements: (a) pious practices like the recitation of the rosary, the wearing of the scapular, the First Friday devotion, Perpetual Novenas, the Benediction of the Blessed Sacrament, etc., (b) organizations like the Confraternities, the Legion of Mary, the Vincent de Paul Society, etc., (c) the habits currently worn by priests and nuns in Kerala, (d) institutions like schools, colleges, hospitals, etc., (e) the current model of the institutional training of the clergy, (f) and even the law of priestly celibacy. I wonder whether the author, in his loyalty to the ideal of recapturing the original identity of the Syrian Churches, will accept such a programme of radical de-Latinization, and, even if he were to do so, whether the faithful and the hierarchy of the Syrian rites will be prepared to back him up. In this respect at least I am more authentically Syrian than Fr. Abraham as I am prepared to view positively the purging out of some of these Latin elements from the Church in Kerala.

Fr. Abraham is of the view — and in this, I agree with him — that in any attempt at adaptation, we should take care, "not to uproot the peoples' devotional life." [32] Here, we might ask whether the return to the original spirituality of the Syrian Churches would not uproot the devotional life of the common man, as it is intimately bound up with Latin elements. If Fr. Abraham answers that the recapturing of what is originally Syrian will have to be a slow, retrogressive evolution, others could similarly argue that a planned progressive evolution of the three rites into one indigenous rite is possible without unduly upsetting the devotional life of the people.

Conciliar Statements

The conciliar statements quoted by Fr. Abraham in no way invalidate my plea for one indigenous rite in Kerala. The demand for the preservation of the Eastern rites cannot mean the perpetuation of structures and institutions which are not rooted in local cultures and are the matrix of conflicts within the Church. For, the council has affirmed unity and catholicity as the fundamental principles that should guide any liturgical reform.[33] True catholicity means not mere pluralism of rites but a pluralism of rites, based on pluralism of cultures. Hence the conciliar statements cannot be applied uniformly to the Eastern rites in the Middle East and to the Syrian rites in Kerala. Besides, the radical reform of liturgy which the Council envisages in mission countries if honestly carried out in Kerala will bring about the convergence of the present three rites into one indigenous rite for the faithful in Kerala. We should also take note of the fact that the solutions suggested by the Council to problems like multiple jurisdictions are more in the nature of provisional compromises than of definitive decisions valid for all times. Vatican II is just a beginning, not the end of all thinking in the Church.

To conclude, what stands in the way of the planned evolution of the present three rites into one indigenous rite for Kerala is not so much the force of ideas and convictions as the power of deeply entrenched vested interests, economic, social and ecclesiastical. But this need not cause any undue pessimism. For, the Spirit of Christ who even today is working in the Church is more powerful than our "ungodliness and wickedness" which seek to "suppress the truth." (Rm.1:18)

(Vaidikamitram, Vol. 2, 1969, p.227-238; *Ingathering*, Chapter 3)

15

Church and the Challenge of Social Revolution in Kerala

The Problem

A well known Marxist revolutionary in Kerala, has a picture of Jesus put up in a prominent place in his home. Asked for an explanation by a Christian, his reply was, "Well, if Jesus Christ were living today he would certainly be with us in our revolutionary movement." Is this claim true? If true, does it not oblige the Church too to be there, where Christ is, namely, with the forces of revolution that are gathering momentum today? Where in reality does the Church stand in relation to the collective demand of the oppressed masses of Kerala for radical social changes? These are the basic questions to which we shall address ourselves in the following pages.

Dynamics of Revolution

Poverty

To answer these questions, we must investigate the causes, the nature and the extent of this revolutionary ferment. The decisive factor here is the appalling poverty and misery of the masses. Eighty-two percent of India's rural population subsist on a meagre income of 70 paise per day. In Kerala, the percentage of those who belong to this category is greater still, namely, 87 percent.[1] We should also note that by far the majority of the population, to be exact 143,49,574 persons out of a total of 169,03,715, live in the 1575 villages of the State (as against 92 towns).[2] Taking the rural and urban population together, 59 percent of households get a monthly per capita income below Rs 25.[3] And this must be seen against the background of the steep fall, over the last twenty years, in the purchasing power of the Rupee. There is a marked disparity in the distribution of land. About one-third of the households in Kerala do not own any land, while a small minority (0.80 percent) own land ranging from 10-acre holdings to vast estates and plantations.[4] Kerala leads other states in the matter of unemployment also. 2.7 percent of persons belonging to the working-age group between 15-59 (excluding housewives and children) are unemployed.[5] As in the rest of India, so too here, we have to reckon with the depressing fact that, after twenty years of planning, the gulf between the rich and the poor is widening. The contrast is particularly marked in the coastal areas where the landscape is studded with miserable huts, the monotony of which is broken but rarely by the bungalow-type buildings of the middle classes or the palatial homes of the privileged few. Equality of opportunity exists more on paper than in reality. College education, which is a prerequisite for the more remunerative jobs, is beyond the financial means of the poorer classes.[6] Even when the poor can afford it, their children cannot compete with those of upper-class families, and this for the following reasons: First, the facilities required for study, like proper food, light, conveyance, and books are denied to them, second, there is no tradition of learning among the poorer classes since in the past learning was the monopoly of the Brahmin caste. Those few who manage to complete their university education have still to cross innumerable hurdles before they can get jobs, like securing recommendations and having to give bribes or forced donations, none of which is within the means of the poor. Thus, the poor are condemned to remain poor, while the rich become richer and richer. However, the mere fact of poverty and social inequality does not explain the contemporary revolutionary ferment. For the poor were always with us, but the urge for revolution is a phenomenon of comparatively recent origin. The root of the present revolutionary fervour lies not in the quantitative increase of poverty but in the qualitative difference in the concrete experience of poverty.

Secular experience

In the past, poverty and inequality were accepted and experienced as part of an order of things sanctioned by the gods or by an impersonal fate. In this sense, the experience of poverty was sacral. Though realized in time, it had its support in the eternal and the immutable. Consequently, it was devoid of any element of inner tension or conflict. Today with the onset of secularization,[7] poverty has been shorn of its sacral, other-worldly halo and reduced to the domain of profane facticity. With this, the immutability and sanctity of the traditional social order, built on the principle of hierarchical inequality is called into question. Emancipated from the sanction of a personal God or an impersonal law (*dharma*), poverty today is viewed as a contingent evil that man is called upon to eradicate through rational means. Thus secularisation has created conditions favourable to the social revolution.

Horizontal Solidarity

This secular experience of poverty has also become socialized. In the past, the pour man experienced his misery as an individual or as a member of a closed social unit like the caste or the joint family to which he belonged. His economic existence was determined by the relationship of subordination to, and dependence upon, the upper castes and his immediate feudal lord. The latter was the 'gods on earth' who bestowed on their dependants favours in kind or cash. Today this vertical social hierarchy is breaking down, the upper castes are becoming demythologized and reduced to the common denominator of ordinary citizens. The collapse of this vertical solidarity synchronizes with the emergence of horizontal solidarity in various forms. The most significant, among these, is the horizontal solidarity on the basis of shared poverty and misery. The poor belonging to various and even opposed castes and confessions are coming together as the exploited, the underprivileged and the downtrodden, on the plank of common misery. In other words, we are today witnessing the formation of a proletariat in varying degrees of cohesion according to the varying circumstances in different places. Every particularistic loyalty, whether it be to caste, religion, or language, is being neutralized by loyalty to the cause of the working class. Education, social legislation, adult franchise and above all the activities of the Communist Party,[8] have played a role in bringing about this change. The revolutionary implications, of this new development, are obvious. In the past, due to the fragmentation of social feeling and the presence of conflicting loyalties, both of which are characteristic of a caste-ridden society, the exploited found themselves helpless in the presence of tradition-bound unjust social structures. Conflicts, if and when they arose, tended to remain micro-social and could easily be stifled by repressive measures.[9] Today, on the contrary, the poor, forged into one on the basis of common interests, have become conscious of their power. They are awakening to the realization that they are not the mere byproducts of history but its very subject.

Expectation without Fulfillment

The experience of poverty, when secularized and socialized, already contains a call to revolt. This inner tension inherent in the experience of the poor is further accentuated by the ever-widening gap between expectation and fulfillment. The level of expectation is constantly rising, thanks to the pattern of living set by the upper classes, to the promises made by political parties, and to the spread of education. The many poor are witnessing the privileged few enjoying values like better clothing, food, entertainment, leisure, modern means of conveyance, aesthetic satisfaction, etc., while they themselves live in subhuman conditions. What is worse, they are well aware that, given the present pace of development, the lot of their children or even their children's children, is not going to be any better than theirs. Thus in the present-day experience of poverty opposites meet power and frustration, optimism and despair, courage and fear.

Moral Indignation

Another aggravating factor is the recognition by the poor that the sub-human condition to which they are condemned is also an injustice. This is by far the most explosive of the elements that make up the revolutionary ferment. The poor have begun to reflect and reflecting they have come to the conclusion that it is their sweat and blood that make the crops grow and factories run and enable the upper classes to enjoy benefits of modern civilization. Thus, they have come to look upon the rich as social parasites, living on the life-blood of those who toil. However, it is not merely individual exploiters but also social structures that stand between expectation and fulfillment. These structures are in part the relics of feudalism, in part those which go to make up the very warp and woof of democracy, in so far as these are being prostituted by vested interests. For the poor, democracy itself, as it is in practice, has become an enemy, the more formidable since it parades itself under the mask of the government of the people, by the people and for the people. They have come to view democracy, as practiced in Kerala, like alienation, a political outgrowth detached from the mainstream of their life. They see corruption, injustice and inequality thrive under its protective mantle. Thus, the poor and the downtrodden are strangled between the sacral tyranny of the past and the profane, pseudo-democratic tyranny of the present. For them, the overthrowing of this tyranny is simultaneously the vindication of justice. Hence, a revolution has become an ethical imperative, a quest after the realization of human, moral values. It is this ethical element that gives the advocates of revolution courage and a sense of mission.

In sum, the contemporary experience of poverty has become secular, collective, in constant tension between expectation and fulfillment, and instinct with moral fervor and indignation. In other words, it has become charged with the dynamism of revolution. The resulting mental climate among the working classes and their thinking elite may be summed up in the following words of a Marxist thinker of Kerala,

> "The growing economic disparity, the gap between the real income and its purchasing power, the rise in prices, food scarcity, corruption, and black-marketing, the growing hardships of the people, the failure of the men in power to bring about radical changes in the social structure and lead the country to the avowed objective of socialism — these have evoked a moral and spiritual crisis and a sense of helplessness, frustration, despair, and cynicism, as also of anger, indignation and revolt."[10]

In the past, the urge for revolution was mainly in the collective subconscious of the masses. Various cultural and religious inhibitions prevented it from emerging to the level of conscious reflection and decision. Besides, the oppressed masses had no effective leadership, no concrete alternative programme for the reconstruction of society. But today the situation is different. The forces of revolution have become organized, their socio-political goals further defined, thanks to the leadership and propaganda of the Communist Party. However, the mood for revolution is not confined to the laboring classes or professed communists. It is found also among the educated youth of the lower middle class who do not profess allegiance to the Party. For, they too are faced with increasing pauperization and economic insecurity. Unlike the masses, they can reflect consciously on the evils of the present social order and formulate concrete programmes of revolt against the establishment. It is this collective urge for revolt that finds expression in the frequent and innumerable strikes, demonstrations, go-slow programmes, and even outbursts of violence, which mark the social and political life in Kerala today.

The Regional Seminar on the Renewal of the Church has taken note of this situation:

> "We cannot afford to ignore the naked economic reality. Nor can we lightly dismiss the explosive social situation created by the prevalence of wailing mouths and hungry stomachs. The agony of the hungry and the anxiety of the jobless beget discontent and despair. These, in turn, would constitute the smouldering lava deep within the womb of a social volcano that could erupt at any time. When it does, all our good and noble work may be washed out in the devastating outflow."[11]

The Role of the Church in Retrospect

The role of the church concerning this revolutionary ferment has been ambivalent. On the one hand, she has a share in sowing the seeds of revolution; on the other, she is today a powerful and well organized counter-revolutionary force. Her Gospel of justice, equality, and universal love has made the poor and the underprivileged conscious of their dignity as persons. The pioneering work she did in the field of education, and of social service for the benefit of all irrespective of caste or creed has been a standing criticism of the injustices built into the traditional social system. The Christian contribution to education is mainly responsible for the fact that there is today an educated elite among the poorer castes and classes. It is this elite that is now giving articulate expression to the inarticulate revolutionary urge of the masses. To this positive influence exercised by the kerygma and praxis of the church must be added that of western literature and philosophies, which have been an important vehicle of Christian values, the assimilation of which posed a positive threat to the status quo. The present transition from tradition to modernity as well as the contemporary mood for revolt derives not a little from Christian inspiration.

This is but one side of the picture. On the other, the history of the church in Kerala since independence is a record of alliance with conservative socio-political forces. Both her kerygma and praxis show a pronounced bias in favour of the status quo.

The Church has yet to become conscious of her true destiny and mission concerning contemporary society. There has been no serious reflection on her part on the Christian significance of the present revolutionary ferment. Her preaching is geared to a past age and has become greatly anachronistic. It usually presents itself as a message of individual salvation, and that too in the spiritualistic sense of the salvation of the 'soul'. It has scarcely any relevance for the social, corporate and historical destiny of man. And even when it deals with social problems, it concerns itself with justifying the status quo and becomes thus an apologia for an unjust social order. Its main theme might be summed up thus: "The existing socio-economic order is just and is willed by God. Hence it has to be maintained at any cost. The most one may do is to rectify certain defects and imbalances in the present set up." The church calls for better social relations between the rich and the poor, between the employer and the employee, while at the same time justifying the social structures which vitiate these same social relations. She preaches charity, whereas what the people want is justice. Her kerygma is so adapted to the requirements of the status quo, that both the exploiting few and the exploited many among the believers go away equally satisfied: the exploiting because they can congratulate themselves on having already practiced that charity which has been proclaimed from the pulpit; the exploited because they have been assured that their reward in heaven will be commensurate with their misery on earth. Similarly, the church preaches a bourgeois morality whose basic norm is conformity to the established order. The poor are deemed morally upright when he does his work for the current wages, even when these wages do not meet the requirements of justice. His conduct becomes unethical, the moment he questions the justice of the existing wage structure, and he is branded a Communist, a threat to peace. Conversely, the rich who indulge in anti-social practices like black-marketing and hoarding is held up as an example of integrity so long as he makes occasional donations to individual poor, to the church or her charitable institutions!

What is true of the church's teaching applies equally well to her commitment in the socio-political field. She has consistently supported the Congress Party in Kerala even though the latter has little support from the poorer classes, is riddled with corruption, and is controlled by the vested interests of the rich and powerful. She has become a plaything in the hands of these same politicians who spare no effort in organizing receptions to ecclesiastical personages to get the votes of the Christian community. In her support to the Congress as well as in her opposition to the Communist Party, her policy has been shaped less by the principles of the Gospel than by her own economic and denominational interests. She has connived at unjust measures initialed by the Congress governments as in the case of the brutal eviction of settlers from Government lands in 1961-64, whereas she has been highly critical of the communist regime, even when the latter initiated legislation and programmes to bridge the gulf between the rich and the poor.[12] In the political field, the church has abdicated her moral responsibility. She has ceased to be a moral force capable of engaging in meaningful social criticism.

The official church and the religious are assimilated to the rich also based on common economic and political interests. The former need the goodwill and financial support of the rich for the maintenance and expansion of their secular institutions and projects. Conversely, the upper classes look to the clergy and the religious as clients, customers or patrons in the field of business.

Here one might point to the social service activities sponsored by the church as an index of her commitment to the welfare of the poor. Even here a more critical evaluation is called for. While we do not question the sincerity of all those engaged in social services, there is no gainsaying the fact that for quite a few social services have become a means for getting money from within and without the country. In any case, objectively speaking such services are nothing but a bourgeois version of Christian love. For social service is here divorced from social living. There is much work done for the poor, but so little living with the poor. In most cases, those engaged in social services themselves lead a comfortable life, a life that is secure, well ordered, and even well provided with the amenities of modern civilization. It is from this world that they step out into the world of the poor to distribute 'favours' to which the poor have no right. Having done so, they return to the world of security where they belong. This type of social service presupposes and needs for its very continuance a social order based on inequality. In essence, it is but a variation of the favours bestowed on serfs by the old feudal lords. The thinking people among the poor are likely to reject in future such distribution of charity, as they have already done in a few cases in Kerala. In the case of some Christians belonging to the upper classes, this brand of social service comes in handy as a suitable means to neutralize the guilt feelings created by their anti-social practices in professional life. They use social service as a religious veil to cover the nakedness of their unjust social dealings, to provide a religious halo to their irreligious life. Besides, most of the social services tend to perpetuate the same social and economic inequality, the evil effects of which they are meant to remedy. By attending exclusively to the immediate needs of the poor, we lull them into a sense of momentary satisfaction and kill the collective urge to reconstruct society. On the one hand, we give food, clothing, and shelter to the poor; on the other, we assiduously maintain the social conditions and structures which make it impossible for the latter to find food, clothing, and shelter. The current forms of social service, divorced as they are from effective participation in social revolution, are self-contradictory and hypocritical. What the poor and the oppressed expect from the church is neither money, nor food, nor clothing but rather involvement in their day-to-day struggle to change the social, economic and political laws, institutions and customs which maintain them in sub-human conditions of life. What they expect is not favours from above or from outside but collaboration from within, effective sharing in their struggle and anguish of existence. This is precisely what the official church and well-to-do Christians refuse to give. And in doing so, they betray the cause of the working class and knowingly or not, impede the radical reconstruction of society.

This assimilation to the bourgeoisie is observable also in the particular ethos that governs the social life of the clergy and the religious. To cite but a few examples: It is quite becoming for a priest or nun to dine in a posh restaurant; it is unbecoming if he or she does so in a cheap eating place frequented by coolies and beggars. It is quite becoming for a priest or nun to teach in a school or college, to administer institutions, to supervise the cultivation of crops, etc., but it is unbecoming for them to till the soil, to harvest the crop, or to wash clothes for a living. The higher one climbs in the ecclesiastical ladder, the greater is one's assimilation to the bourgeoisie. For instance, it is all right for a layman, nun or priest to walk long distances; not so for a bishop. He must always travel by car, preferably in one imported from abroad. The appurtenance of the clergy to a higher social class is so much taken for granted by the poor people themselves that when a priest visits their homes, they would not dare to offer him the ordinary food they eat or invite him to sit on the bare floor. They will have special food prepared and a chair brought from a neighbouring house for the occasion. With the poor, the clergy and the religious do not feel at home, whereas with people of the upper classes they regain their sense of belonging and find their proper human climate. This explains why most priests and nuns have real friends only among the rich. Finally, it is only the rich and the powerful who have any say in determining the policies of the church in religious as well as secular matters. Thus most bishops and priests in Kerala have around them a set of advisers exclusively drawn from among important, lawyers, land-owners, and businessmen, who form their aristocratic brain trust. The poor are reduced to mere objects of charity or recipients of ministerial service. In short, the clergy and the religious in Kerala tend to form a class apart that is alienated from the poor people and assimilated and subservient to the upper classes.[13]

The social conservatism of the clergy and the religious has percolated to the rank and file of the people of God and created a climate of opinion that is opposed to any radical transformation of the existing social order. The poor who are taught to accept the existing order as sacrosanct have reconciled themselves to an attitude of resigned hopelessness and frustration. The more progressive elite among the Christian youth who feel committed to the eradication of all inequality is forced to emigrate, at least in their hearts, from the church. This is true also of thinking sections among the working class believers. They are becoming disillusioned with a church that stands in the way of their economic salvation in the name of the salvation of their souls. For these people the only alternative is communism. Today the cross of social revolution is borne mainly by those of the working class who have opted for communism. The church is standing on the wayside criticizing and denouncing as this proletarian way of the cross passes by. But it may well happen that, in utter disillusionment with the church more believers cross over to the side of the revolutionary movement led by the Communist Party. The church will then find her ranks depleted and herself made the target of a violent revolution. Hence the very need for survival imposes on the church the obligation to revise radically her present policies. The scope of this essay does not allow us to explain how such a reorientation in view of effective participation in revolution is equally demanded by her God-given mission.[14] In what follows we shall do no more than indicate the main lines which such a reorientation should take.

The church in Kerala should commit herself anew to her original prophetic mission. She should retrace the steps she has taken in the direction of making her message into an ideology at the service of the rich and the powerful, and preach the universal message of the gospel. She should proclaim the Kingdom of God, the kingdom of justice, love and peace, as the future of all men, of the rich and the poor alike, as the future of this concrete world with its laws, structures, and institutions. She should preach the Kingdom not only as God's gift but also as man's creation. She should impress it upon all believers that their very faith demands them to commit themselves to the task of making the present social relations and structures more and more conformable to the demands of the Kingdom, i. e. to the demands of justice and love.[15] It should be her constant concern to show that the Christian hope in the eschatological Kingdom contains historical imperatives for man, here and now, that it is the basis of his earthly hope. Only thus can her preaching become the good news to the poor, a blessing to those who hunger and thirst for justice. In the concrete situation existing in Kerala, the church should not be satisfied with demanding merely a gradual evolution of the present social order into a more equitable one but go a step further and call for the radical and rapid transformation of society. In other words, her prophecy should take the form of a call to social revolution, which however does not mean that she should necessarily advocate the use of violence. If, on the contrary, she were to opt for a gradual eradication of injustice, she would be a party to condemning numberless poor either to premature death or to a life unworthy of man.

As an integral part of her prophetic mission, she should also engage in social criticism.[16] Whereas in the past she exercised such criticism only when her own institutional or denominational interests were at stake, in the future, she should raise her voice against every form of injustice, whether it is committed against believers or not. Her criticism should be directed above all against the injustice embedded in social structures, for instance, against the present unequal distribution of land, the shocking disparities inherent in the wage structure, the denial of equal opportunity to all especially in the matter of higher education and employment, the practice on the part of the rich of evading progressive social legislation by having recourse to legal loopholes, against profiteering, hoarding, black-marketing and various other forms of corruption. The Church's criticism should cover also the revolutionary forces operative in socio-political life. For, these forces and the concrete activities through which they find expression are ethically ambivalent. They are inspired not only by the desire for a just and equitable society but also by hatred, vengeance, and lust for power. Failure to criticize the antisocial elements inherent in the contemporary revolutionary ferment will have fateful consequences, as the new social order brought about_ by revolution may turn out to be more unjust than the one it will have replaced, one in which the exploiters and the exploited of today will have only exchanged their roles. Hence revolutionary criticism by the church must become a criticism of the revolution itself. The church, therefore, while identifying herself with every manifestation of authentic longing for justice, must dissociate herself from those sentiments, policies, and programmes which betray the revolution from within.

Neither prophetic preaching nor prophetic protest will be of much significance if the church fails to commit herself to revolutionary praxis. The greatest scandal in the history of the church in Kerala has been her failure to translate her message into action. Hence the communist claim that they are putting into practice what the church preaches without practicing. It is perhaps here we should seek the reason why precisely in Kerala, where there is a socially dominant Christian community, we find also the strongest communist movement of India. Communism breeds on the Christian impotence to bridge the gulf between theory and praxis. Hence the need for a concerted attempt to make the message of the gospel practically relevant to the aspirations of the poor for more human and humane conditions of life. However, to avoid the emergence of new forms of hierocracy, the task of translating the social message of the church into revolutionary action must be left to the laymen as members of the church and citizens of the country.[17] Drawing inspiration from the prophetic ministry of the official church, Christians should commit themselves to programmes aimed at the elimination of unjust social structures.

In facing this challenge the church will have to reckon with the fact that the present revolutionary movement is inspired and guided by communism. Here one could envisage two possible approaches: the first would consist in creating a non-communist revolutionary front enlisting the support of all men of goodwill irrespective of caste or community, excluding however any collaboration with the Communist Party. Such a front will have for its aim also the weaning away of the working class from the hold of communism. The second approach would consist of critical collaboration with the revolutionary movement guided by the Communist Party, without any intention of creating an alternative revolutionary movement. Neither of these two approaches will be adequate in the present situation. As for the first, it will take a long time before such an anti-communist revolutionary movement can take shape and establish its bona fides before the eyes of the poor. In the meantime, it will be condemned to socio-political impotence. Besides, it is futile to think that the future of the state can be shaped leaving the communists out. Communism has come to stay and is likely to become more and more powerful over time. For, it is the only political movement that is rooted in the masses, that can count upon a band of committed workers and has consistently stood for the poor and oppressed classes. It is mainly the communists who have made the poor aware of their rights, of their claim to a life worthy of man. It is sheer illusion to hope that the poor classes will throw away communism to join any other movement relying merely on its promises.

Hence any Christian action should include within its scope some form or other of collaboration with the communists. Neither will occasional, selective collaboration with communists without creating an alternative democratic revolutionary movement, be fully satisfactory from the Christian point of view. For those engaged in such collaboration may eventually become absorbed into the communist movement, since they are not organized and lack the support of a movement of their own. Such a danger is all the greater since the average educated catholic is ill-equipped intellectually and spiritually to face the fascination of the communist ideology. Hence a combination of both approaches is necessary for the Christians to play any meaningful role in the present crisis. On the one hand, the Christians should form a democratic revolutionary front together with the adherents of other religious beliefs based on commonly shared ideals; on the other, they should offer critical collaboration to the Communist Party. In other words, they should judge each measure, each programme, sponsored by the communists on its own merits and offer or withhold support according to whether the objectives aimed at and the means to be employed align with the demands of justice and equality.[18] Only such critical collaboration within the framework of a democratic revolutionary movement will be able to liquidate centres of reaction and reconstruct a just social order. To promote such collaboration the church should initiate dialogue with all those committed to social revolution.[19]

Ecclesial Revolution as Condition for Social Revolution

Any significant participation of the church in the revolutionary movement requires as a *conditio sine qua non* a revolution within the church itself, both in her thinking and acting, as is clear from the analysis we made earlier in this essay. What should be the nature and the scope of this revolution?

The church should learn to read the signs of the times, to understand history in the light of the gospel, and to understand the gospel in the light of history. Her theology should derive not only from above but also from below, i.e. from the concrete life of the people. In other words, she should listen not only to the word as contained in the Bible but also to the Word operative in historical situations, events, and movements. Such an attempt at revision should extend also to her traditional ethics, especially to the prevailing conceptions regarding private property, nationalization, individual rights, and social peace. She should ask herself whether these conceptions do not contain elements that are conditioned by a social order which served the interests of a privileged few.

The present mode of seminary formation, which turns out every year numerous priests who are uprooted from their own culture and alienated from the common people, must undergo a radical change. During their very formation, seminarians should be made to experience the economic insecurity and the existential anguish of the poorer classes and share their aspirations for a just social order. Only such a generation of priests will be able to give leadership to those who hunger and thirst for justice.

To engage in effective social criticism the official church must be inwardly free from vested interests and bourgeois loyalties. And she should lack this freedom so long as she clings to her educational, charitable and developmental institutions. Hence she must make a determined effort shortly to get rid of the socio-economic empire she has built for herself. The vast landed properties owned by the official church and by religious orders must be distributed among the poor[20] or transferred to duly erected trusts under the control of competent men drawn from the different communities. Money coming from abroad for socio-economic projects must be directly made available to such organizations or trusts without having to go through ecclesiastical hands.

Priests and nuns who engage in secular activities should take care not to undertake administrative or financial responsibilities.

In the past, the bishops lived in their glass houses and issued statements and directives on socio-political situations of which they had no real knowledge. What little they knew reflected the biased version supplied by lay leaders belonging to the upper classes. In the future, they should consult laymen representing all classes within the church before they issue official statements and pass judgments. Hence the need for occasional as well as institutionalized dialogue between the clergy and the laity. It is from such dialogue rather than from preaching alone that the laity in the future will draw inspiration for truly Christian action in the political field.

Bishops, priests, and nuns should recapture the authentic spirit of evangelical poverty. This means not merely the giving up of all pomp and luxury in the matter of dress, housing, conveyance, etc., but also a sincere identification with the economic insecurity of the common man. Like the poor, they too should work to live. Else their claim to represent the Christ of the Gospel will lack credibility, and they too will be counted as social parasites. All that makes the clergy and the religious today a sociologically distinct class assimilated to the bourgeoisie must be eradicated. They should be with the people so that the problem of 'going to the people' will not arise in the future. All this will demand not only a personal renewal on the part of individual bishops, priests and nuns but also a fundamental change in ecclesial structures.

Will the church in Kerala be able to face this challenge and bring about the necessary renewal given her task in the world of today? Realism forbids us to expect any significant change to come from the top, i.e. from ecclesiastical authorities. For since the Vatican council there has been if anything, a hardening of reactionary attitudes on the part of the official church. But there is a strong minority of the younger clergy and the laymen who are fully aware of the need for a radical change in the church's policy. Unfortunately, these are disorganized and lack the courage of conviction to air their views in public, much less to translate them into action. Much would depend on whether they will muster enough courage to organize themselves in the future to bring their influence to bear upon the renewal of the church. There is yet another source of hope. Though those who are in charge of the destiny of the church do little to give it a new direction and purpose, they may eventually be forced to do so by God working in and through historical events and forces, perhaps even in and through the revolutionary movement gathering strength in Kerala. For Christ and his cross are not absent from this collective urge of the poor masses to revolt against an unjust social order and usher in a new order of things in which it would be possible for them to live a life worthy of man.

(Vaidikamitram, vol. 3, No. 1, pp. 25-44; *Ingathering*, Chapter 4)

16

The Role of the Church in National Development

Introduction

The Pastoral Constitution on the Church in the Modern World, marks the beginning of a new awareness on the part of the Church, of her role in the promotion of the earthly wellbeing and development of man. Implicit in this new awareness, is an evaluation of the current practice of the Church in this respect and a call to reorient Christian action, in the temporal sphere, in the light of the socio-cultural changes taking place today. Correspondingly, the aim of this article is two-fold: to evaluate the role the Church in India in the promotion of man's earthly welfare, especially in the field of education and socio-economic development, and to explore the new direction, her activity should take in the future.

Any scientifically accurate evaluation should be based on the relevant data regarding both the extent and the consequences of the Church's present secular commitments. Unfortunately, there is a dearth of such data especially where the consequences of the temporal action of the Church are concerned, little socio-religious research has been done in this field in India. And yet we cannot afford to wait till all the relevant data are forthcoming, as any delay in assessing the present situation, may lead to the Church's evolving along wrong lines and consolidating irrelevant structures and institutions. Hence even a tentative assessment like the present one can serve a useful purpose.

The Extent and Nature of the Church's Secular Commitments
The activities of the Church in the temporal sphere may be grouped under three heads: educational, charitable and developmental, leaving out her action in the political field, as this has not assumed any institutionalized form. Under the first category come kindergartens, schools, colleges, technical institutes, etc.; under the second, crèches, orphanages, homes for the destitute, homes for fallen women, dispensaries, hospitals, boys towns, etc.; under the third, co-operatives, industrial estates, schemes for the production, storage and distribution of food grains, irrigation projects, etc.

In 1964 there were 7382 Catholic educational institutions in the whole of India, ranging from kindergartens to university colleges.[1] Of these, 724 are secondary schools.[2] The number of university colleges totaled 76 in 1967.[3] Charitable institutions including hostels for boys and girls numbered 1743 in 1964.[4] In the Catholic Directory 1964, developmental activities are grouped indiscriminately under, either educational or charitable institutions. During the last three or four years innumerable Church-sponsored developmental projects have sprung up, of which we have no statistical data. On a rough estimate, the total number of educational, charitable and developmental institutions and projects sponsored by the Church in India, may come to 10,000. While certain charitable institutions like orphanages, homes for the destitute, etc., do not show any appreciable increase in number over the last decade, we are witnessing a vast proliferation of educational and developmental institutions and programmes.

Recent years have also witnessed a considerable increase in the clerical-religious personnel, engaged in these activities. While, in the past, it was mainly those who were destined for teaching, who underwent specialized training, today priests and nuns are seeking professional training, also in social service and developmental activities. The quantum of foreign aid also has assumed gigantic proportions during the last decade. We notice also efforts to co-ordinate and centralize these secular activities of the Church both at the diocesan and national levels. How are we to evaluate this ever-growing temporal institutional complex? Is this whole development something to be welcomed? Does it contain elements, which militate against the true nature and mission of the Church?

Positive Gains

The increasing commitment of the Church, to the secular well-being of man, bears witness to the awareness that she should not confine herself to the sacristy but should become involved in the destiny of the common man. Implied also is the realization — though often confused and inarticulate — that the building up of the Kingdom of God here on earth is not to be identified with the numerical expansion of the visible Church. The various activities initiated for the welfare and development of man have also served to project the image of the Church as a people dedicated to the service of mankind, especially of the poor and the underprivileged. Christian institutions have contributed not a little to the leveling down of caste distinctions by not recognizing caste-superiority as a title to preferential treatment. They have played a significant role also in defending and fostering values like the equality of all men and the dignity of the human person. We may reckon as a positive gain also the secular achievements of the Church. The type of education imparted in our schools and colleges is recognized as superior to that given in other educational institutions. Catholic hospitals are well known for the quality of professional service rendered. These positive gains, however, should not make us blind to the evils inherent in the present trend and to the serious pastoral-missionary problems it creates.

A Question of Survival

Before we examine these negative aspects, a word about the economic-political future of the Church's activities in the temporal order. Economically, our educational institutions are on safer ground than our other activities, as in their case the expenses are met either with the fees collected from students or/and grants from government or university agencies. The same optimism cannot be voiced with regard to their political future. One should take into account the tendency, on the part of the government and the university, to pass laws which would severely curtail the autonomy of private educational institutions, in the matter of the choice and payment of teachers, of determining the curricula, etc. It is now realized that "with every academic year, the Christian colleges throughout India are increasingly restricted in the exercise of their individuality and their ability to function as Christian institutions."[5] This problem has become acute in Kerala and may become so also in other States depending on the ideology of the government in power. In respect of economic and political security, Christian charitable and developmental activities, pose a greater problem. For one thing, these depend heavily on material help from Christian and secular sources abroad, and in this sense, their economic base is mainly outside the country. For another, the influx of money from abroad is becoming more and more suspect in the eyes of the government. The course of events in the recent past, especially in North India, seems to indicate that the government is moving to a policy that would demand that, in the future, all financial help sent to the Church from abroad should be channeled through governmental agencies. If that comes true, many of our charitable and developmental activities will have to be given up. Even those institutions which do not depend heavily on foreign help, like hospitals, have to compete with government-aided institutions and may cease to become financially viable. The prevailing sense of complacency has, therefore, little ground for justification.

The Church, a Sign of Division?

One of the most significant points of crystallization of the Church's self-awareness today is to be found in the affirmation that she is "by her relationship with Christ, both a sacramental sign and an instrument of intimate union with God, and of the unity of all mankind."[6] The Church in her existence and activity must be a unifying factor. Any of her activities which promote disunity must be held as spurious and unauthentic. Seen in this light, the temporal activities of the Church in India, present a disturbing picture. Do they not generate conflicts between various sections of the people of God? To begin with, they seem to create tension between the clergy and the laity. The activities and institutions under consideration are predominantly secular in character. They are secular in their goals insofar as they pursue the well-being and advancement of man here on earth; they are also secular in the methods employed since these are derived from various profane sciences. The fact that they are occasionally or even regularly associated with religious activities and services should not obscure the intrinsically secular character of the bulk of the work that is done. Though secular in aims and methods, these institutions are in varying degrees and in different ways under the control of the official Church. Usually, all responsible positions are held by the clerical-religious personnel. To cite but one example, out of the 724 secondary schools, only 92 have lay principals.[7] This applies also to charitable and developmental activities. This is a stumbling block and a scandal to the educated laity, as in their opinion priesthood and religious vocation should not entitle one to secular status and authority. They see in this a form of clerical domination and criticize it in the strongest terms. If the tensions inherent in this situation often remain underground and seldom take the form of open conflict, it is partly due to the tradition of unquestioned acquiescence in which the laity, especially of the older generation, have been brought up. But with the coming of age of the laity and with the growth of secularism within and outside the Church, the present tensions and conflicts are bound to increase.

The Church's present mode of involvement in the temporal order introduces a division even within the ranks of the clergy, and religious sisters. These tend to fall into two classes: those priests and religious who have power, prestige, and money associated with temporal institutions, and those others who are deprived of these because they devote themselves to the less prestigious activities like pastoral ministry, catechetical instruction and the more humble type of social services. In the contemporary Indian Church, the business-minded, fund-raising type of priest seems to have a marked ascendency over the charismatic priest and has established himself somewhat as an ideal, others may aspire to.

Some of our secular institutions tend to alienate also the poorer classes — Christians as well as non-Christians — from the clergy and the religious, and this for two reasons. First of all, many of our educational institutions at the higher levels are of benefit primarily to the upper and middle classes and only marginally to the poor.[8] This applies also to many of our better-equipped hospitals in urban areas. Secondly, the maintenance and expansion of these temporal institutions are not possible without money and influence, both of which are the prerogative of the rich. Hence the understandable concern of priests and nuns to cultivate assiduously the friendship of the rich and the powerful. This is offset to a great extent by the fact that the Church is sponsoring a large number of institutions and projects throughout the country, which directly help the poorer classes. But even here there is a need for self-criticism. Are we not treating the poor and the under-privileged merely as objects of charity and not enough as 'subjects', who too have something to share with us? Will not such a mode of service, in the long run, create collective resentment in the very people we are trying to help since we render help as it were 'from outside' without really identifying ourselves with their anguish of existence and experience of insecurity? Moreover, by providing massive economic assistance, do we not create the impression that we really belong to the category of the 'haves' as opposed to the 'have nots'?

The divisive forces, inherent in the temporal activities of the Church, affect also her relationship with non-Christians. This relationship has undergone a change since independence. A decade or two ago, Christian service in the educational and social sphere was accepted and welcomed by the majority community as a means of social and economic emancipation. Today, this is no longer the case. The frequent questions raised in the Parliament criticizing the religious and socio-economic activities of missionaries, the attempts made to bring about legislation to control the flow and utilization of money sent from abroad for the activities of the Church, the violent anti-Christian propaganda carried on by militant Hindu groups like the Jan Sangh, the expulsion of missionaries engaged in welfare and relief work; all these are indices of a significant change in the Hindu attitude towards the Christian community. In this mounting hostility to Christian action in the educational and socio-economic field, we should recognize the signs of the times. It is true that such hostility is not uniformly present everywhere in India nor shared by all. There are still vast numbers of people who are grateful for the work we do. It is equally true that political hostility often co-exists with a personal appreciation of our services. Yet the trend itself of growing antipathy to Christian enterprises is something to be reckoned with. Its causes must be analyzed and its missiological implications studied.

The problem must be seen in its historical perspective. In the pre-Independence days Hindus could afford to view Christian presence and action with tolerance as they were in a position of relative security, and as the secular-institutional complex within the Church had not yet assumed such proportions as today. The last two decades, however, have witnessed a progressive disintegration of the sociological base of Hinduism, namely of joint-family, caste and village economy.

The collapse of the sociological infrastructure of Hinduism and the impact of Western ideology have undermined also Hindu beliefs and practices. This has reduced Hinduism to a position of insecurity and put its followers on the defensive. Hinduism is today faced with the problem of survival. This sense of insecurity is heightened by the phenomenal growth of Christian institutions and activities and by the socio-economic-political power which is its essential concomitant. There is the fear that this mighty religious-secular build-up might engulf and eventually eliminate a tottering Hinduism and that it may be used to lure the backward classes into the Christian fold. This fear-complex — along with other socio-cultural factors — explains much of the militant anti-Christian propaganda carried on especially in the north. The historical resentment against the 'Christian' domination of British colonialism, today, feeds on what looks to the Hindus like the subtle — and therefore more dangerous — neo-colonialism of Christian secular-institutional domination. We shall not be far from the truth, if we assert that it is partly the desire to counteract the increasing socio-economic power of the Christian Churches that has led to the policy of Hindu organizations and groups to open parallel institutions like schools, colleges, hospitals, etc. This parallel development, in its turn, breeds jealousy, rivalry, and tension between the two communities. It would seem therefore that the Hindu opposition is not so much to Jesus Christ as to the concrete historical form of Christianity in India, which professes allegiance to him; it is not even so much to the Church as to her socio-economic power. But it is not power alone that divides. Many Hindus see in the type of education we give in our schools and colleges a divisive factor insofar as it produces an elite that is uprooted from Indian culture and alienated from the masses.[9] Hence it is incumbent on us to revise radically the present policy of the Church so that she really becomes what at present she is not fully, namely, an effective sign of the unity of all men among themselves.

The Church a Leaven or a Ghetto?

The Church is called to serve "as a leaven and as a kind of soul for human society."[10] A true leaven must be in close contact with, and somehow connatural to, the mass to be fermented. Further, it must have the capacity to cause fermentation. Similarly, the Church must be in vital contact with Indian society and assimilated into its culture. She must also be filled with the leavening spirit, so that the face of Christ may shine through her. How does the emerging secular complex stand in relation to the Church's contact with the world and to her own authentic religious existence and mission?

The secular set-up in question has the appearance of an artificial world which the Church has built up on the margin of the real world, as a soil of secular annex to her properly religious existence and pseudo-religious annex to the secular world. This 'world' stands between the Church with her religious activities and institutions on the one side, and the real world where the destiny of the country is shaped, on the other. One might, however, argue that it is precisely through the mediation of this 'world' that the Church as an organization is able to come in contact with the various strata of Indian society. But it is necessary to ask whether this contact is as it should be. The Church, even as a socially organized body, has to fulfill the function of being the sacrament of salvation. Hence the specific contact she seeks with the world must be at the inter-personal, existential-religious level. When one views the Church's temporal activities and institutions as a whole, one cannot but conclude that they do not create the conditions for such a truly dialogical contact with the world. The factors responsible for this are, among others, the mass character of the services rendered with its concomitant anonymity and impersonation, the possession of secular authority by priests and religious which reduces the beneficiaries to a position of dependence, the dissociation of the helping deed from the revealing 'word', the cult of efficiency and the climate of legalism that prevails in many of our institutions,[11] and the disparity in culture and standard of living between the clerical-religions personnel and the common man. In consequence, the temporal concerns of the Church act more like a protective shell than as an instrument of dialogue with Indian society.

The very factors which prevent the Church's redeeming contact with the world also distort her image in the eyes of non-believers. These naturally tend to identify the Church with her imposing secular facade. For them, the Church is something like the United Nations Organization, a worldwide association for the cultural and economic development of man. It is only secondarily, if at all, that they think of her in terms of her belief and religious mission. Moreover, the Church's gospel of the primacy of love is often neutralized and contradicted in practice by the legalism prevailing in our institutions. Her catholicity is compromised by a culture and an ethos that is alien to the people.

Her Diakonia does not appear as unselfish service as it is coupled with power and prestige. Her striving for human welfare does not appear convincingly genuine as it is divorced from living with the people. She does not project herself as a truly uncompromising moral force as much of her secular activity is ethically neutral and as her moral judgments are often vitiated by secular vested interests.

The practices and policies currently followed with regard to temporal action have also a secularizing influence on the Church. The secular recoils on the religious sphere and stifles the pneumatic within the Church. This is seen in the conscious or sub-conscious use of secular criteria in determining priorities, in evaluating the success or failure of local Churches, in the excessive preoccupation of priests and religious with raising financial resources, and in the mobilization of the human and material resources of the Church for temporal activities to an extent which cannot be justified on pastoral or missionary grounds. Has not all this led to the neglect, on the part of the official Church, of its priestly, prophetic and pastoral mission? Have not liturgical services fallen into empty formalism in many places? Is not the teaching of catechism and religion neglected in our schools and colleges?[12] Have not pastoral visits fallen into disuse or been reduced to merely social or business calls? Can the Church in India honestly say that she is above all the place where Jesus Christ can be encountered and his message heard by non-believers? As for the very poor, do not priests and religious act on the assumption that their only obligation is to feed them, as though the injunction Christ gave to his disciples, "Preach the gospel to the poor", has become outdated, as though the words of Peter that he has neither silver nor gold but only the power of the name of Christ, have no relevance for his successors today?

The secular preoccupations of the clergy and the consequent neglect of pastoral work have repercussions also on the laity. Not being nourished adequately on the word and the sacrament, and deprived of suitable pastoral guidance, the laity becomes incapable of bearing witness to Christ before non-Christians. More and more educated laymen are drifting away from the Church and succumbing to the religion's indifferentism and materialism that are in vogue today. Even the Church-going laity have not awakened to their being the Church. The Church for them is the hierarchy and its institutions. As a result, they understand their Christian vocation in terms of approximating to the clerical-religious world or of associating themselves with it. They shunt their specific responsibility to promote the earthly well-being of man and to consecrate the secular city on to the all too willing shoulders of the clergy and the religious and to foreign benefactors. Thus the average layman has acquired two faces: one religious and the other profane. The first is turned exclusively to the hierarchical-institutional Church; the second alone is turned to the world of their secular professions. In other words, insofar as they are Christians, they are not citizens of the country; and insofar as they are citizens, they are not Christians. Thus as a community, they fail to be a redeeming leaven in the secular city.

To sum up, our analysis thus far has shown that there are certain elements inherent in the present mode of secular commitment on the part of the clergy and the religious which make the Church a sign of division and prevent her being a divinizing leaven in India.

The Dynamics of the Present Trend

Before we attempt to define the role of the Church in the temporal sphere, it would be worthwhile to ascertain the factors and attitudes which go to form the dynamics of the present development in the Church. The increasing involvement of the Church in secular matters is partly a continuation of her traditional policies, partly a reaction to her experiences in the past. Latin Christianity came into existence in India as a colonial extension of the Church in Europe, which subsequently influenced also the Syrian Christian communities. It brought, along with it, the ethos and the structures of medieval theocracy which found a favourable soil in India, where the priestly class of the Brahmins enjoyed also socio-economic privileges. The activity of the Church was therefore shaped by the conviction that, over and above her religious mission, she has also a properly secular mission, that the secular should be subordinated to the religious as a means to an end. This attitude is still prevalent among many priests and bishops. The theocratic ethos found a further incentive in the objective need for the Church to engage in secular tasks like education and charitable activities, as there were in the early days no other agencies willing to undertake them. This was particularly the case with education.[13] The Church thus did pioneering work in the socio-economic and cultural fields. The institutions she started were understandably under clerical control, as there was a certain confusion of the roles of the official Church and the laity, and as there were not enough competent laymen to undertake such activities. Their denominational character too was strongly marked mainly due to the wrong missiological ideas prevalent in those days. The early missionaries, with a few exceptions, had a negative approach to Indian culture as it was identified with 'pagan' Hinduism and was rejected as hostile to Christianity. Hence one of the main concerns of the official Church was to protect the Christian community from the 'pernicious' influence of Hinduism and Indian culture. As a result, the Church in India developed its own psychological variation of distance pollution so characteristic of caste-ridden Indian society and became something like a pseudo-caste among other castes. This pollution complex was also extended to other Christian Churches as these were considered the embodiment of heresy. Consequently, the Church in her religious-secular activities was caught up in a process of involution, which was further facilitated by the identification of the Church of Christ with her historical expression in the West. It is in this process of involution that we should seek the root of the contemporary tendency of the Church to create her own institutional ghettos.

The development of the Church during the last decade or so reveal also certain features that are new. What strikes one first is the phenomenal rate of growth of secular institutions sponsored by the Church. But this quantitative growth reveals, on deeper analysis, a qualitative change, which consists in the fact that the axis of ecclesial activity ad extra has shifted from conversion to development.[14] In the earlier days, schools and colleges were opened primarily to educate Catholic children and

— though this was not openly admitted — to promote the conversion of non-believers. Even social work was considered a means of securing conversions. However, this policy eventually proved a failure, at least when we measure the results against the expectations. For converts came only from the poorer castes and even their number declined in course of time for various socio-political reasons. There have been only very few converts from the upper castes and from the intelligentsia. This gave rise to a poignant sense of frustration and defeatism among the clergy and the religious, Indian as well as foreign. Such pent up frustration has today found a convenient outlet in commitment to educational, charitable and developmental activities. For here, at last, one sees concrete results: crops raised, wells dug, houses built, patients healed, children educated, etc. Missionary zeal is reborn as zeal for the welfare and development of man. The Church in India today is in the process of transition from a theocratic to an almost secularist concept of her mission. If in the past temporal activities were considered a means for the fulfillment of her religious mission, today they are made into a means to promote man's earthly welfare, "as though the divine teaching of Jesus Christ and his work itself were simply a recipe to be used to achieve a purely human result".[15] However, the momentum of tradition and the mystique of development do not exhaust the dynamics of the secular commitments of the Church. Once a temporal process is set in motion, it gathers strength by a certain immanent law of supply and demand. It is also accelerated by extraneous factors like considerations of prestige and power. The present development of the Church, along secular lines, is therefore motivated not so much by serious pastoral-missionary thinking as by historical, psychological and existential factors.

Orientations for the Future

Our analysis thus far has shown that a reorienting of the Church's action, in the temporal sphere, is urgently needed in India. What are the principles that should guide such a reorientation? Which are the policies that call for a radical revision? In the following pages a tentative, exploratory attempt is made to answer these questions.

1. There is first of all the need for a shift in emphasis in the very self-understanding of the Indian Church in relation to secular realities. The Church should realize that her true mission is "to proclaim and spread among all peoples the Kingdom of Christ and of God and to be on earth the initial budding forth of the Kingdom." [16] She should muster enough courage to be herself, to be true to her identity as the sacrament of salvation for all. She should not ask to be anything more or anything less. In relation to the secular, this means two things. Negatively, she should not seek to supplant the autonomy of man, of society and of earthly realities. She has not come to be a substitute for the State or to be a State alongside the Secular State. She has "no proper mission in the political, economic or social order."[17] Besides, she should not fail to distinguish clearly between earthly progress and the growth of the Kingdom of God.[18] This means that she should not act on the assumption that men are brought nearer to God merely by being better fed, better clothed or better provided with the amenities of modern civilization. "Grace is grace, and profane history is not the source of salvation. Evangelization is of a different order from that of civilization. To feed man is not in itself to save them, though my own salvation obliges me to feed them. To promote culture is not the same as converting men to faith."[19] More positively, the temporal action of the Church must be guided by the realization that her role consists not so much in continuing the work of creation as in leading it to its eschatological fulfillment in Christ, not so much in constructing the earthly city as in shaping it according to the mind of God, not so much in improving the living conditions of men as in leading them nearer to God and to one another. To achieve this end, the Church should bring the light of the Gospel to bear on the world of men and things, inject into Indian society the energy "which consists in that faith and charity put into vital practice, not in any external dominion exercised by merely human means."[20]

2. In the fulfillment of this social mission, the proper roles of the official Church and the laity must be respected.

> "As regards activities and institutions of the temporal order, the role of the ecclesiastical hierarchy is to teach and authentically interpret the moral principles to be followed in temporal affairs. Furthermore, it has the right to judge, after careful consideration of all related matters and consultation with experts, whether or not such activities and institutions conform to moral principles. It has also the right to decide what is required for the promotion of values of the supernatural order." [21]

It is not normally the task of the hierarchy to translate the social message of the Church into concrete prescriptions or to initiate specific programmes for the Christian ordering of the earthly city or for the development of human society. Such direct involvement, coming from the official Church, smacks of clerical triumphalism implying, on the one hand, an over-estimation of the role of the hierarchy in shaping the world and, on the other, an underestimation of its properly religious mission (Rahner). It leads in practice to the denial of the autonomy not only of the secular but also of laymen, in the exercise of their Christian responsibility for the consecration of the earthly city.

The official Church, therefore, should give up the illusion that it should or even can promote national development and Christianize the temporal order over the heads of the laity. Besides fulfilling its primary function, which is "so to preach the message of Christ that all earthly activities of the faithful will be bathed in the light of the Gospel" [22], the official Church should concentrate its efforts on the dissemination of the Christian social message among the masses and the intelligentsia, on social evaluation and social criticism, and on dialogue with the secular city so that the latter will take shape according to the mind of Christ. These services rendered by the Church will fulfill a real need in India, where the traditional dichotomy between religion and ethics is having adverse repercussions on various aspects of national life, where the factors, retarding development, are not so much economic as ethical, like corruption, nepotism, power-politics, and exploitation of the masses. It is ironic and even tragic that the Church in India, which is going all out to promote economic development, is doing so little to create the rational and ethical infrastructure of development that she is eminently qualified to do. The time has come for the Church to give up its all too material preoccupations and emerge as a moral force guiding the evolution of Indian society at this critical period of its history.

3. The official Church should recognize in practice that the consecration of the secular city and the promotion of human development, is primarily and properly the task of the laity.

> "From priests, they may look for spiritual light and nourishment. Let the layman not imagine that his pastors are always such experts, that to every problem, which arises, however complicated, they can readily give him a concrete solution, or even that such is their mission. Rather, enlightened by Christian wisdom and giving close attention to the teaching authority of the Church, let the layman take on his own distinctive role." [23]

This role they are to fulfill on their own responsibility and in collaboration with all men of goodwill. [24] The recognition of such lay responsibility also demands that the bishops and priests respect the healthy pluralism that may exist among laymen where there is a question of finding concrete solutions to socio-economic and political problems in the light of the Gospel.

4. In order to bring the temporal action of the Church into greater conformity with these principles and to solve the pastoral-missionary problems discussed earlier, it is necessary to aim at a progressive withdrawal of Church-sponsored temporal institutions and projects from direct ecclesiastical control. These temporal undertakings should be not more under the control of the hierarchy than the similar secular activities of ordinary laymen. They should eventually be entrusted to duly erected, autonomous trusts or associations of laymen. Here it could be objected that there are not enough reliable and competent laymen to undertake these jobs. This is largely a convenient myth created and perpetuated by clerical vested interests. How else could we explain the fact that the other Christian Churches, though numerically smaller, have been able to find competent laymen to run most of their educational and other institutions? Moreover, if there is a shortage of competent laymen, that very fact is indicative of a vicious circle in which we are caught up:

There are not enough such laymen because the clergy refuse to share responsibility with them and are too engrossed in temporal matters to be able to attend to their Christian formation; and because there are not enough capable laymen, the clergy feel justified in devoting themselves more and more to secular activities and monopolizing all responsible positions. This vicious circle can be broken only if the clergy take the initiative in progressively handing over responsibility to laymen and make every attempt to create a responsible lay elite in the Church. In the long run, such a policy will be beneficial to the Church, though in the immediate future it may — even this is doubtful — lead to a certain decline in the standards of efficiency.

In our educational and other institutions, priests should normally undertake only those functions which are related to their priestly ministry, like the teaching of catechism, religion and moral science, student counseling and spiritual guidance. Priests should engage in secular activities only where such involvement is called for by the pastoral-missionary needs of the Church. The Council too views the direct involvement of the clergy in secular matters rather as the exception than the norm.

> "It is true that those in holy orders can at times engage in secular activities, even have a secular profession. But by reason of their particular vocation, they are chiefly and professedly ordained to the sacred ministry."[25]

In the case of those priests who may continue to work in temporal institutions under lay administration, the principle should be strictly followed that religious authority does not entitle one to secular power and that priestly office does not seem to confer additional competence in secular matters.

5. However, declericalization alone will not solve all the problems we raised at the beginning of this essay. It is necessary to make Christian activity, in the temporal order, progressively more ecumenical. Such activity should not only express the unity that is already there among Christians of various denominations in India but also promote and bring about the unity that is willed by God. The Church should explore all

avenues of co-operation with our non-Catholic brethren in her effort to shape Indian society according to the mind of Christ. The ecumenical collaboration that has already been initiated at the national level through structures like Afpro (Action for Food Production) and The National Board of Christian Higher Education in India should be extended also to the regional and local levels. Vatican II considers such collaboration particularly necessary in developing countries.[26] Collaboration with other Christian denominations will be an enriching experience for the Church especially because the former has set an example by promoting lay responsibility in secular matters.

Ecumenical collaboration should cover also our relations with non-Christians. Though Christian denominational institutions may be found necessary in some places and under certain conditions, the missionary needs of the Church and the socio-cultural changes, taking place in India today, demand that we further expand the base of our action in the temporal order by enlisting the co-operation also of non-Christians. At a time when elemental forces of disintegration are breaking out throughout the country and the whole nation is in search of a unifying soul, we Christians cannot afford to withdraw into our institutional shells and refuse to fulfill our Christ-given mission to be an instrument of union and reconciliation. The need for co-operating with non-Christians has been emphasized also by thinking non-Catholic Christians in India.[27] The time is now ripe for such joint Hindu-Christian commitment to the right ordering of the secular city, as the ethical values we are trying to incorporate in Indian society are no longer the monopoly of the Christian community, but have become the common property of all right-minded Indians and have been enshrined even in the Indian Constitution. A reorientation of Christian action along these lines will eliminate the ghetto character of the Church and create the conditions for meaningful dialogue between Christianity and non-Christian religions in India.

6. Finally, the clergy and the laity must give up their almost exclusive reliance on separate institutions, whether they be strictly denominational

or ecumenically structured, for the promotion of the well-being and development of man and for the Christian ordering of Indian society. This task devolves primarily upon the vast majority of individual Christians who are employed in the various services of the State, in independent professions or in institutions sponsored by other secular or religious agencies. For it is these laymen who are in immediate contact with the various structures and institutions where the future of our country is shaped. It is chiefly they who can truly achieve the synthesis of working for the people and living with the people. Bishops and priests should, therefore, give top priority, in the years to come, to the moral and religious formation of an adult laity, who will, in turn, infiltrate the various structures and institutions of the country and guide their future development from within. Thus the entire people of God will bear witness to Christ who came not to be served but to serve (Mt. 20:28).

Such a shift in emphasis from separate institutions, be they wholly or partly sponsored by Christians, to the individual or organized lay activity within the framework of the various structures of national life will in no way bring about a diminution of the influence of the Church as some seem to fear. Rather the opposite is the truth. The short history of Communism in India should act as an eye-opener to us in this regard. Though the followers of Marx and Lenin have not set up their own communist schools, colleges, hospitals, etc., they are today perhaps a more dominant ideological force in India than even Christianity, with its long history of institutional activity. While Christians remained enclosed in their institutional ghettos, the Communists managed to infiltrate into every sector and stratum of national life. Here too "the children of this world are more astute than the children of light" (Lk. 16: 9). Besides, those who entertain the fear that such a shift in policy will diminish the influence of the Church, usually confuse the mission of the Church with the exercise of secular influence through socio-economic-political power and prestige. Further, they identify the influence of the Church with that of the official Church. They forget that the laity too is the Church and that their Christian action in a secular society "is truly an activity of the Church, not, it is true, wholly directed by the Church's hierarchy, but inspired and guided by the spirit of the Church."[28]

The reorientation of ecclesial activity in the temporal sphere along the lines indicated above will make the Church what Christ willed her to be, what the people of India expected her to be, a unifying leaven in the Indian Society and the sacrament of salvation. On the contrary, if the Church were to perpetuate the status quo and continue with the present policies, she would eventually become more in need of redemption than the world she is meant to be an instrument in redeeming. In trying to be all things to all men, she would cease to be herself; in her effort to gain the whole world she would run the risk of losing her own soul. This is the anguishing choice that faces the Church in India today.

(Clergy Monthly, Feb. 1969, pp.59-75; *Ingathering*, Chapter 6)

17

Christianity as Liberation

The Quest after Freedom

Our age is marked by a universal quest for freedom. This quest has more than one dimension. Man is today striving to overcome his bondage to nature. Through science and technology, he is trying to fight disease, senility, famine, floods and other natural calamities. He is engaged also in freeing himself from social evils like injustice, inequality, and exploitation. He wants to overthrow the structures, institutions, and laws that reduce the many to being slaves of a favoured few. These efforts at self-emancipation are today assuming vast proportions. They are also drawing inspiration from various ideologies of liberation, the most important of which is communism.

Finally, at the deeper level, there is man's attempt to free himself: from the ambivalence of freedom, from the possibility of individual and collective suicide. What is the ultimate end of all this striving for liberation? What is its Christian meaning and value? What ethical imperative does it contain for the Christian?

The Liberation That Is Yet to Come

Unlike the philosophies of despair, the Christian faith projects a horizon of hope, the hope that all human striving for liberation will find fulfillment in the realization of absolute freedom in the eschatological Kingdom of God. This hope finds symbolic expression in the Book of Revelation:

> "Then I saw a new heaven and a new earth, for the first heaven and the first earth had vanished, and there was no longer any sea ... I heard a loud voice, proclaiming from the throne: "Now at last God has his dwelling among men! He will dwell among them and they shall be his people, and God himself will be with them. He will wipe every tear from their eyes, there shall be an end to death, and to mourning and crying and pain; for the old order has passed away! Then he who sat on the throne said: Behold, I am making all things new!" (Rev. 21:1-5).

In the Kingdom, man will forever dwell in God, and God in man, in the communion of love. He will be thus freed once and for all from the ambivalence of freedom and the possibility of sin. All men, living from the same centre of infinite love, will form one community of love, the eschatological people of God. The Kingdom as the "home of justice"(2 Pet 3:13) will be the final liberation of man from every social alienation. It will be the inauguration of a 'classless society', in which all will be equal without being uniform, in which each individual will exist "as the totality of society as thought and experienced" (Marx).

Finally, the reign of God will mean also the definitive liberation of man from every bondage to the world of things. The old order, in which material things, whether originally given or produced through human labour, tended to enslave man or divide man from man, will be replaced by one in which matter will embody man's love for God and for his fellowmen. Thus "the universe itself will be freed from the shackles of mortality and enter upon the liberty and splendour of the children of God." (Rom 8:21)

The Liberation That Already Came

The Christian looks to absolute freedom as the future of man. His hope is grounded in the faith that absolute freedom has already appeared in our midst in the person of Christ. Jesus of Nazareth is God's liberating initiative made manifest in history. He is the truth that sets man free: "If you dwell within the revelation I have brought, you are indeed my disciples; you shall know the truth, and the truth will set you free" (Jn 8:31-32).

The liberation, Jesus proclaimed, is primarily a spiritual one. His mission was to free man from sin and the ambivalence of freedom. Hence his call: "Repent and believe in the Gospel" (Mk 1:15). Repentance requires that man centre his life not on himself but on God.

Jesus came to free man from sin in order to make him free for love, free to love God in his fellowmen. "This is my commandment: love one another, as I have loved you" (Jn.15:12). The radical love he demanded cannot coexist with an unjust social system. It tends, by inner logic, to justice, individual as well as social. It seeks to find expression in a society in which there is "no such thing as Jew or Greek, slave, and freeman, male and female" (Gal. 3:28). It comes to rest only in a fellowship of equals:

> "At the moment your surplus meets their need, but one day your need may be met from their surplus. The aim is equality" (2 Cor. 8:14).

The love Jesus preached is, therefore, a subversive element planted in the heart of humanity. That is why his message is good news and a blessing to the poor (Lk. 6:20). The poor in this context means not merely the pious and the humble, but also, and above all, that class of people who are deprived of the goods of this world, are bent under the weight of oppression, and have none to defend their cause. To them, Jesus proclaims not only spiritual but also social liberation.

The message of Jesus contains also the good news of man's liberation from the world of things. For the absolute character of the love he demands, makes every earthly good relative. It implies the call to man to safeguard his transcendence vis-a-vis the products of civilization and to use them only as instruments of love.

The liberating initiative of God, revealed itself not only in the saving words of Jesus but also, and above all, in his dying and rising from the dead. His death means a 'yes' and a 'no'; yes to the absolute demands of love, and no to all that enslaves man, to sin, to every form of evil, personal as well as institutional. Raised from the dead, he represents that privileged, focal point of humanity that has already crossed over to the realm of absolute freedom. The risen Christ is the ultimate guarantee that all human striving for liberation will come to a successful issue.

The Liberation that is Coming Here and Now

Jesus Christ, whose life and death contains, in principle, the liberation of man from every bondage, is still at work in history through his Spirit. "And where the Spirit of the Lord is, there is liberty"(2 Cor 3:17). The Spirit is mysteriously at work, enlarging the sectors of freedom and preparing mankind for the coming of absolute liberation.

This activity of God should not be conceived as taking place outside the current of our history, as if man's self-creation in time, is of no relevance to the Kingdom of God. God frees man by calling him to free himself. Man's 'yes' forms an integral part of God's liberating activity. In other words, the reign of freedom that is emerging is essentially dialogical. And our concrete history is the expression, in time and space, of this theandric dialogue. Hence it is not only in the realm of man's soul but also in his economic, social and political life that we should look for the footprints of Him who goes ahead sowing the seeds of freedom.

Seen in this light, the social and political movements of today, which aim at the emancipation of man from hunger, ignorance, oppression, and exploitation, assume religious significance. They are but so many ways in which the man of today is responding to God's invitation to integral freedom.

Liberation as an Ethical Task

These reflections go to show that the Christian will be failing in his duty if he were to show indifference to the various liberation movements that are gathering momentum today especially in economically backward countries. He may not stand by the wayside, as a passive onlooker, while vast masses of men are struggling to cast off the shackles of injustice and exploitation. To do so would amount to denying his allegiance to the Spirit of Christ who is at work renewing man and society. Faith should rather impel him to enter the field of action, and co-operate with all men of goodwill, in creating a society in which "the free development of each is the condition for the free development of all" (Marx).

The Christian of the future is required to practice a new form of asceticism, consisting in selfless commitment to the reconstruction of society:

> "Is not this what I require of you as a force: to lose the fetters of injustice, to untie the knots of the yoke, to snap every yoke and set free those who have been crushed? Is it not sharing your food with the hungry, taking the homeless poor into your house, clothing the naked when you meet them and never evading a duty to your kinsfolk?" (Is 58: 6-7).

For this, he has to develop a new sensibility which enables him "to experience as dealt with himself every blow dealt with his neighbor" (Che Guevara).

Christian commitment to the task of liberation will have to take a revolutionary form in countries like India, where manifest and long-standing injustice and exploitation exist together with an increasingly articulate consciousness on the part of the oppressed masses, of their right to a life worthy of man. It must become both revolutionary criticism and revolutionary action, aimed at the radical and rapid transformation of the existing social order. In such conditions, the Christian shares the prophetic mission "to pull down and to uproot, to destroy and to demolish, to build and to plant" (Jer. 10).

Towards Critical Participation

In committing himself to the creation of the family of man, the Christian should not forget the ambivalent character of socio-political movements for liberation. These may be motivated not only by the desire for economic and social equality, but also by self-interest, lust for power, and class-hatred, all of which are factors which betray revolutions from within. Where this is true, the new social order, which such movements bring into existence, will be nothing but an inverted copy of the one they will have replaced, one in which the exploiters and the exploited of today will only have exchanged their roles.

Consequently, revolutionary criticism and action must go hand in hand with criticism of revolution. While identifying himself with every just cause, the Christian should dissociate himself from those programmes and projects that are detrimental to the common good. Through criticism of the revolution he should bear witness to the fact that, in the final analysis, it is not possible to achieve liberation from socio-economic alienation without a sincere effort on the part of man to free himself from sin, in response to the grace of God.

It is therefore in the destiny of the Christian to be never fully at home either with the revolutionaries or with the reactionaries. His lot is to be like Christ, who said of himself: "Foxes have their holes, the birds their roosts; but the Son of Man has nowhere to lay his head" (Mt 8.20).

(Rally, Dec. 1970, Vol. 47, No. 6, p.12-13; *Ingathering*, Chapter 7)

18

The Christian and the Call to Revolution

Introduction

The Problem

The Christian is today confronted with many challenges of which the most pressing, especially in economically developing countries, is the one posed by revolution. He lives in an atmosphere charged with revolutionary elan. He sees all around popular movements aimed at the eradication of economic and social inequality, at the demolition of socio-economic structures embodying the tyranny of the privileged few over the underprivileged many. In this situation, he feels the irresistible urge to participate in such movements. For he knows well enough that justice is on their side, and that they hold the key to the future. But, for the average Christian, to throw in his lot with the forces of revolution would look like a betrayal of his faith, of his loyalty to Christ. For the faith he imbibed from early childhood has instilled in him an instinctive reverence for order, peace, and security. He has been taught to see the will of God in existing social evils and to submit himself to them in a spirit of resignation. Besides, he asks: what does it profit a man to gain the whole world and suffer the loss of his soul? He, therefore, concludes that his faith demands of him non-participation in, if not opposition to, revolutionary movements. He has thus to choose between his loyalty to Christ and loyalty to the cause of the oppressed masses. Confronted with this anguishing choice, many believers opt for revolution, sacrificing in the process their allegiance to Christ and his Church. Others withdraw into the privacy of their Christian existence or take refuge in bourgeois conformism. Still, a third group lives in a state of permanent spiritual conflict with the resulting loss of creativity. Is this polarization a necessary consequence of the Gospel? Is it possible for the Christian to commit himself to revolutionary action, not in spite of, but because of his faith in Christ? What follows is a tentative attempt to solve this problem.

The Approach

Revolution, understood as the rapid and radical transformation of an existing social system (as a system of structures and values) into a more humane one, is one of the modes of social change whereby humanity strives to move forward to a fuller realization of its possibilities, and, as such, is one of the modes of development. Hence, it is in the broader framework of human development that we should conduct our inquiry into the Christian meaning of revolution. Development may be defined as the humanization of man through the humanization of 'nature'. By 'nature' we mean not only the material world but also the socio-cultural conditions of life as given at any particular point of history. Today, the process of development implies something more than the fact that changes are taking place in the world. It means above all that the world itself is moving forward, and that too at a vertiginous speed. This new existential situation has thrown up also new questions. Formerly when man lived in a relatively static world, he could afford to stand still with his eyes focused on an equally immovable firmament, all lost in contemplation. His question then was: Whence came I? How shall I return to my original home? Today, with man reduced to the condition of a pilgrim, the all-important question is: Where are we moving to? For, in the final analysis, it is the point of arrival of the collective march of mankind that can give meaning, content, and orientation to man's historical decisions here and now. This question regarding the unknown Ahead has to be answered in the light not only of reason but also of faith. How does faith envisage the end of all human development?

The Kingdom as the Future of Mankind

It is no use looking in the Bible for a detailed description of the end-result of history. The end remains shrouded in mystery. Yet we do find in the Bible a veiled vision of the ultimate fulfillment. We have a prophetic, symbolic description of it in the Book of Revelations: "Then I saw a new heaven and a new earth, for the first heaven and the first earth had vanished, and there was no longer any sea. I saw the holy city, new Jerusalem, coming down out of heaven from God, made ready like a bride adorned for her husband. I heard a loud voice proclaiming from the throne, Now at last God has his dwelling among men! He will dwell among them and they shall be his people, and God himself will be with them. He will wipe every tear from their eyes; there shall be an end to death, and to mourning and crying and pain, for the old order has passed away!" (Rev 21:1-4)

The end-fulfillment of history is pictured here in terms of a universal reconciliation - the reconciliation of man with God, with other men, and with the world of things. The Kingdom is above all the togetherness of man and God, the indwelling of man in God, and of God in man. But, for God to take man into his heart is to make him fully human, in other words, it is to personalize him. This ultimate flowering of the human is at the same time the liberation of man from every form of human alienation - from sin and the ambivalence of freedom, from suffering and death. The personalization of man, however, should not be conceived in purely individualistic terms. For God, in personalizing him, also socializes him. In as much as all men begin to live from the same personal centre of infinite love, they begin to exist in and for one another. In other words, they become a people, God's people. This means the definitive overcoming of all class-antagonisms. The Kingdom 'as the home of justice' (2 Pet 3:13) is the realization of a 'classless society', in which all men will be equal without ceasing to be different, one without being uniform, in which personal existence will encompass and be encompassed by the life of the community. The new community brought into being by God will not be one of the disincarnate souls.

On earth, man enters into communion with other men and with God, only through the mediation of his body and of other material things, whether originally given or produced by him. This mediation will not be suppressed in the Kingdom. Rather it will reach its supreme sublimation. The "new heaven and the new earth" is the universe, "freed from the shackles of mortality" and endowed with "the liberty and the splendour of the children of God"(Rom 8:21). The world of things will be then the perfect medium of expression of the love that binds man and God into one theandric community. Man will then possess things without their becoming 'mine' or 'thine'. The end of all human development will transcend both collectivism and individualism, and usher in the true socialism of being and having.

The Kingdom as Already Present

The eschatological Kingdom is something radically and totally new: "Behold! I am making all things new" (Rev 21:5). However, it comes into being not by annihilating but by renewing the old: "I am making all things new." More, this renewal is already at work at the heart of history. The Christ-event marks the inbreak of the Kingdom into this world. "The time has come; the kingdom of God is upon you; repent and believe in the Gospel." (Mk 1:15). The God-related, communitarian, and cosmic dimensions of the Kingdom are realized in the life and message of Jesus. The life of Jesus was one of abiding communion with the Father: "As thou, Father, art in me, and I in thee" (Jn 17:21). In dying and rising from the dead he passed over from the realm of the 'already' into the realm of the 'not yet'. He did so carrying humanity in his heart. Here is the basis of our hope that the human pilgrimage will come to a successful issue. All men, in so far as they are open to the invitation of truth, are already sharing in Christ's togetherness with the Father, in his passing over into the newness of the risen life.

The Christ-event inserted into the world also a new principle of human togetherness, namely, love - a love that gives itself ("For this is my blood ⋯, shed for man, for the forgiveness of sins." Mt 26:28) even to the point of self-emptying unto death (Phil 2:8). This love is not a weak well-wishing, that can coexist easily with any social system however unjust. It is a dynamic force, one would say, a subversive element, planted in the centre of history. For by an inner logic it tends to justice. If to love is to give, the first gift one can bestow on one's neighbour is to recognize his unique value as a person with inviolable rights. The justice inherent in love seeks to create equality: "At the moment your surplus meets their need, but one day your need may be met from their surplus. The aim is equality." (2 Cor 8:14). This is the reason why the message of Jesus is really good news to the poor: "Blessed are the poor" (Lk 6:20). The poor here means not merely the pious and the humble but also, and above all, that class of people who are deprived of the goods of this world, are bent under the weight of oppression and exploitation and have none to defend their cause.[1] To them, the Messiah comes as one who routs the arrogant of heart, pulls down princes from their thrones, exalts the lowly, fills the hungry with good things, and sends away the rich empty-handed (Lk 1:51-53). Though the salvation brought by Jesus is essentially religious, it has implications also for the economic and social liberation of man, since the law of love he proclaimed and sealed with his own blood, cannot coexist with discrimination against any particular class, and can be truly 'at home' only in a society in which there is "no such thing as Jew or Greek, slave, and freeman, male and female." (Gal 3:28). The love that Jesus inserted into the course of history is now silently at work overcoming the powers of hatred and demolishing the structures that divide man from man. Seen in this light, all social movements which have for their aim the promotion of justice, equality, and brotherhood, are ways in which the Kingdom of God realizes itself here on earth.

The Christ-event means also the insertion of the Kingdom into the world of matter. The word in becoming flesh became one with the cosmos. He took the material world into his heart and gave it the possibility of sharing his own destiny of dying and rising from the dead. Through his death and resurrection, he made matter the 'sacrament' of man's love for God and his fellowmen. In him and through him the material world including the products of human activity has become radically reconciled to God. (Col.1:20). The Kingdom is, therefore, growing in the womb of the universe which now "groans in all its parts as if in the pangs of childbirth." (Rom 8:22). The 'new heaven and the new earth' is germinally present in our earth and in our heaven.

The Kingdom as an Ethical Task

The Kingdom both in its end-fulfillment and in its germinal presence is the gift of God, "the new Jerusalem coming down out of heaven from God" from whom comes every perfect gift (Jn 1:17). However, the sheer gratuity of this gift does not make it any less the fruit of the action of man, since God's gift takes the form of man's free decision and action. The Kingdom as it grows in history is the result not only of the action of God who calls from the unknown Ahead but also of the trembling response of man to the same call. In other words, it is dialogical in its very nature. Its dialogical character is finally rooted in the dialogical structure of the very being of the God-Man. In Jesus Christ God's saving Word and man's response fuse into one to form but one personal existence. As was his being, so too was his earthly life essentially a dialogue with the Father, a truth that stands out clearly in his death: "The Father loves me because I lay down my life, to receive it back again. No one has robbed me of it, I am laying it down of my own free will. This charge I have received from my Father" (Jn. 10:18). What is true of Christ is true also of the Kingdom as it emerges in history. It demands man's response, his personal decision here and now. Hence the urgency of the call: "The Kingdom of God is upon you, repent and believe in the Gospel" (Mk. 1:15). The Kingdom, therefore, grows not alongside but in and through the course of history as shaped by man. The history of salvation and 'profane' history do not run along parallel lines. They form but two dimensions of the same reality.

The realization of the Kingdom is therefore also an ethical task, a 'charge' that man has received from the Father. What then is the content of this ethical task? The Kingdom demands from man, first of all, spiritual conversion, a change of heart so that his spiritual forces become centred on God rather than on his own self. This conversion is not something that is accomplished once for all. It unfolds itself in the form of one's individual history in response to the ever-renewed invitations of God. To march forward not knowing fully where one is going to, to have to choose between the many paths that lie ahead, not to be able to settle down anywhere for good - that is the destiny of the man who has turned to God once and for all. Fanatical conservatism, therefore, stands at the opposite pole of the spiritual revolution demanded by the Kingdom.

In the past, Christians tended to interpret the metanoia demanded by the Kingdom almost exclusively in individualistic and spiritualistic terms, without taking into consideration the social and corporeal dimension of man. Man is social and corporeal not only in what he is here and now but also in what he is called to be in the eschatological Kingdom. Hence to be converted to God implies being committed to the reign of absolute love, justice, and peace beyond history and to the reign of ever greater love, justice and peace here on earth. It demands commitment to a constant renewal of society so that the latter conforms more and more to the eschatological Kingdom. Before the demands of the Kingdom in its absolute fulfillment, every existing social order assumes a provisional character. To absolutize it by refusing to go beyond it is a sin against our hope in the Kingdom that is 'to come' and against our faith in the Kingdom that is now emerging. Conversion requires also a new relationship to the world of things. Negatively, the believer must see to it that he does not become a slave to the machine and its products, to the world of his creation. Positively, he must strive to make the production, exchange, and use of goods subservient to the growth of universal love and fellowship in society.

The Christian, in virtue of his very faith in the Kingdom, is put in a situation of the dialectical tension between a commitment to concrete secular goals economic, social, and criticism of all social systems whether existing or yet to be realized. He has to commit himself to concrete goals since there is no other way to make the existing social order harmonize with the end-fulfillment of history. He has to be critical of every social goal and system lest he should make them absolute, and thereby 'freeze' mankind's march to the Kingdom at one cross-section of time. His faith in the kingdom that is already emerging calls for commitment; his hope in the Kingdom that is yet to come calls for criticism and detachment. Both commitment and criticism have to be safeguarded. Commitment without criticism breeds fanaticism, intolerance, and utopianism; criticism without commitment empties the Christian life of any meaningful content here and now. However, commitment and criticism are not two separate functions. They are immanent in each other. Hence the Christian attitude to all human development may be described as a critical commitment or committed criticism.

Revolution for the Sake of the Kingdom

Social criticism may have to take a revolutionary form in certain conditions. Such conditions exist in economically developing countries like India, where there have been wide-spread and longstanding injustice and inequality, and where the masses have become painfully conscious of their subhuman conditions of life, of their right to a life worthy of man. These conditions are in violent contradiction to the requirements of the Kingdom and call for a rapid and radical reshaping of the social order. In such conditions, the Christian is inspired by his faith not only to co-operate with already existing revolutionary movements but also to initiate them. He is urged on by his hope to translate his criticism into practice, into concrete programmes of subversion directed against the existing social order. Like the prophets of old, he is "set over nations and kingdoms, to tear up and to knock down, to destroy and to overthrow, to build and to plant" (Jer. 1:10). In fulfilling this task he is not alone. For God is at work in history awakening the conscience of men and calling them to a richer and fuller being. Hence the Christian who co-operates with all men of goodwill in the reconstruction of society is, in fact, cooperating with the Spirit of God that makes all things new. However, faithfulness to the logic of the Kingdom demands that he criticizes also the revolution to which he is committed. For revolutionary movements may harbour factors like vested interests and class hatred that betray their own cause and foredoom them to failure. Revolutionary criticism and action divorced from self-criticism may usher in a social order which is nothing more than an inverse copy of the one it replaces, in which the oppressor and the oppressed of today will only have exchanged their places.

An existing social order is overthrown in view of building up another one more in harmony with the demands of justice. To achieve this, it is necessary to project into the future a model to be realized. Here the Gospel can give the believer only a general orientation. For, if it is relatively easy to determine what is at variance with the Kingdom, it is in most cases impossible to derive from the Gospel any concrete model of society to be realized here and now. There may be many possible 'projects' that are equally in harmony with the requirements of the Kingdom. Or it might happen that the ideal project is not practicable in existing conditions. Here the Christian is thrown back on his own resources. He has to enter into dialogue with other citizens and make use of the data provided by the secular sciences like economics, sociology, political science, etc. Besides, the compatibility of more than one project with the Gospel obliges him to respect pluralism of opinion and action among believers as well as unbelievers. Like any other citizen, the Christian too shares the human condition of having to take leaps into the unknown future at the risk of failure. It follows from this that where there is a question of building up the future, faith can provide him nothing more than an eschatological horizon of hope that acts as a source of motivation and as a negative criterion for the choice of projects.

In his commitment to the revolutionary reconstruction of society, the Christian should beware of identifying earthly progress with the growth of the Kingdom. The new social structures and institutions he brings into existence are delivered up to the judgement of sinful man, to the ambivalence of his freedom, and to the judgement of the living God. They can be used by other men either for or against God, either as an instrument of love or as an instrument of hatred. Besides, what man creates is subject to the redeeming fire of God, who judges both in history and at the summing up of history. The Christian, therefore, has no guarantee that all that he helps in creating will be gathered up into the Kingdom. Yet he knows that something of what he creates will somehow be gathered into the "home of justice" (2 Pet 3:13) by God who has reconciled and is reconciling the universe to himself in Jesus Christ.

Revolution Under the Sign of the Cross

What maintains any existing social order is power, secular or religious. Hence no social order can be radically transformed without breaking the power-structure inherent in it. Now power can be broken only through power. Can Christian use any kind of power including physical violence to overthrow unjust social systems? The answer, it seems to us, must be sought in Jesus Christ, who not only is the Kingdom but also the Way leading to it. The mission he received from the Father was in a sense revolutionary. He came to bring down the walls that Jewish formalism had built between man and man, and between man and God, and to lead Judaism and humanity back to the very source of true religion, namely, the personal decision of man in favour of total self-giving to God in his fellowmen, which is made possible by the gracious, redeeming initiative of God himself. In other words, he came to insert into the world love as the fundamental principle of secular as well as religious life. In accomplishing this task, he had to face the opposition of a twofold power-structure: the socio-religious power of official Judaism, and, indirectly, the political power of the Roman Empire. In such a situation the temptation to follow the way of violence would have been quite natural. For in Jesus' lifetime, there was already the extremist movement of the Zealots, who hoped to overthrow Roman supremacy and restore the old theocratic state through armed rebellion. It is also likely that among the disciples, besides Simon the Zealot, Judas Iscariot and Peter who originally belonged to the Zealot group, there were also others who nursed the hope that their master would declare himself a political Messiah and take up arms against Rome.[2]

Yet Jesus rejected both political Messianism and the use of violence. His rejection of violence seems to be unconditional, for he says: "all who take the sword will perish by the sword" (Mt 36:52). The path he chose was one of nonviolence: "Do not resist one who is evil. But if anyone strikes you on the right cheek, turn to him the other also" (Mt 5:39). He rejected violence because it is the child of hatred which is diametrically opposed to the love that seeks to redeem all including one's enemies. The Kingdom cannot be brought into being through a principle that denies it.

However, the refusal of Jesus to resort to violence does not mean that his attitude to evil was one of passive acquiescence or abject capitulation. What he rejected was not resistance but violent resistance. He did resist evil and that too passionately. His bold and incisive criticism of the hollowness of the Jewish religious formalism ("you hypocrites," "you vipers' brood" Mt 23:33), and of secular authority ("Go and tell that fox". Lk 13:32) proves the tenacity with which he held on to truth. It was his determined 'no' to the evil that cost him his life. He sealed his resistance with his own blood. He replaced the weakness of violence – for all violence is an expression of weakness – with the power of suffering. He thus made the cross the weapon of all revolution and the ultimate guarantee of its success.

The Christian, therefore, has to apply the methodology of the cross to his revolutionary commitment. In eschewing all hatred, he must hold on to truth and organize collective resistance to unjust structures and institutions so that these cannot any longer continue in existence. In this, he will find an inviolable guide in Gandhi, who was the first to transform the power of love unto death into a weapon for the socio-political revolution. He was also the first to show that collective non-violent resistance is capable of overcoming even well-organized military power. The effectiveness of *satyagraha* (which means precisely 'holding on to truth') contrasted with violence consists in this: that while the latter can bring about change only in objective structures of society and not in the hearts of the opponents, the former is better calculated to achieve both. Finally, it was Gandhi who interpreted for the modern man the 'political' power of the Cross. He was convinced that "nations like individuals, could only be made through the agony of the Cross".[3]""

Clearing Up a Difficulty

We have tried thus far to draw out the revolutionary implications of our hope in the Kingdom. But the Christian revolutionary who looks to the Jesus of the Gospel for inspiration is confronted with a certain disconcerting ambivalence in some of his words and attitudes regarding the social problems of his day. On the one hand, Jesus places himself on the side of the revolutionaries with his message of love as the mainspring of religious and secular life, with his criticism of the rich, of the merciless, and of those who pervert the law of God, with his refusal to be a conformist as is shown by his dealings with the Samaritans, with women, with sinners and publicans. On the other hand, he manifests a certain indifference to the affairs of this world. For instance, he refuses to identify himself with the political hopes of the Zealots, or to get involved in settling disputes over property rights: "My good man, who set me over you to judge or arbitrate?" (Lk 12:14). He seems to take for granted the unjust social practices of his time, not excepting slavery (Lk 17:7-10; Mk 10:42ff). How to explain this ambivalence? A detailed treatment of the problem is beyond the scope of this essay. We shall do no more than briefly indicate the principle that should guide our search for a solution.

The solution should, it seems to us, be sought in the dialogical structure of the being and life of Jesus to which we referred earlier. Jesus is, above all, God's saving Word to man. Now the redemptive initiative of God made visible in and through him does not annul the autonomy of man as constituted by the creative initiative of the same God. Jesus came into the world not to take over the work of creation proper to man, but to lead it to its eschatological fulfillment. In other words, his mission was to save man, and not to create a new social order. He did not come to open a short cut to the "new heaven and the new earth" by dispensing man from the anguish of creating his own history. The transcendence of his salvific mission demanded of him that he did not identify himself with concrete socio-political programmes like that of the Zealots. The relevance of his mission for the reconstruction of the earthly city is only indirect (i.e. requiring the mediation of human freedom) in so far as he gave man a new faith, a new love, and a new hope, without which his commitment to the creation of a better world would be deprived of ultimate meaning and value.

The ambivalence in question must be interpreted also in the light of the fact that Jesus, God's saving Word to man, is at the same time humanity's 'yes' to the same Word. And as such he shared the human condition. He appeared on earth at a particular stage of history and had the limitations of his age, of his culture. His being invested with a universal mission does not make him any less the product of his environment. Hence we would not be taking his humanity seriously if we were to expect him to pose our problems and propose our solutions. The concrete actions and reactions of Jesus need not necessarily be the norm for our actions today. What we must do is to assimilate the core of his message and the spirit that governed his life, and reinterpret them in the light of our contemporary situation. The ethical imperative of critical participation in social revolution, which we have derived from Jesus' central message of the Kingdom, is the fruit of one such reinterpretation. In a sense, therefore, we are called upon to do greater things than he did, though this 'greater' will always fall short of what he was and what he did, since in him alone was realized the plenitude of divinity and humanity.

[This essay is to be read more as a meditation on the Gospel than as a systematic theological treatise. Hence the paucity of references. However, the author claims no originality, and gladly recognizes his indebtedness to contemporary theological writings.]

(Jeevadhara, 1971, pp.29-45; *Ingathering*, Chapter 8)

19

Christianity and India's Development

What is development?

Development may be defined as the humanization of man through the humanization of 'nature'. By 'nature' we mean not only material nature and its resources but also the complex of those objective conditions given at any particular stage of history. These conditions may be economic, social, political, ethical or religious. The integral development of man demands the humanization of all these conditions in such a manner that he is enabled to unfold all his possibilities and aspirations harmoniously. But development may also be understood in a narrower sense to mean the humanization of man through the humanization of his socio-economic conditions. Understood thus, it comprises not merely a quantitative increase in the production and consumption of goods and services, but also, and above all, a qualitative improvement in the network of human relationships within which production, distribution, and consumption take place and in the type of man that emerges. It is in this narrower sense that the word is taken in this paper. We shall, therefore, deal with cultural, political and other aspects of societal life only in so far as they have a direct bearing on economic development.

The crucial word in our definition of development is 'humanization'. In respect of the world man creates through work, it means the incorporation of his intelligence, of his rationality, in the material things around him and in the socio-economic structures into which he is inserted. In respect of man who fashions his world, it means the progressive maturation of the human in him. And the 'human' in him consists above all in his transcendence, i.e. in his capacity to be what he is not, and not to be what he is. But what is the content of his self-transcendence? It can be nothing other than the realization of values like creativity, equality, justice, love and fraternity, the quest after which is an integral element of man's global experience. Self-transcendence in freedom implies further that no set socio-economic conditions, however perfect, can adequately express the fullness of man. No sooner has he created new conditions of life than these evoke in him new and more complex needs, the satisfaction of which calls for a further transformation of them. Besides, every socio-economic system he brings into being is likely to create in its turn fresh forms of alienation, which can be overcome only through further changes, whether superficial or radical, in society. Development, therefore, is not a goal, an optimum to be attained, but essentially a process, an unending quest in search of the ever-widening horizon of the humanly possible. In this sense, all nations are developing, and no nation is developed. The distinction between the developed and the developing nations is valid only where development is viewed in terms of 'having' and not of 'being.'

When, in the light of the above reflections, we assess the situation of any particular country, either of the following possibilities is likely to present itself. The social system of the country in question may be sound and needs nothing more than minor reforms to remedy functional imbalances and inadequacies. Or it may be the case that the existing system is essentially unjust and calls for radical and rapid transformation. In the first case, development can be achieved through planned evolution: in the second case, it is possible only through a revolution. Even a rapid glance at the Indian situation will show that here nothing less than a revolution can ensure socio-economic development.

Structures of Unfreedom

The evils of underdevelopment in India are obvious to anyone who cares to see: the denial of even the minimum means of subsistence to millions, the appalling poverty and misery of the masses, the ravages wrought by under-nourishment, diseases and premature senility, the extent of infant mortality, the growth of underemployment and unemployment and the exclusion of vast sections of the population from a share in the goods of civilization and culture. But to grasp the extent of the dehumanization these imply, it is necessary to go deeper and reflect on the system that produces them, and, above all, on the man who creates and is created by the system. In other words, we should try "to grasp things by the root. But for man, the root is man himself."[1] The socio-economic system existing today is such that man is enslaved by the world of things, by his fellowmen and finally, by the State itself.

Man and Material Nature

The vast majority of the Indian people belong to the working class, whether agricultural or industrial, salaried or self-employed. In one way or another, they are engaged in the tasks of producing goods and services to meet the varied needs of society, like food, clothing, housing, roads and means of communication. In doing so they are remoulding nature in their linage, incorporating their mind and spirit in the world of objects, and thereby extending their existence in time and space. The goods we see around us, the products of civilization available in the market, are the concretization of their toil, the solidification of their being and willing. If this is so, it is but natural that these goods should belong to them in reasonable abundance. What happens is the opposite. About eighty percent of the rural population, which in turn form eighty-two percent of the total population of the country, are living on a meager per capita income of seventy paise per day.[2] This has to be viewed against the steep rise in prices during the last twenty years. With such a paltry income the working classes cannot buy even a fraction of the goods they produce in the sweat of their brow.

The producer is thus deprived of his product. Those who construct palatial homes for the privileged minority live in miserable huts. Those who produce various types of sophisticated foods (Amul milk powder, Lactogen, Horlicks) cannot afford even one full meal a day. Those who produce beautiful sarees have to be content to see their daughters going about in tattered rags. Those who produce cars and scooters are unable to have them. Those who produce works of beauty are doomed to live in absolute dirt and squalor. Those who work on the land and raise crops are often not the ones who own them. Those who produce costly antibiotics have often to be satisfied with less effective remedies when they fall ill. Those who through their labour put up mighty buildings for colleges, institutes of science and universities, are given only a marginal share in the services provided in them.

If the working classes are denied the fruits of their labour, to whom do these accrue? To the privileged classes. A third of the entire national income is appropriated by the richer ten percent of the population.[3] Much of our industrial production is geared to the consumption of the upper or middle classes. Every day the market is flooded with more and more sophisticated luxury goods: cosmetics, various brands of foreign liquors and cigarettes, etc. which only a small minority can afford to buy, while the large majority lack even the necessities of life. One, therefore, is faced with the conclusion that the present economic system is such as enables the rich minority to exploit the labour of the majority for the production of goods which they alone can consume.

Deeper than the alienation of the product from the producer is the alienation he experiences in the very process of work. For the toiling masses in India, work is nothing but a process of self-alienation, or to use a Marxian phrase, of 'spiritual self-castration'. Far from being the act of self-realization, work is for the vast majority, the prostitution of their physical and spiritual powers for the benefit of the privileged classes. Day in and day out the labourer sells his work, or rather, his capacity for work, to the employer for a salary that is scarcely enough to keep his body and soul together. During the hours of work, he belongs not to himself but the employer. In other words, he is not a man insofar as he is a worker; and insofar as he is a man he is not a worker. He can have dominion over himself - and that is what constitutes the human - only outside the hours of work. Thus work which ought to be an end in itself becomes only a means to an end, the end being a few coins. Since work is the essence of man, this implies that man himself is reduced to the position of a means. If so, it is clear that the system of salaried labour as it exists in India is essentially dehumanizing. Even if we were to accept it as provisionally valid, still we have to question the criterion of assessing remuneration. The criterion currently used is not that of the contribution one makes to society. It is derived from the bourgeois conception of the superiority of intellectual over manual labour. Thus while an executive is paid a salary of, say, Rs 2,000 a month, a municipal scavenger is paid around Rs 150, though the service rendered by the latter is as essential to society as that rendered by the former.

The supreme expression of the alienation of the laboring masses consists in this; that these have no control over the economic system, no say in the matter of shaping their economic future. It is not the workers that decide what they should produce, how they should produce it and how the products have to be distributed. The prices even of essential commodities are determined either by the arbitrary decisions of commercial exploiters or by the impersonal law of supply and demand. This means that the working classes are degraded to mere byproducts of history, whereas in justice they should be its subject and creators. The above analysis shows that the present system of production, distribution, and consumption is such as to keep the working classes of India in a permanent state of material and spiritual underdevelopment. But behind this system stand the exploiting classes. A brief survey of them would be in order here.

Man and Society

The privileged classes who benefit from the existing socio-economic system are of two types: one originating from feudal society, and the other, created by the capitalistic system imported by the colonizers.

1. The dominant castes

The modernization of India through industrialization and western types of education led to the breakdown of the vertical solidarity proper to caste. The lower castes broke loose from the domination of the ritually superior castes. At the same time modernization contributed to the birth of a new form of cohesion based on horizontal solidarity among sub-castes sharing a common culture. This, along with universal suffrage, invested the numerically dominant castes with tremendous social and political power over the numerically inferior castes. Among such dominant castes are the Nairs of Kerala, the Gounders, Padayachis and Mudaliars of Tamil Nadu, the Lingayats and the Okkalingas of Mysore, the Marathas of Maharashtra, the Patidars of Gujarat, the Rajputs, Jats and Ahirs of North India.[4] These have a vested interest in keeping the lower castes and the outcastes in their present economic backwardness. "The dominant castes are fighting hard to retain the privilege of being classified as backward classes. The low castes and the Harijans are becoming increasingly aware of what is happening. They are finding that the lion's share of the jobs, scholarships, seats and free studentships reserved for the backward castes are going to members of the dominant castes.[5] In this context, we may also mention the rural elite which has inherited the tradition of the earlier Janmis and Zemindars. Though not necessarily belonging to the dominant castes, they are, in many ways, exploiting the rural population. They control most of the panchayats which offer them opportunities for political office and patronage.[6] They are devouring much of the government assistance made available to the backward classes through community development, co-operative farming, etc.[7]

2. The modem bourgeoisie

To this category belong the industrial, commercial and professional elite. They embody the ideology of private interest, competition and the survival of the fittest. In many parts of the country, it looks as if they have entered into a tacit alliance with the rural elite on the one hand and with the bureaucrats and politicians, on the other. This middle-class axis controls much of the national press, and to some extent, even the police, if not the judiciary. The big industrialists have succeeded in concentrating excessive economic and political power in their hands. The report of the Mahalanobis Committee, 1964, has admitted that "the working of the planned economy has contributed to the growth of big companies in the Indian industry."

Man and State

If the dominant castes, the rural elite, and the modern bourgeoisie have been able to maintain and strengthen their privileged position in the country, it is in part since they have found a willing accomplice in the Stale itself. Although, with the introduction of universal suffrage and democratic elections, power passed into the hands of the people at large, in practice it is concentrated heavily in the middle classes. The educated middle class formed the backbone of the ruling party even in pre-independence days. However, this middle class had one thing in its favour, namely, that it was predominantly urban, and had assimilated, in varying degrees, the principles of socialism. But today the rural elite, which did not grow up in the tradition of socialism, are playing an ever-growing role in the affairs of the ruling party. They obstruct the framing as well as the implementation of progressive social legislation. What is worse, even when the government opts for bold socio-economic reforms, its efforts are frustrated by the concerted resistance of the emerging bourgeoisie. The situation is further aggravated by the conservatism of the bureaucracy. The latter is fast growing into a gigantic tumor in the body politic that eats up a good part of the revenue. For instance, the bureaucracy in Kerala, which constitutes only 1.5 percent of the population is devouring 70 percent of the state revenue. The members of this class are the secular version of the Brahmins of yesterday and have all rights and few obligations as against the people who have all obligations and few rights.[8] The collusion between the politicians and the bureaucrats on the one hand, and the neo-feudal and the bourgeois elite on the other, has made a farce of democracy itself, which is by and large the government of the privileged classes for the privileged class.

We have thus far analyzed some of the economic, social and political structures that enslave the masses of India and keep them in a state of economic misery and stagnation. They find a favorable soil in the system of ideas and values prevalent among the elite as well as the masses.

The Tyranny of Ideology

It is clear from the preceding analysis that both feudal and capitalistic structures exist side by side in contemporary India. Correspondingly we find also the coexistence of feudal and capitalistic ideas and values among the people. Leaving aside the ideology of capitalism, we shall briefly indicate some of the intellectual and attitudinal vestiges of feudalism, which prevent India's march to socialism.

The traditional spiritualistic conception of religion as the way of liberation from the historical conditions of human existence cannot inspire commitment to the creation of a better social order within the pale of history. Besides, religion has for long been divorced from ethics.[9] This makes it possible for persons to be excessively scrupulous in religious matters and at the same time unconcerned about moral values, especially in social life. Similarly, undue stress on individual salvation has eclipsed all ideas of collective salvation and universal human solidarity. It has prevented the emergence of a truly social humanism, which alone could provide an adequate basis for a socialistic society. We may also mention here the theocratic conception of the world, which views the existing social order as willed by the gods, and the attitude of fatalism and resignation created by the belief in *karma* and *samsara*, all of which act as a brake on social revolution. Coming to the domain of ethics we find again the same individualism as was noticed at the level of religiosity. The stress is mainly on personal virtues like austerity, self-control, detachment, and chastity, and only marginally on one's social obligations.[10] Paradoxically, individualism in ethics grew within the framework of the collectivism of the joint family, caste and village economy. The authoritarianism of these traditional structures did not favour the development of personal responsibility and decision. At the level of social consciousness, there still exists a hierarchically ordered society based on status rather than on function. Consequently, the social inequalities existing today go unquestioned. No less entrenched in the minds of the people is parochialism. Loyalty to limited groups like the family and the caste takes precedence over loyalty lo society as a community of persons. This has led some Indians to entertain the extreme view that "the traditional Hindu mind is incapable of feeling a civic responsibility or wider secular loyalties for any length of time beyond its kinship group."[11] Finally the occupational satisfaction inherent in caste is at the root of the prevailing contempt for manual labour and the search for white-collarr jobs.

The Challenge of Revolution

Our reflections thus far lead us to the conclusion that nothing less than a structural transformation can create the conditions necessary for economic development in India. Further, the structural change envisaged here has also to be rapid. To resign oneself to the present pace of development would amount to condemning generations of men, women, and children to a subhuman mode of existence and premature death. And a radical and rapid transformation of the social system is precisely what we understand by revolution. Hence the word revolution sums up the challenge of the hour. Such a revolution must be fought on two fronts: on that of socio-economic structures and on that of ideas and attitudes. In other words, the country needs both a structural and mental revolution. These two are not to be thought of either as consecutive phases of the global process of social reconstruction or as running parallel to each other. They are complementary and dialectically interrelated. A revolution of structures is ineffective without a corresponding change in the ideas and attitudes of people. Likewise, it is not possible to bring about a mental and moral revolution without the transformation of socio-economic structures. It is in overthrowing the structures of unfreedom and exploitation that the masses will rid themselves of the feudal and capitalistic ideology and assimilate the values proper to socialism.

The social revolution understood thus is today an objective need. And it is increasingly becoming also a subjective need, i. e. a need felt by the oppressed classes and by the intelligentsia among the youth. The prevailing mood in the country has been aptly expressed by a Marxist intellectual in the following terms:

> "The growing economic disparity, the gap between the real income and its purchasing power, the rise in prices, food scarcity, corruption, and black-marketing, the growing hardships of the people, the failure of the men in power to bring about radical changes in the social structure and lead the country to the avowed objective of socialism - these have evoked moral and spiritual crisis and a sense of helplessness, frustration, despair, and cynicism, as also of anger, indignation and revolt."[12]

It is this frustration and anger that are finding an outlet today in violence and the destructive instability pervading the country. To all appearances, the country seems to be heading towards chaos and disintegration.

This is the context in which we should study the role of Christianity in India. I have elsewhere tried to show the theological basis of Christian commitment to development [13] and social revolution.[14] My aim in what follows is limited, namely, to indicate the forces of reaction in Indian Christianity and also to suggest some guidelines which might be of use in orienting Christian commitment in the future.

Indian Christianity - A Reactionary Force

Christianity has played an ambivalent role concerning the socio-economic reconstruction of India. It has indirectly sown the seeds of social revolution (1) by creating through its educational services an elite which is capable of giving articulate expression to the mute aspirations of the masses, (2) by heralding a new humanism based on the dignity of the human person and the equality of all men, (3) by bearing witness to the truth that authentic religiousness expresses itself in service to one's fellowmen, and (4) thereby inspiring Hindus to launch similar projects for the welfare of the masses. It has thus played a significant role in helping India pass from feudalism to modernity. But the problem facing India today is a different one, namely, that of passing from the vestiges of feudalism and from the modernity of the capitalistic type to true socialism. In respect of the new challenge, Christianity in India acts less as a catalyst of change than as a defender of the status quo, and this both at the level of theory (a blanket term meaning beliefs, ideas, and attitudes) and of practice. When we say this, we have in mind not the idea of Christianity that we find crystallized in the documents of Vatican II and the teaching of the recent popes, but the one professed by the majority of Christians in India today.

Christianity as Ideology

Though Christianity has brought to India much that is new, yet it has also served to reinforce those ideas and attitudes in traditional Hinduism that is uncongenial to the requirements of social reconstruction. Conversely, the conservative elements in traditional Hinduism have reinforced the retrogressive elements in Christian theology, spirituality, and ethics. The spiritualistic bias of the religious Hindu finds an ally in the Christian idea of the salvation of the 'soul' and the spirituality nourished by the same. The attitude engendered by belief in *karma* and *samsara* agrees well with the spirituality of resignation prevalent among many Christians. The traditional hierarchism of caste and the contemporary hierarchism of wealth find their counterpart in the hierarchism of authority in the churches.

Above all, it is in the field of ethics that Christianity joins hands with feudalism to buttress the forces of capitalism. Among Christians, ethics tends to be reduced to a demand for integrity in personal life while it leaves intact even the most dehumanizing social structures. Even where it deals with social relations, its fundamental norm is that of conformity to the status quo. It takes the prevalent conceptions of rights and obligations as natural and sanctioned by God. To give a few instances: the right to private property, understood as the right to use and to misuse it, is even today considered sacred and inviolable. So too, Christian leaders are wont to laud the present form of government as democracy, though in reality, it is chiefly government of the privileged classes. Likewise, they sing the praises of social order and peace, oblivious of the fact that order, as it exists, is maintained by the use of permanent violence on the part of a privileged minority against the mute majority. They tend to forget that what the country needs today is neither stability nor anarchy but creative instability. In sum, the collective consciousness of the Christian Community is marked less by the urge to create the future than by the desire to conform to the past, less by hope in 'the not yet' than by submission to 'the already'. Christian beliefs have lost their eschatological tension and have assumed the nature of an ideology of legitimization. They, therefore, merit in large measure, mutatis mutandis, the criticism that Karl Marx leveled against the Christianity of his time:

> "The social principles of Christianity have justified slavery in ancient times, have glorified medieval servitude, and are capable of approving the oppression of the proletariat, if need be, even if with a slightly contrite air. The social principles of Christianity transfer to heaven the compensation for all infamy, and thereby justify the perpetuation of this infamy on earth. The Social principles of Christianity declare that all infamies committed by oppressors against the oppressed are the just punishment for original sin or other sins, i. e., that they are trials imposed by the Lord, in His infinite wisdom, on souls that are saved. The social principles of Christianity preach cowardice, contempt of self, lowliness, submission, humility - in a word, all the qualities of the rabble. The proletariat that refuses to be treated like a rabble needs its courage, its self-respect and its taste for independence much more than its bread. The social principles of Christianity are crafty; the proletariat is revolutionary.[14]

Reaction in Practice

Christian commitment in the secular field falls roughly under three heads: education, social service, and other socio-economic projects. Seen from the angle of development through revolution their relevance needs to be questioned today.

1. The present educational system in the country is geared to the creation of a middle class of government servants, businessmen, politicians, and professionals. This is especially true of university education. Neither schools nor colleges give the students an adequate understanding of the real problems and needs of the masses, let alone equipping them intellectually and morally to fulfill the task of social reconstruction.

The values they represent and disseminate are derived from western capitalism, which stands for private interest, competition, aggressive self-assertion, and disdain for every form of manual work. And Christian schools and colleges are no exception. Their managements use their religious authority, wherever possible, to buttress and sanction the present system of education, just as they employ the latter to prop up their religious authority. No wonder that no creative initiative has come so far from them for the reform of education.

2. Social service is a valid form of Christian witness in society in any age. But where it is divorced from a commitment to radical social reconstruction, as in India, it serves as a kind of opium for the people, as a palliative that dampens revolutionary fervour and inhibits the urge to revolt. Besides, with the steady flow of financial resources from abroad, those who organize these services tend to become an aristocracy in the Christian community.

3. The positive gains accruing to the masses from Christian socio-economic projects like co-operatives, irrigation works, cottage industries, and industrial estates are marginal, considering the minority status of the Christian community and the colossal needs of 560 million people. In any case, they are inadequate attempts at improving the living conditions of the people while leaving intact the present exploitative socio-economic system.

There is another reason why the present mode of institutional commitment on the part of the Christian community is detrimental to true development. India is becoming progressively secularized. The various sectors of life like education, science, and politics, are freeing themselves from the domination of organized religion and reasserting their legitimate autonomy. This process is to be welcomed as a sign of man's coming of age. From this point of view, the attempts of the Christian community to bring within its control, secular sectors of life through its institutions is essentially reactionary. We may sum up this section by saying that in respect of India's development, Christianity has sinned both by default and by excess. By default, since its commitments aim merely at improvements within the system without transforming it radically; by excess, since it has overstepped its competence by trying to control secular spheres of life. Hence the historic task of Christianity today is to find a formula of commitment which, on the one hand, meets the objective demands of revolution, and on the other, respects the legitimate autonomy of secular man. In what follows we shall give a few guidelines for the reorientation of Christian praxis in the secular sphere.

Towards a Subversive Christianity

Prophetic Proclamation

Unenlightened enthusiasm for economic development and capitulation to materialism are bringing about the death of prophecy in the Indian Churches. And this in an age when even Marxism itself is striving to recapture its original prophetic mission and hope. It is often forgotten that development, as the humanization of man through the humanization of his socio-economic conditions, is possible only within the framework of a prophetic hope for the future of mankind. The primary task, therefore, of Christianity is to proclaim its hope that mankind is called to the eschatological community of love, to the classless society of the new heaven and the new earth, (Rev 21). It must awaken and sustain hope in the ultimate success of the human venture on this planet. It should likewise awaken and sustain the faith that the eschatological community of love is germinally present and mysteriously taking shape already in the realities of secular history. Only such a faith, instinct with hope, can release the creative energies of the masses for the building up of the future, and inspire the generosity and courage required for demolishing the structures of unfreedom. Only such a faith instinct with hope can save man from the tyranny of the past and the present and thus ensure his transcendence.

Social criticism

To hope for the end-community of love as the absolute future of man is to accept the relativization of all historical stages of development.

Furthermore, it is to be inwardly compelled to reject everything in the present that mutilates man, or erects barriers between man and man. Social criticism, therefore, is an integral function of Christian hope. For such criticism to be effective, it must have the following characteristics: (1) It must be radical. It is not enough to bring to light the superficial inadequacies of the existing social system. It is necessary to go deeper and lay bare the underlying structural causes. Criticism must concern itself not only with the denunciation of personal sins but also with the elimination of structural sins, i. e. sins embodied in social institutions and laws. (2) It must be universal, i. e. directed against all alienations of men whatever the community or religion they belong to. (3) It must be scientific. Its methodology must be at once inductive and deductive, i. e. based on the data not only of revelation but also of the empirical sciences: economics, sociology, demography, cybernetics, and so on. For this, it must make use of interdisciplinary and truly ecumenical consultation. (4) It must be permanent since, in any social order man may create, new alienations are bound to crop up which in their turn will have to be eliminated. (5) It must be institutional. Though individual criticism on the part of Christians is legitimate and necessary, only the organized expression of the Christian conscience will have enough moral weight to influence the masses as well as centres of decision in society.

Politicization

For social criticism to be a dynamic force in reconstructing society it must percolate to the level of the masses. The under-privileged must be made conscious of the nature, the extent, and the mechanism of the exploitation to which they are being subjected. They should also be made aware of their rights as human beings and as citizens of the country. But a mere awareness of one's rights without a corresponding awareness of one's obligations can lead only to irresponsible agitation. It is here that the Marxist-inspired movements for liberation have failed. Politicization must therefore also include the education of the masses in the values of the new society envisaged, namely, the dignity of work, concern for the common good, the sense of solidarity, etc. The project of constructing a socialistic society cannot be accomplished by men and women whose system of values is derived from feudalism or capitalism. What is needed today is nothing less than a mental revolution among the masses.

(Jeevadhara,1972, pp. 47-62; *Ingathering*, Chapter 9)

20

Dialogue with Non-believers

The aim of this article is not to explain the object or nature of dialogue but only to pinpoint some of the essential prerequisites for it. The first prerequisite is that we have something to say of our own and that we do so in our own language. But do we, Indian Christians, have our own thoughts about God and the universe, thoughts that have the taste, smell and colour of our earth, of our flesh and blood? No. The thoughts that we so dutifully proclaim and even the language in which we couch them come from abroad. So far we have been thinking alien thoughts and uttering alien words. Though political colonialism came to an end, theological colonialism still continues. It is perpetuated through seminaries, through publications and associations. So long as this situation continues no meaningful dialogue is possible with non-believers. The latter want to know what we think on our own, not what we think by proxy. The time has, therefore, come for Christians in India to think their thoughts and pose their questions. They have to vindicate the freedom to be themselves, the right to their own existence instead of being mere relaying stations for ideas broadcast by Christian sources in the west.

Need for Criticism

The second prerequisite is preparedness on our part to subject to severe criticism our usual habit of classifying people as believers and non-believers. Such classification, though unavoidable, may imply that those who profess atheism are necessarily devoid of any faith, and the others have no share in unbelief. These assumptions do not stand the test of critical analysis. For it may well happen that those who deny God at the level of rational discourse, affirm him in practice, i.e. existentially, in so far as they are committed to absolute values like love and the brotherhood of men. In fact, one of the fruits of dialogue is the unveiling of the theist in the atheist.

It is also possible that the God who is denied is only a false image of God that the believers themselves have projected. Conversely, many of us who profess to be believers are existentially atheists in so far as we disown God in practice. Or it may be the case that the God we believe in is one we have made in our own image to legitimize our interests, to sanction our unholy deeds and to guard our purse. If so, the dividing line between belief and unbelief runs not so much through two neatly distinct classes of people as through the heart of every man. To realize this is to have the basic openness necessary for dialogue.

Eschew Dogmatism

The third prerequisite is the eschewing of all dogmatism. Dogmatism is the child of pride. It is man's attempt to imprison God in limited concepts, to render the relative absolute, the conditioned unconditioned. For the dogmatist, God is a possession, a private property. Being in possession of truth, he is capable only of teaching, not of learning. He talks but never listens. And if he listens it is only in view of refuting, confounding and anathematizing. The very structure of his being and thinking is monological.

If dogmatism is the enemy of dialogue what about dogma? The crystallization of faith into dogma had relevance in the earlier pre-scientific age when the universe appeared to man as a fixed order. It was an eternal and immutable cosmos that gave birth to eternal and immutable formulations of faith. But today we are living in a world that is subject to radical and rapid changes, in a world that is marching forward, thanks to the advance of science and technology. Hence in the present age, the crystallization of faith into dogma is neither possible nor meaningful. The age of dogma is over. We are living in the post-dogmatic age. Henceforth terms like 'eternal' and 'immutable' have meaning only as qualifying the ultimate horizon which beckons us from beyond the beyond. Seen in this light, past dogmatic formulations are not tents in which we may settle down for good but mere signposts that point to the ever-receding horizon of absolute truth. To recognize this is to accept our condition as pilgrims on the march. In doing so, we are but recapturing the original attitude of Jesus for whom God was not a possession but one who is to come, the time of whose coming neither the Son nor the angels know. The recognition of the provisional character of all formulations of faith makes it possible for us to discover the element of truth in the unbelief of others and the element of untruth in our belief. If the non-believer too is equally willing to engage in self-criticism, dialogue becomes a common quest, and the common quest the basis of a new brotherhood.

Non-Conformism

The fourth prerequisite is responsible non-conformism. And this for the following reason: Thought is conditioned by life. And life in the Church is still by and large monological. All thinking starts from above and seeps down to the lower ranks. The clergy are expected to say amen to what the bishops say, and the laity to what the clergy say. Thought and expression may not trespass the narrow circle drawn by the official Church. In this setup Christians react in three different ways.

Some choose to conform and remain within the circle. They are barred from true dialogue. For they can only try to draw the listener into their own orbit of intellectual unfreedom. And in the process, they become the object of amused pity from the part of the very people they speak to.

There are others who find a way out by evading any confrontation with the non-believers. They know well enough that they cannot explain the meaning or relevance of the formulae they learned by rote. Not to make fools themselves they take refuge in silence.

There is still a third group, a minority, who dare step outside the circle and start questioning the thus far unquestioned. They opt for responsible non-conformism and for freedom of thought and expression. This does not mean that they reject the teaching of the Church. They accept it for what it is worth, namely, as historically conditioned expressions of the truth of the gospel. In a Church, whose ethos and structure are largely monological, only this third group is intellectually equipped to initiate authentic dialogue.

Involvement

Let me conclude by indicating yet another pre-requisite, which has to do with our concrete involvement in the world. The most convincing proof of theory is practice. The truth of our claims has to be verified on the basis of their ability to change the world. To proclaim God from housetops carries little conviction if we ignore the God who dwells under leaking roofs. To preach the new heaven and the new earth is a great thing, provided we strive to make it a reality instead of clinging to the old heaven and the old earth. a belief that justifies the old order, stands already refuted before an unbelief that tries to usher in a new one. Creative unbelief is truer than impotent belief.

Let us not, therefore, go in for dialogue unless we have declared war on the existing unjust social system and are actively committed to the cause of the oppressed. Let us show in deed that our faith carries good news to the poor, brings release for prisoners and recovery of sight for the blind, and lets the broken victims go free. Let us not forget that it is our alliance with the oppressors that has driven many to the fold of atheism. Looked at from this angle, the Church in India is still in the pre-dialogical era. Only those few Christians who are actively engaged in constructing a better home for the human family have a valid claim to initiate dialogue with non-believers. In the case of the rest, dialogue is an exercise in sham modernity.

(New Leader, Dec.1973; *Ingathering*, Chapter 10)

21

The Future of Christian Education and Christian Education of the Future

The term 'Christian education' is an ambiguous one. It may mean the process whereby the young are mentally and spiritually equipped for Christian living. In this sense the content as well the aim of education is specifically Christian. What is imparted is the message of the Gospel and the aim is the growth of the young into Christian maturity. Under this category of Christian education, may be grouped preaching, catechesis and the teaching of theology. Christian education may also mean secular education in arts and in the sciences either of nature (physics, chemistry, biology, etc.) or of man (history, psychology, sociology, etc.), which is in one way or another controlled by the Christian community. Here the 'Christianness' in question is external to the content and the aim of education. To this category belong Christian schools and colleges in India.

In this article, we shall first consider the future of Christian education as characterized by Christian control in order to arrive at a clearer understanding of what Christian commitment in the field of education should be in the future. But the future of any social structure is determined by the confluence of objective socio-historical forces and the subjective decision of man. We shall, therefore, analyze the main socio-historical forces and trends, which Christian education is exposed today, with a view to answering the question, how the Christian community has to respond to the challenges they pose. Our method consequently will be both descriptive and prescriptive.

Christian Education in a Secular World

Secularization is a process that affects both the mode of thinking and the mode of social life of a given people. In relation to thinking, it means the eruption of rationality and the vindication of its autonomy vis a vis mythical-religious conceptions. In relation to societal life, it means the progressive emancipation of the this-worldly spheres of human activity, from the control of organized religion. In either sense, secularization forms a significant aspect of the cultural change in contemporary India. In bringing about this change, the western type of education has played an important role. It freed the Indian mind from the tyranny of magic, myth, and religion over the personal and social life of man. It also undermined the priestly monopoly of learning. But the domination of secular society by religion still persists, though in an attenuated manner, in the form of schools and colleges controlled by religious agencies. However, in the more politically conscious States like Kerala, such domination is being vehemently challenged by student movements and political parties. This indicates an irreversible trend in social evolution and will inevitably spread also to other parts of the country.

Far from being alarmed at this development, Christians must welcome it as an index of the maturity of secular society and gladly relinquish their control over secular education. However, giving up her own schools and colleges does not mean that the church will have to keep away from such a significant area of life as education. What she should do is rather to seek a new mode of presence. Since it is mainly through priests and religious that the official church exercises her presence in the domain of education, their future role needs to be clarified. In a secular society, those priests and religious, who choose to work within the present system of education, will naturally have to seek employment as teachers in socially controlled schools and colleges. the concept of social control implied here is broader than nationalization. Nationalization of all educational institutions is an evil. It will kill all initiatives from below and will only produce standardized human beings. Neither will it allow room for legitimate ideological and cultural pluralism. Hence the good of the country requires that most educational institutions be run by duly constituted secular bodies responsible primarily to the people they serve. In such institutions, governmental control should not exceed what is strictly needed for national coordination and planning. This, of course, means a restructuring of the entire educational system which Christians as a minority cannot bring about. They should, however, work for it in collaboration with other citizens. In the meanwhile, priests and religious, who want to go in for systematic education in the arts and sciences, will have to work in State-owned schools and colleges.

Pluralism of Christian Commitment

Another significant change taking place in contemporary society is the diversification of the agencies of education. In traditional India, the family was the fundamental agency of education, understood in its triple function of teaching the young how to do things (technical education), how to explain the phenomena of nature and of man (scientific education), and finally how to be a person in the community (humanistic education). With the onset of modernization and the break-up of traditional social structures, all these three functions of education were taken over by schools and colleges. Modernization brought about also a change in the content of education. This is particularly true of its humanizing function. Formerly humanistic education consisted of initiating the young into the symbols, beliefs, traditions, and institutions of the caste or the community to which they belonged. In the colonial era, it meant nothing more than equipping pupils to become petty government servants and instilling in them the ideology and the value system of the western capitalist society. It is this empty humanism that is even today embodied in our educational system.

But modernization generated another process, which today is challenging the monopoly of education by schools and colleges, namely, the explosion of communication media and the emergence of new types of socially educative groups. The press, the radio and the world of publications are becoming increasingly powerful factors in the education of the masses. Equally important is the role played by socio-cultural associations and political parties. For want of a better term, we shall call these new modes of education para-institutional. This pluralism of educational agencies roughly coincides with a functional differentiation. Schools and colleges still monopolize systematic education in the natural and human sciences. But they are becoming increasingly dysfunctional in regard to humanistic education, which task is fulfilled mainly by para-institutional agencies. The boys and girls of today assimilate their system of values less from schools and colleges than from newspapers, popular reviews, novels, and films. They derive their civic and political education from socio-cultural associations and political parties representing a wide spectrum of ideologies.

We must also note the significant fact that the values and ideas imbided from outside the campus tend to become disruptive of the educational system itself. This is borne out by the strikes and agitations that frequently paralyze institutional education. It is equally beyond doubt that, of the two modes of education, the para-institutional is the more powerful agent of social change. We may mention here three reasons for this new development. First, in educational institutions, the stress is more on imparting information than on formation. In other words, there is little involvement in the subject taught either on the part of the teacher or of the pupil. Secondly, in these institutions, it is not dialogue or discussion but authority that is the primary principle of knowledge. The impersonal authority of the textbook has taken the place of the personal authority of the guru in ancient days. Thirdly, the present system of education is the product and the guarantor of an unjust social system. In the measure in which the student community becomes conscious of this fact, they become automatically insulated against the value system it represents. It is outside the campus that these limitations are to some extent overcome. There, truth becomes a matter of involvement and the search for it conducted in the context of dialogue with one's peers. It is also there that students acquire weapons for social criticism and become radicalized.

We do not, of course, mean that institutional education cannot be so radically renewed as to become an effective agent of humanization. But the social pressure necessary for any such renewal will come not from within the system but from without, i. e. from the world of para-institutional education.

The fact that the primary vehicle of humanism is no more the traditional type of school and college provides the Church with a challenge and an opportunity. In her concern for maintaining and expanding institutional education, she has woefully neglected the important area of para-institutional education. This is all the more deplorable since humanization is an integral part of her mission in society while teaching mathematics or chemistry is not. In the future, her primary concern should be to be a critical and creative force in the world of literature, the press, the radio, and the film. She will have also to evolve new methods for being present in the equally important realm of social, cultural and political associations. For this, we need a new type of priest and religious who would be writers, novelists, poets, radio artistes, film critics, scriptwriters, trade union leaders, and even politicians. However, this should not be interpreted to mean that the Church should create her own world of communication media or her own communal political party. That would be nothing more than a new version of the old hierocracy. Her aim should be rather to utilize the existing secular media of communication and to infiltrate educationally significant associations and movements. Where new organs of presence are created it should always be on an ecumenical basis in the broader sense of the term.

Education for Socialism

We have seen that the Church should be effectively present in the area of para-institutional education. The question now arises: what should be the content and function of this presence? Christians have been present in the educational field, in one way or another, for over a century. Yet their presence has not in any way hastened the march to socialism. It has, it would seem, even contributed to the strengthening of the existing exploitative social system, and to the perpetuation of the values of western bourgeois civilization. What is needed, therefore, is a new mode of presence. To define it more clearly, we must once again consider the concrete historical situation in which Indian society finds itself today. For Christian commitment has always to be in the manner of a response to questions which society poses to itself.

Here we come up against the most fundamental problem facing the country as a whole, namely, the conflict between goal and ideologies. The avowed goal that the nation has set for herself is socialism. This is implied in the Constitution which envisages the creation of social order in which there will be, "justice, social, economic and political; liberty of thought, expression, belief, faith and worship; equality of status and opportunity; and ... fraternity assuring the dignity of the individual and the unity of the nation." (The Preamble) This socialistic goal, however, is contradicted by the system of goals, norms, values, and legitimizations embodied in the educational system. The ethos characteristic of our schools and colleges is one of private interest, competition, aggressive self-assertion, the superiority of intellectual over manual work, peace at the cost of justice, and stability at the cost of change. This is partly true even of the ideology represented by the para-institutional agencies. The national newspapers, on the whole, reflect the vested interests of the giant capitalists. The small press is either the organ of parochial interests or is guided by mere profit-motivated expediency. All India Radio which could become a powerful instrument for the education of the masses in socialism is more often than not utilized for justifying the policies and doings of the powers that be. There is, of course, a socialist press controlled by the leftist political parties. But the socialism it propagates is vitiated by an all-too-blind acceptance of the Soviet or the Chinese model, both of which are but aberrations of socialism as originally envisaged by Marx. Besides, the revolt against the capitalist system, which the leftist parties foster among students and workers, is often sham and hypocritical in so far as it is motivated by values of the same system, i. e. private interest and the lust for power. Seen from this angle, the student revolt in the country is directed not so much against the capitalist system, as against its exclusive character which bars them from becoming capitalists themselves. Similarly, when workers strike their aim is not so much to abolish the dehumanizing system of salaried labour but to secure higher wages so that they too can eventually belong to the bourgeoisie. Seldom, if ever, do they agitate for participation in decision-making or in management. Their aim is almost always a quantitative improvement in terms of material amenities, not a qualitative change in the social system.

If our analysis is correct, neither institutional nor para-institutional education is geared to the task of ushering in socialism. This state of affairs bodes ill for the future of our country. To project socialism as the national goal and at the same time perpetuate educational forces that are counter-productive of the same goal can only lead to collective frustration. Fortunately, more and more people are becoming critical not only of the existing social system but also of the revolutionary movements engineered by leftist political parties. But they have still to become a significant socio-political force. Hence the historic need today is to create a socio-political movement genuinely committed to true socialism.

To meet this need is the task of Christian education in the future. Christians working in the field of education, whether institutional or para-institutional must have for its principal aim the creation of the proper cultural infrastructure for a socialist society. By socialist society, we do not mean any one historical model existing anywhere in the world. What we have in view is a society in which the development of each individual will be the condition for the development of society as a whole, and, conversely, one in which the development of the society will be the condition for the development of the individual. Only in such a society will we be able to overcome the dehumanization inherent both in collectivism and individualism.

Here one might ask: What is Christian about such commitment to education for socialism? Will not the giving up on the part of the Church of her schools and colleges, mean the end of Christian education? It is true that Christian commitment of the sort we have suggested would mean the end of Christian control of the educational system. But then such control historically came into being when Christian leaders parted company with the Jesus of Nazareth and chose to reconcile the irreconcilable, namely, the cross and the sword. Hence in providing educational service without the exercise of secular power, Christians will only be recapturing the original vision and hope of Jesus. Besides, education for a truly socialist humanism will have an authentic Christian content inasmuch as it prepares the ground for the coming of God's reign in history which is a reign of justice, love, peace and universal brotherhood. However, the 'Christianness' in question will not be an exclusive characteristic of the education undertaken by Christians but will be common to all men of goodwill, engaged in the same field. From the point of view of our eschatological hope, such education will be more genuinely Christian than much of what parades under the name of 'Christian' education today.

Need For an Attitudinal Revolution

To fulfill the task of Christian education as described in the foregoing pages, there is a need for a revolution of attitudes in the Church, of which we shall now pinpoint the more salient aspects.

1. Hitherto Christian thinking has been the victim of what we might call the ecclesial bias which made the Church the be-all and the end-all. The world was Christian only if it somehow came under the control of the Church. Today, the time has come to effect a reversal of attitude by putting God and his Kingdom first. And the Kingdom of God is there where human beings grow into maturity and into one another to form a community of persons united in mutual esteem and love. And this precisely is the aim of all humanistic education. Seen from this angle, education is not just one among the many activities of the Church but her mission par excellence. Only an approach like this can save

the Church from the danger of reducing her mission either to one of making converts or at the other extreme, to one of being an instrument of mere economic development.

2. Christian educators must rid themselves also of the dogmatic bias which sets up authority as the primary principle of truth. Such bias inhibits all radical questioning and even methodical doubt. It prevents Christians from effectively participating in the contemporary quest after the ever-new horizons of truth. It also condemns them to the pitiable condition of having to reject every new idea, but only to be forced to relent in their opposition as the idea in question becomes widely accepted, and finally to come on the scene to sanction and legitimize it. Such an approach can only make them suspect, in the eyes of the younger generation. Authority as the principle of truth, therefore, must be subordinated to the principle of obedience to reality, i.e. to the global experience of man. Christian educators should learn to regard truth not so much as a possession but as the distant horizon, which beckons man from beyond. This implies that they give up their false intellectual security built on the foundations of western rationalism and on a pre-scientific static view of the world.

3. Yet another barrier to be overcome is the capitalist bias, which often coexists with feudal attitudes. The capitalist bias manifests itself both at the level of ideas and values. Take for instance the word 'justice.' It is commonly assumed that it stands for a universal value, transcending particular historical periods. But what is really meant by the word bears the stamp of its capitalist origin. Thus, for instance, if the worker and the employer are given what is respectively their due, Christians would call it a just order of things. But they easily forget that this type of justice presupposes and in no way calls into question the injustice inherent in the bourgeois mode of production. The concept of freedom is another example. For most Christians, it means the ability to do (to own and to produce) what one chooses, unhindered by any other person. Here the 'other' is considered the limit of one's possibilities. This again is a capitalist concept of freedom. From the socialist perspective, on the

contrary, the 'other', far from being the limit of one's possibilities, is the condition for the possibility of overcoming one's limits. Similarly, the much-hymned idea of peace means, in reality, the institutionalized disharmony characteristic of capitalist society.

The same capitalist bias pervades also the value system in the Church. The bourgeois ideology of private interest and competition is an important factor underlying the proliferation of institutions in the Church. The capitalist cult of efficiency has its counterpart in the high value which Christian schools and colleges attach to efficiency and discipline, judged solely in terms of first classes secured and trophies won. With the explosion of development consciousness among Christians, money, that symbol of capitalist alienation, is fast becoming almost the equivalent of 'grace', and 'grace' itself is being monetized. One could go on multiplying instances. What has been said is enough to show that bourgeois prejudices and preferences colour much of what we are used to qualifying as Christian ideas and values. All this shows that nothing less than a radical attitudinal change is required if Christians are to become a significant humanizing force in the domain of education.

(Jeevadhara, 3, Jan. 1973, 57 - 65; *Ingathering*, Chapter 12)

22

The Jesus-Fellowship

The Approach

Our understanding of the Church is determined by the angle from which we look at it. Traditionally, we viewed the Church as 'emanating' from the risen Jesus in whom dwells the fullness of the divinity. In consequence, we tended to identify the Church with the Kingdom of God. Outside the visible community of Christians, we saw only imperfect participations of the spiritual riches which we, its members, possess by right and in abundance. We cordoned off the Church from the rest of mankind, but all the same, claimed as ours whatever was true and good in the latter by labeling it 'anonymous Christianity'. This way of thinking is at the root of that Christian triumphalism from which we have not yet fully broken loose. Besides, it is essentially hypocritical. For we know well enough that the grandiose claims we make are not sociologically verified, that there may be as much evil in the Church as outside it. Moreover, the traditional approach has rendered any attempt at dialogue with non-Christians fruitless, since our claim to possess the fullest revelation has relegated them to a position of inferiority, and thereby put them on the defensive. Hence the need for a new understanding of the Church.

The approach I have followed in this paper may be called historical. It consists of viewing things from the point of view of the Jesus of history.

The following are the positive reasons for this shift in perspective: First, what is distinctive about the Judeo-Christian world-outlook is precisely that it is in history it sees the revelation of the truth regarding God and man. It is also the only outlook that is in harmony with the contemporary quest for truth, which has for its point of departure man's collective historical experience. Second, the image of Jesus and his Church projected by the community of believers at different stages of history is itself in need of a criterion by which we may judge its validity. And this criterion can be nothing else than the life and teachings of the Jesus of history, understood in the light of our present experience of the living God. Third, the historical approach restores the man Jesus to His rightful place in theological thinking and will lay the basis for a new humanism in tune with the self-understanding of man today.

I am fully aware of the problems posed by the quest of the historical Jesus, knowledge of whom has come down to us only as mediated through the faith of the early Christian community. However, I do not share the view that this faith is so opaque a veil as to totally hide the visage of Jesus. Rather, the historical truth, regarding Jesus, was itself a central concern of the early Christian faith (See Lk 1:1-4). Hence it is possible for us today to gain an understanding of Jesus, adequate enough to make our Christian existence meaningful. It is this conviction that has inspired me to engage in a new search for the meaning of the Church, of which this paper is but a tentative formulation.

The Reign of God

The all-absorbing concern of Jesus was the reign of God. He lived in the hope that God would come to rule over the world and to gather in, his people. "The right time has come, and the Kingdom of God is near! Turn away from your sins and believe in the Good News!"(Mk. 1:15). It was for the sake of the Kingdom that he gathered around Him disciples who form the historical nucleus of the Church. Hence in order to understand the meaning of the Church, it is necessary to grasp the nature of the reign of God, Jesus announced.

The Not Yet and the Already

Jesus, like the prophets of old, looked forward to God who would come to bless the poor, comfort the mourning, show mercy to the merciful, satisfy those who hunger and thirst for justice, give the promised land to the meek, reveal his face to the pure of heart, gather into his family all who work for peace among men, and thus bring history to its fulfillment (Mt 5:3-11). But the absolute future, he announced, though it transcends history, does not reduce it to a total void. For the God who is to come, is also one who is coming and in a sense is already come in our midst. He is already at work in the here and now of history: "If it is by the finger of God that I cast out demons, then the Kingdom of God has come upon you" (Lk. 11:20). The Kingdom emerges in human society wherever people love one another, and in so loving meet the God of love (Mt 7:21; 25:40).

By inviting us to look to God who is beyond the beyond as our absolute future, Jesus freed us from the tyranny of time. The future that is God, relativizes all the achievements of the past as well as the institutions, laws, and customs, which condition our existence in the present. He thereby made us free for the future, for the working out of the mysterious plan of God in history. On the other hand, by proclaiming the reign of God as already emerging in the world, he showed the way to freedom from all false dualisms - of this world and the other, of this age and the age beyond, of matter and spirit, and of the temporal and the eternal. He likewise liberated us from all Utopian hopes which, by focusing our thoughts on an imaginary beyond, deflect our energies from the challenges of the real world.

The Total Man

The Reign of God in its final flowering as well as in its emergence consists of salvation not merely of individuals but of the entire family of man. It is above all to gather people and to abide by them that God comes and is at work in our midst. Jesus uses many and varied symbols to express this truth, he speaks of this new humanity as the flock (Mk. 14:27; Lk.

12:32), the throng of wedding guests (Mk. 2:19), God's planting (Mt. I3:24ff), the net (Mt. 13:47), the city of God (Mt. 5:14), the people of the New Covenant (Mk. 14:24), the new family of God (Mk. 3:34-35; Mt. 23:9; 25:40), the eternal home (Lk. 16:9), the New Temple (Mk. 11:17), the festal meal (Mk. 14:25; Lk. 22:30). The Kingdom of God is the realization of the Total Man as a theandric community of love.

The new people of God break all bounds set by birth, status, race or religion. It is open to all who have faith in God. It is significant that nowhere in the Synoptic Gospels does Jesus explicitly demand faith in Himself. The reference to faith in Jesus in Mt.18:6 and 27:42 is considered to be an addition by Matthew to the Marcan text.[1] What Jesus demands explicitly or implicitly is faith in God (Mk. 11:22). This faith could coexist with membership in any ethnic or religious group. We find Jesus imputing faith to the Samaritan leper (Lk. 17:19), the Syro-Phoenician woman (Mk. 7:25-30), and to the gentile nobleman (Mt. 8:5ff). His vision of the universality of the Kingdom finds clearer expression in His words: "Look! Here are my mother and my brothers! For the person, who does what God wants him to do, is my brother, my sister, my mother" (Mk. 3:34-35). The new brotherhood He envisages has for its basis neither kinship nor cult nor any set of doctrines but solely man's absolute concern for the will of God, in other words, faith manifested in deeds of love. And the love of God in question is shown in the love of one's neighbour. Hence on the last day of reckoning, it will be solely by the standard of brotherly love that God decides whether man should be awarded or denied entry into the Kingdom (Mt. 25:31ff).

The Jesuan vision of the Kingdom as accessible to all who have faith active in love liberates us from sectarianism and religious bigotry. It makes us free for encountering God in all men of goodwill irrespective of their caste, community or even religion. He opens our eyes to the truth that the dividing line between the Kingdom of God and that of Satan runs not through social classes or communities, but through the heart of every man. It so broadens our mind and heart that we can enfold within a cosmic WE, all those who seek the face of God in sincerity. It poses also a challenge for us to pull down all barriers, we have created between man and man in the name of religion.

The Free Man

God is at work in history forming a community of men, united in love. And love is the matrix of freedom. The irruption of the God of love in the person of Jesus is marked by freedom from the cosmic powers which hold man in bondage: the blind see, the lame walk, lepers are made clean, the deaf hear, and the dead are raised to life (Lk. 7:22-23). So too the poor, that class of people bent under the weight of oppression and having none to plead their cause, hear the good news of freedom from injustice (Lk. 4:18-19). Jesus also brought the good news of freedom from religious formalism (Mt. 5:24) and from the legalism that cripples the spirit and kills love (Mk. 2:17; 7:1-17). By criticizing the practice of Corban, which dispensed men from the obligation of loving their parents, and the law of Sabbath which barred them from doing good to their fellowmen. He proclaimed the truth that no law or custom that goes against the demands of love, can ever bind in conscience (Mk. 3:4; 7:9-12). All this shows that for Jesus the reign of God meant the reign of freedom.

The reign of God which brings into being the Total Man, free from every alienation and free for the fullness of love, was the focal point upon which all the energies of Jesus converged. His whole being was in tension towards the God who comes to rule over man and the universe. His words, "Set your mind on God's Kingdom and His justice before everything else, and all the rest will come to you as well" (Mt. 6:33), sum up his own fundamental attitude to life. Everything else, including the new fellowship, He initiated, takes on its full meaning only when seen in the light of his commitment to the Kingdom.

The Jesus-Fellowship

Every great man, committed to a cause, gathers around him, disciples. This is what Jesus too did, as all the Gospels attest. "I have chosen you to stay with me. I will also send you out to preach and you will have authority to drive out demons." (Mk. 3:14-15) These words, addressed to the Twelve, give us the substance of discipleship in general.

Staying with Jesus

Jesus chose those whom he wanted, so that they might stay with him, i.e. share his faith, his hope, and his destiny. In the measure in which the disciples were open to God, He initiated them into the mysteries of the Kingdom. He revealed to them the truth that history is tending to its consummation and that in His word and deed they were already witnessing the beginning of the end. He also strove to instill in them the values of the Kingdom. "You know that in the world the recognized rulers lord it over their subjects, and their great men make them feel the weight of authority. That is not the way with you; among you, whoever wants to be great, must be your servant, and whoever wants to be first must be the willing slave of all" (Lk. 10:42-44).   Similarly, in the Sermon on the Mount, He instructed the disciples in the ethics of the Kingdom. When asked by them for a prayer that would distinguish them from the many religious sects in Palestine, He taught them the 'Our Father', which is a vibrant expression of hope in the reign of God to come. In all his teaching the aim was not so much to reveal Himself as to reveal God's purpose in history. Even where He reveals himself, the stress is on His role in making present the reality of the Kingdom. Finally, Jesus demanded from the followers that they should identify themselves with His destiny. They are equally under the divine must as their master. "The Son of Man must suffer much and be rejected by the elders, the chief priests, and the teachers of the Law"(Mk. 8:31). The question that Jesus asked the sons of Zebedee is addressed to all disciples: "Can you drink the cup that I must drink? Can you be baptized in the way I must be baptized?"(Mk. 10:39) It follows from what has been said that 'staying with Jesus' has to be understood as essentially oriented to the reign of God.

The new fellowship, which Jesus formed, may be understood also in a broader sense so as to include, besides the disciples, all those who shared his expectation of the reign of God. He sought the company of the marginalized in society, the publicans and the sinners, contact with whom was forbidden by orthodox Jews. By inviting them to table-fellowship (Mk. 2:15-17; Mt. 9:10-13) He attacked the distinction between the sacred and the profane, which was a fundamental tenet of Judaism. This could well be one, if not the most important reason why the religious establishment decided to get rid of Him.[2] Though He believed, He was sent only to the lost sheep of Israel, He did not deny the Gentiles who had faith in the benefits of his ministry of healing. In fact, His table-fellowship with publicans and sinners is to be understood as an anticipation of the eschatological meal open also to the Gentiles: "Many, I tell you, will come from east and west to feast with Abraham, Isaac, and Jacob in the Kingdom of Heaven" (Mt. 8:11). The universality of the Kingdom finds its reflection in the universality of the Jesuan Fellowship.

By Word and Power

Jesus did not form the circle of disciples so that they might sit around and contemplate Him or offer Him worship. He demanded that they should follow Him, in His march to the Father. For His face was set on Jerusalem where he had to meet his destiny. Before that he had to tread the highways and by-ways of Palestine, preaching the good news from God and vanquishing the powers of evil opposed to the Kingdom. This He commanded his disciples to do. They were to preach what they heard their master preach, namely, that God's rule had already broken into history and that the time had come for a decision either for or against Him. They were to announce the emergence in the history of the Total Man reborn in freedom. But this was only one aspect of their mission, Equally decisive was the task assigned to them to drive out the demons. To grasp the full meaning of this mission, it is necessary to keep in mind that, in the time of Jesus, demons were thought to be responsible for evil in general, physical (storms, floods, accidents, diseases, etc.) as well as moral (moral blindness, disobedience to God, etc.). 'Driving out demons' is, therefore, a comprehensive term, which means declaring war against everything that militates against God's dominion over man and the universe.[3]

The Jesus-Fellowship and the Church of Today

The fellowship, which Jesus created is the nucleus of the Church of later times. In any renewal of the Church, the structure and dynamism of its origins have to play a normative role. If so, certain conclusions impose themselves on us.

The basic conclusion, we arrive at, is that the Church is not something that is intelligible in itself. Nor does it exist for itself. It derives its being and meaning from the fact that it exists for the reign of God. It is not so much an institution as a community straining itself towards the realization of the new humanity envisaged by Jesus. It is a collective longing and search for something greater than itself, namely, the full revelation of the reality of God in the visage of man. It is true to its essence only in the measure in which it commits itself to promoting the interests of the Kingdom. Those, who reduce it to a sort of tent in which we may settle down for good, deserve the same rebuke which Jesus administered to Peter: "Away with you, Satan, you think as men think, not as God thinks" (Mk. 8:33).

The full realization of the Kingdom, as a theandric community, is something yet to come. It is no more than a horizon of hope. To live in this hope is to accept having to grope in the dark, to take risks and to live without the security this world can provide. To leave behind all secure moorings and march ahead to the unknown, is the destiny of the Church. Fidelity to this destiny demands that the Church should resolutely reject every temptation to absolutize the relative or to use past standards to judge the present and the future. Where the living God demands, she should be prepared to go even beyond Jesus, recognizing full well that He too was a product of His culture.

In Jesus we have the irruption of the divine in the already here and now of history. It was the spirit of God that descended upon Him at the time of His baptism, which drove Him into the desert, sent Him on the mission of preaching and healing, and finally led Him to the Cross. Similarly, the Church can fulfill its mission only if it has already come under the power of the spirit of God. How can it in honesty preach the Kingdom of God, if it is not itself governed by the ethics of the Kingdom? How can it work for the reign of freedom, if it suppresses freedom of thought and expression in its own ranks, if its leaders lord it over their subjects and make them feel the weight of authority? How can it proclaim the primacy of love, if its own life is characterized by the primacy of cult and law? How can it be an instrument in the hands of God for the realization of the Total Man, if it is a house divided against itself? How can it drive out demons by the finger of God, if it has already entered into a concordat with the demons of money, prestige and political power?

We saw that the universality of the Kingdom Jesus proclaimed, found expression in His table-fellowship with publicans and sinners and in His openness to the Gentiles. If so, the structure of the Church, which is but the continuation in the history of the Jesuan fellowship, must also be open to all men of goodwill committed to truth, justice, and love. This is especially true of the Eucharist which, on the one hand, looks back to the table-fellowship of Jesus, and, on the other, looks forward to the festal meal of the end time, when Jew and Gentile shall sit at the table of God.

Finally, a word about the mission of the Church today. The task, which Jesus entrusted to his disciples, has in no way lost its relevance or urgency. Our task, as disciples of Jesus, is to preach the reign of God, to interpret and proclaim God's will as manifested in the situations, events, forces, and trends of the world we live in. It is to work for the birth of a new humanity in which men will live in and for one another, in which the freedom of each individual will be the condition for the freedom of all, and conversely, the freedom of all will be the condition, for the freedom of each. No less relevant and urgent is the task of driving out demons. Expressed in non-mythical terms, it means that we have to engage in a constant struggle against the economic, social, political, ideological, and other forces which enslave man. The demons of today are not only power for evil inherent in human freedom but also the sins embodied in social structures, customs, and false systems of values and ideas, like social exploitation, inequality, casteism, communalism, corruption, prostitution, materialism, hedonism, etc. A Church that does not fight against these 'demons' is nothing less than an institutionalized betrayal of Jesus.

(Jeevadhara, pp.190-198,1974; *Ingathering*, Chapter 11)

23

Jesus Today

Our age is marked by a profound concern for the future. Envisaging the future, planning for it, projecting alternatives - these have become matters of absorbing interest. Not merely interpreting history, but creating it, occupies the minds of men. Paradoxically, this concern for the future has generated its opposite, namely, a concern for the past, a tendency to return to the origins. In philosophy, this tendency has found expression in the slogan 'Back to things themselves', i.e. back to the world of our original experience, the matrix of all truth. This trend is also observable among the Marxists, especially of the West, who are trying today to return to the early writings of Marx. This can also be noticed among the adherents of various religions: Hindus today are striving to recapture the original insights of the rishis and seers of old. Christianity is no exception. Luther's was the first attempt to free faith from the accumulated traditions of the past and to root it directly in the message of the Gospel. In our own times, Catholics are returning to the New Testament writings, to drink there from the clear spring of the earliest traditions. This trend has of late become further radicalized in so far as the aim is to get behind the Gospels to the original phenomenon of the historical Jesus and his teaching.

Why this tendency especially at a juncture when our primary concern is with the future? It can only be because it has dawned on us that we cannot leap into the unknown future unless our feet are solidly planted in what is perennially valid in the past. Implied is also the recognition that for us today the origins of historical movements are more relevant than their subsequent developments and accretions. This means further that the history of ideas and movements has not been one only of progressive clarification but also of self-alienation and deviation. This is true even of contemporary Marxism, which has developed along lines which Marx would never have approved of. The deviation had in fact set in even during his lifetime, as is clear from a letter he wrote to a friend, in which he pleaded not to be called a Marxist and disclaimed being one. A process of alienation can be discerned also in the history of the Christian faith. Would not Jesus of Nazareth, if he were to come in our midst once again, disown much of what today is being done in his name by Christians?

Jesus Bound

The alienation of Christian faith and practice from the historical Jesus took place along three principal lines - cultic, dogmatic and institutional. For an adequate grasp of this process, it is necessary to go back to the very sources of Christianity and from there trace its development right up to our own day. This is not possible within the limited scope of this article. What is attempted here is nothing more than a schematic and, admittedly, a simplified outline of the salient features which even a cursory study will reveal.

Cultic alienation was the first to set in. The historical Jesus devalued cult by subordinating it to justice, mercy, and love. He did not project himself as an object of worship. He did not institute any rite which may be called cultic in the traditional sense of the term. What we call the Eucharist today was originally a prophetic gesture that looked forward to the end of present history when God would invite his children to sit at table with him. But no sooner had Jesus died than there developed a cult centred upon him. However, the focal point of this cult was not the Jesus of history but Jesus risen from the dead and seated at the right hand of the Father. Jesus who was part of our history was replaced in Christian piety by the risen Christ who is thought of as above history, as eternal and immutable. The same piety removed him from our midst, from the common run of everyday life, and installed him in the tabernacle. It built a separate home for him furnished with flowers, candles, holy water, incense and the like. It projected him as a stickler for ritual purity, who avoided publicans and sinners and looked down upon the 'profane' world of everyday life. Cult also started a process of abstraction. The death of Jesus was dissociated from his historical life or reduced to a mere prerequisite for resurrection. Jesus was further fragmented into many formal aspects, each of which in its turn became the object of a new 'devotion'. Thus we had a plethora of devotions having for their objects, 'The Precious Blood', 'The Crown of Thorns', 'The Five Wounds', 'The Sacred Heart' etc. By the Middle Ages, Christianity had become a cult-centered religion. Mercy, justice, and love took second place to the Eucharistic cult and the devotions. The circle was complete. A non-cultic prophetic movement ended up as a cultic religion.

The history of dogma and catechesis shows a parallel process of alienation. Jesus, as pictured in the Synoptic Gospels, is a man among men, a member of the family of man. He was less word made flesh than flesh become word, matter endowed with a tongue. The flesh of our flesh, blood of our blood, bone of our bones, he learned to love in being loved by others and gained knowledge of himself in being acknowledged by others. It is in meeting his kind that he learned kindness and compassion. He loved man. He struck roots in others to such an extent that all this became a need for him, especially in moments of crisis. Exquisitely attuned to everything human, he valued the friendship of women; he loved children, wine and flowers. He could rejoice with those who rejoiced and weep with those who wept.

Like any man, he too had to grow in wisdom and in favour with God and man. He was a quester after truth: after the God who made him; and he found Him on the banks of Jordan. On the day of his baptism at the hands of John the Baptizer, he was taken hold of by God. He was swept off his feet, uprooted from his familiar world and transplanted into the realm of the divine. There he was given a new mind and a new heart, and he began to see the world in a new light, in the light of the reign of God. But his search did not end there. He had still to come to terms with God and reach a point of clarity regarding his mission in life. The consequent inner struggle with light and darkness is represented in the Gospels as the temptation in the desert."Jesus was also fully conscious of his limitations. Asked about the final coming of the Kingdom, he replied, "But about that day or that hour no one knows, not even the angels in heaven, not even the Son, only the Father" (Mk. 13:32). So too he admitted openly that he could not dispense the blessings of the age to come just as he liked. The sons of Zebedee who sought from him the favour of being allowed to sit in state one on his right, the other on his left, were told bluntly that to sit on his right or left was not for him to grant, such privileges were for those to whom it had already been assigned (Mk. 10:40). Though the divine in him radiated its power, he did not think of snatching at equality with God (Phil. 2:6). When a stranger called him 'good master' his answer was: "Why do you call me good? No one is good except God alone" (Mk. 10:17-18)."Like any man, he too was subject to varying and conflicting emotions. The woes he uttered against the hypocrites of his day betray a spirit that was quick to flame with indignation. He was filled with anger at the sight of the trafficking that went on in the temple, the house of his Father. The destiny he was to meet in Jerusalem set every fibre of his being in tension. "I have a baptism to undergo, and what constraint I am under until the ordeal is over" (Lk. 12:50). The prospect of death was to him a source of infinite sadness which he tried to share with his friends: "My heart is ready to break with grief" (Mk. 14:34). It filled him with fear and anguish. To quote the writer of the Letter to the Hebrews: "In the days of his earthly life, he offered up prayers and petitions, with loud cries and tears, to God who was able to deliver him from the grave" (Heb. 5:7)

What a far cry from this Jesus, who is so much like us and in his very likeness stands out as the wholly 'other', to the Christ of dogma! The latter is Jesus transmuted as he was made to pass through the Greco-Roman mould of thinking. He came out of this mould fragmented into abstractions like person, nature, hypostasis, body, soul, substance, quality, quantity, essence and existence.

What cult did at the level of action, theology did at the level of thinking. Jesus was reduced to a mere sum of formal concepts. Seen from the human side he is a man with two natures subsisting in one divine person. Seen from the divine side he is the second person of the Trinity identical in nature with the Father and the Holy Spirit. Controversies raged as to whether the Spirit proceeds from the Father only or from the Father and the Sun. What is worse, in this process of sterile philosophical reflection the humanity of Jesus was downgraded. Of course, dogma as well as theology affirmed his human nature but not without denying him the status of a human person, a mode of reasoning which sounds so odd to us. This had its repercussion in popular catechesis. For the mass of believers, Jesus appeared as God under the guise of man. In their eyes he did not really grow in wisdom, for being God, he knew from early infancy all there is to know. Though they recited the official creed which said that Jesus suffered under Pontius Pilate, they assumed well enough that he could not have really suffered, endowed as he was on earth with the beatifying vision of God. If ever they read the Gospels they slurred over the passages which affirmed the human condition of Jesus or, if they were clever enough, managed to put dishonest interpretations on them. In short, if cult segregated Jesus from the company of man and settled him down in churches on the fringe of the real world, dogma banished him to the world of ideas. In the process, the real Jesus of history became a forgotten person.

No less than cult and catechesis, institutionalism distorted the image and the teachings of Jesus. The Gospels picture him as one who right from the outset of his public life rejected power, whether economic or political, as a means to usher in a New Age. The historical movement he set in motion was supposed to be for the poorer classes in Palestine and the Greco-Roman world who had no political ambitions.　But with Emperor Constantine who declared Christianity the state religion, the leaders of the Christian community began to enjoy economic and political privileges. The temptation Jesus overcame in the desert his disciples succumbed to, all too easily. The Church began to exercise control over every sphere of life. This led to a proliferation of institutions. Though in course of time political life regained its autonomy, the Church held on to its institutions, its schools, colleges, hospitals, and orphanages, and even started new ones. Every local church today has its institutional empire. What is still more saddening is that most of these institutions have not even an umbilical bond with the Gospel of Jesus. By and large, they embody the values of capitalism - private interest, competition, aggression, and lust for power. Besides, in so far as they violate the legitimate autonomy of secular spheres of life, they have become many instruments of domination. Thus by a curious development, the 'good news' of liberation preached by Jesus gave rise to structures of unfreedom. Institutionalism has in this manner disfigured the image of Jesus and neutralized the revolutionary, disruptive force of his teaching.

The tragic consequence is that he is the most forgotten person among the very people who claim to be his disciples. He lies buried under the weight of accumulated layers of rituals, rubrics, laws, concepts, legends, myths, superstitions and institutions. He lies bound hand and foot by innumerable cords that tradition has cast around him. His voice is smothered, his spirit is stifled. If he still acts and makes his presence felt in history, it is less through the official church than through honest dissenters among Christians.

It is the duty of all who cherish the vision and hope of Jesus to set him free from the prison-house of cult, dogma, and institutionalism so that he can freely go about pointing, as of old, his accusing finger at the Scribes, Pharisees, elders, priests, and Herods of today. To this end, it is necessary to remove the many veils which historically conditioned faith and tradition have put on him, and let his visage shine forth in its original splendour, and his words ring out in their untamed incisiveness.

What we have said thus far should not be interpreted to mean that the history of Christianity until now has been one only of progressive alienation. Admittedly the development of Christian theory and practice in the West contains, also positive elements in harmony with the teachings of Jesus. These have to be clearly distinguished from others at variance with them. A critical study of this question may be useful, and even necessary, up to a point, but should never be made an absolute for people who do not share the Western tradition. If we Indians have no other way to meet God as revealed in the life and teachings of Jesus than by mentally reenacting the history of Western Christianity we are, of all men, the most to be pitied!

It is necessary to go back to the historical Jesus. But is not the attempt doomed to fail, if the Gospels are not historical documents in the usual sense of the term but the expression of the faith of the early Christians? This is a serious problem of which an adequate discussion, though necessary, is not possible here. This much, however, may be said. It is true that the nature of our sources renders futile any attempt to write a biography or to describe the psychology of Jesus. It is impossible to reconstruct the sequence of events in his life. But to go further and say that no understanding of the historical Jesus at all is possible is unwarranted. The Gospels are the concrete embodiment of the response of the early Christians to historical reality, namely, to the life, words, and deeds of Jesus of Nazareth. Hence, it is possible for us to have a real encounter with the historical Jesus in and through the Gospels. Using the criteria provided by contemporary Biblical criticism, we can arrive at an adequate grasp of the person and teaching of Jesus, which are themselves events in history, and perhaps also, of a very broad outline of his life. Nothing more is presupposed here.

However, this is no plea for rediscovering the historical Jesus in order to mimic him or to repeat his teachings parrotwise. For he was a product of his culture, and his thinking bears the mark of the world that bore him. Both his message and the language in which it is couched need to be brought up to date in order that they may be relevant for us.

Jesus Beyond Jesus

To appreciate fully the need for such a reinterpretation a preliminary reflection, of a general nature, on the dialectics of change affecting ideas and beliefs may be useful. No man thinks in a vacuum nor is he born into the world with innate ideas. He finds himself inserted right from the dawn of consciousness into society with its own specific system of ideas, values, norms, and goals. These he assimilates from early childhood as mediated by the institutions of society like the family, school, and temple. He internalizes the ideas and beliefs currently held by the people at large. What was objective thus becomes subjective and influences his attitudes and decisions.

But the ideas and beliefs of a people at any given time are intimately interwoven with everyday practical life - with the prevalent mode of production, the structures and institutions of society, the political organization, and cultural activity. Ideas influence the social base and are in turn influenced by it. In other words, they mutually condition one another. In normal times there is a- certain equilibrium between ideas and their social base. Crises, however, may develop during which this equilibrium is disturbed and society is thrown off its balance. This may happen in two ways. The first is when ideas change without any corresponding change in the social base. It happens when people assimilate new ideas either from outside sources or from an internal elite. In such conditions, one begins to question the value of the existing social structures and institutions. The other mode in which a crisis develops is when the social base undergoes radical change without a corresponding change at the level of ideas. In such a situation what is called into question is the relevance of traditional ideas. In either case, society is in birth pang bringing forth a new truth. It is in periods of crisis that exceptional individuals arise who play a prophetic creative role. They give articulate expression to the revolt against the past and the longing for the new, which exists inarticulate and confused among the masses. In the tensions maturing in the heart of society, they discover the call of God. Thus masses on their part love and hate the new, at the same time. The burden of the past makes them welcome the new, but the fear of the new drives them to conform to the past. The same ambivalence is found also in their attitude to the prophets in their midst, these being heralds of the new. They slay the prophets and then hasten to erect monuments to the memory of the slain.

The prophets who rise up in periods of crisis are essentially heralds of the future. They are men who dream new dreams and see new visions. Their destiny is to leap into the unknown future and carry the masses with them. They are gripped by an ultimate concern, and their message necessarily has something of the unconditioned. Both in their revolt against the status quo and in their commitment to the 'not-yet' there is much that is valid for men of all times. All the same in the very breakthrough they achieve at the level of a total vision of man, they remain conditioned by the status quo they revolt against. The new they can envisage only in the language of the old. The very content of their message exhibits this tension between the 'not-yet' and the 'already', between the absolute and the relative, between the perennially valid and the historically conditioned. Lonely in the sweep of their vision and in the passion of their commitment, they remain very much men of their age.

Jesus of Nazareth was one such prophet, transcendent in his vision, immanent in his world, perennial in his appeal, rooted in his age, absolute in his demands, yet conditioned by his environment. The universal in his message comes to us, cast in a cultural mould we have long left behind. This poses a two-fold challenge to us: We have first to ascertain in the teachings of Jesus the perennially valid aspects as distinguished from their historical conditioning. Next, we have to bring to light their deeper implications for the man of today and clothe them in our idiom. To do this is to set free the spirit and thought of Jesus from their original mould and thereby release their revolutionary energies for the creation of a better world. This is to allow Jesus to respond to our historical situation in our patterns of thought and speech. Only then can the Jesus of yesterday be a creative force in the world of today and tomorrow.

But in trying to re-interpret Jesus for the men of today, are we not committing the same mistake as the early and subsequent generations of Christians? Are we not distorting his image to suit our tastes and safeguard our interests? That there is such a danger cannot be denied. And the only way to avoid it is to see to it that our interpretation is not naive but critical. But what are the criteria that should guide such criticism? They are twofold: fidelity to the original Jesus-phenomenon and responsiveness to the God who reveals himself to us in history. The Christians of the first centuries could not have applied the first criterion, for they lived in an age in which the boundary between myth and reality was blurred. Reality tended to be mythicized, and myth, to be looked upon as history. Consequently, it was natural for the early Christians to raise Jesus to the status of a mythical person. Criticism in our sense of the term was therefore not possible to them. Our situation is, quite different. We have gone beyond the stage of myth. We also know that any valid interpretation has to be in the nature of a response to historical phenomena as we encounter them. This obliges us at every stage to subject our subjective prejudices and preferences also to criticism lest they colour our interpretation of reality.

As for the second criterion, in the message of Jesus, there is an absolute and a relative dimension. The absolute dimension can be explained only on the basis of his encounter with the Absolute, with God. But, precisely because this encounter was enfleshed in a historical situation, it is possible and even natural that the total significance of it overflowed the limits of what was explicitly perceived by Jesus himself. This is, in fact, true of all aesthetic and religious encounters with truth.   That is why the truth of a work of art is often perceived more fully by the viewer than by the artist himself.   Similarly, it is only subsequent generations that understand the total meaning of a great thinker or a religious genius. However, any further interpretation has to be in line with the fundamental thrust and implicit dynamism of the original datum. Now the fundamental dynamism of Jesus'message pointed to God working in history. If our reinterpretation of Jesus is to be authentic,   it is essential that we encounter in history the same God whom he encountered two-thousand years ago.   It is our responsiveness to the God of today that guarantees our fidelity to the original Jesus-phenomenon. The demands which God in history makes on us today help us understand the deeper meaning of the teaching of Jesus. Conversely, the demands of Jesus help us interpret the signs of the times and decipher the divine challenges inscribed in history. In this way, the   Jesus of history enters into dialogue, in and through us, with the God of today.

However, the encounter with God is not to be understood solely in a mystical, or esoteric sense. Any man gripped by an absolute concern for his fellowmen has encountered God. It is possible, even likely, that the extreme radicals who are in prison today for the sole crime of having opposed an unjust society had a more authentic encounter with God than many professedly religious men and women who devote themselves to prayer and penance. For the same reason, the former may understand the significance of Jesus much better than the latter.

If we retrace our steps to Jesus of Nazareth, it is not to pitch our tent with him in the past but to go beyond him. We go beyond him when we free him from the historical conditioning of the Judaism of the first century, re-interpret his message in the context of our contemporary concerns, and translate it into today's language. Put differently, we can make it possible for Jesus to go beyond himself and discover his true identity in our age. He can slough off the past in order to come alive in the present, with whatever in his past has an abiding value. Thus we raise him from the dead and give him a new name and habitation. Seen in this light, the resurrection of Jesus is a continuing process achieved through our re-interpretation of his message and our commitment in response to it.

A reinterpretation of the entire message of Jesus along the lines indicated is an urgent need of our times. This, however, is beyond the scope of this article. No more can be done here than to illustrate, by way of conclusion, the approach set out here with a few reflections on the Kingdom of God which is central to the preaching of Jesus.

He believed that God would come to free man from every kind of bondage and usher in a new age of justice, freedom, love and universal brotherhood. His concern for the ultimate future is of supreme relevance for us today and will be so for men of all ages. But to be fully operative it has to be stripped of its historical conditioning. One form of conditioning concerns the belief in the imminence of the Kingdom which most scholars attribute to Jesus. If he entertained such a belief, it might possibly have been under the influence of the apocalyptic literature of his days, which found a favourable soil in frustrated nationalism. Be that as it may, for us today, the horizon of ultimate fulfillment has receded into the unknown future, a future handed over to the mysterious working out of two freedoms - the freedom of man and the freedom of God. However, belief in the imminence of the Kingdom brings out a truth that is valid for all times, namely, that the ultimate destiny of man will be settled by his decision here and now. In this sense, God and his Kingdom are always imminent.

Historical conditioning can be traced also in Jesus' conception of the manner in which the reign of God comes into being. Though he called for human response in the form of repentance, faith, and love, the stress is, perhaps unduly, on the character of the Kingdom as a gift of God. Nowhere does Jesus explicitly call upon his hearers to collaborate with God in constructing the Kingdom. All that he demands is that they dispose themselves inwardly for it and pray for its coming. Should this attitude be normative for his disciples today? Probably not, for he lived in a pre-scientific age when the conditions which make it possible for man to envision and create the future did not exist. Hence he could not have realized fully the role of man in bringing about the reign of God. In this scientific age, we are in a better position to understand that the future of mankind depends on our freedom as much as on God's. We know that God's gift comes to us not as something ready-made but as a call addressed to us to create the future, which when responded to, brings freedom and creativity to fulfillment. Therefore, when we today call upon men to commit themselves to the creation of a new Heaven and new Earth we are, in a sense, going beyond Jesus, but going beyond him in the spirit of creative fidelity to him.

It is along these lines that we have to reinterpret his response to the challenge of the Kingdom which, in more than one respect, will be found embarrassing by contemporary radicals. For Jesus did not condemn slavery though he knew of its existence among the Jews. Though there was, in his time, accumulation of wealth in the privileged classes, on the one hand, and unemployment and poverty, on the other, he did not call for any economic revolution. Nor did he join the nationalist liberation movement led by the zealots. From all this, it has been argued, by many Christians, that revolutionary commitment of any sort is opposed to the Gospel. They err because they set up a historically conditioned attitude of Jesus as normative for all ages. Jesus who lived two thousand years ago could not have envisaged a social revolution since its socio-economic and cultural pre-conditions did not exist. As for political liberation, his non-involvement probably resulted from his own reading of the times and from his understanding of the divine challenge as revealed at that particular juncture of history. But this is no justification for social conformism today. On the contrary, the basic thrust of his message demands radical commitment where the social system is unjust and oppressive, as in India. One cannot believe in the reign of God as the total liberation of man from every kind of bondage, a liberation to be brought about by human initiative, and at the same time remain neutral to structures of oppression. Similarly, Jesus' affirmation of the primacy of man over the Sabbath can in no way be reconciled with perpetuating the domination of man by structures. When, therefore, Christians commit themselves to social revolution today they are not going against, but along with Jesus. It is through them, only through them, that Jesus comes alive in the twentieth century.

(Jeevadhara, May-June 1975, pp. 169-181; *Ingathering*, Chapter 13)

24

Jesus' Message of Freedom

The Message of the Kingdom

According to Mark, the entire message of Jesus may be summed up in the words: "The time is fulfilled and the Kingdom of God is at hand; repent and believe in the Gospel" (Mk. 1:15). For Jesus, the Kingdom meant, negatively, the definitive liberation of man from all his bondages and, positively, his total reconciliation with nature, with his fellowmen, with God, and, so, with himself.

The Kingdom, in its fullness, will be realized only in the future. That is why Jesus taught us to pray: Thy Kingdom come. Further, he explicitly affirmed the Kingdom as the future when he said, "Many will come from the east and west to feast with Abraham, Isaac, and Jacob in the Kingdom of heaven" (Mt. 8:11). The future, when considered in its fullness, is already present, though but germinally, in the world. Jesus saw in the mighty deeds of God done through him, the inbreak of the Kingdom into the world of human experience. "If it is by the finger of God that I drive out the devils, then be sure the Kingdom of God has already come upon you" (Lk. 11:20).

God's reign is, at the same time, a gift of God and a task for man. It is a gift which man must receive with the openness of a child (Mk 10:13-15). That it is also a task follows from the many demands Jesus made on his hearers, for instance, for repentance, renunciation of wealth, reconciliation with others, etc. (Mk.1:15; 10:21; Mt. 5:3-10). The new humanity, of the future, will, therefore, be the fruit of man's action in response to the creative, saving call of God.

Finally, the Kingdom is at once continuous and discontinuous with our world. The new heaven and the new earth are nothing but our heaven and our earth filled with and transformed by human-divine love. It is nor a spiritual world situated somewhere above, which God will create after the destruction of our world (Mk. 10:29; Mt 5:5).

With authority, greater than of a prophet, even of the Law, Jesus called upon the man of his day to respond to the challenge of the Kingdom. More, he himself responded to the same challenge, and his response took the form of a NO to everything that fetters man and a YES to everything that furthers his fullness.

Freedom from Cosmic Bondage

We read in the Gospels that Jesus performed many cures and exorcisms and thereby freed men from their servitude to the forces of death and decay, operating in the world. His miracles have a threefold meaning. First, they rendered men whole, both physically and spiritually. Second, the healed were reintegrated into society as equals among equals (Mk. 1:44; 2:11). Third, the miracles restored the image of God in man and thus brought him nearer to his maker (Mk. 2:5). This work of liberation, Jesus initiated, will be completed only with the final coming of God's reign, when man will rule over nature and the products of man will act as the vehicle and the sacrament of man's love for God and for his fellowmen.

Justice For the Poor

The message of Jesus was in principle subversive of the unjust and oppressive economic system that prevailed in his days. This is borne out by the story of the rich young man (Mk. 10:17-31). The latter was one who strictly observed all the commandments of God while remaining within the system of private property. And it was precisely attachment to his property that barred him from entry into the Kingdom. Hence Jesus' words: "You lack one thing; go, sell what you have, and give to the poor, and you will have treasure in heaven; and come, follow me." And this the young man was not prepared to do, and he departed with a sad face. Commenting on his behaviour, Jesus went on to say: "It is easier for a camel to go through the eye of a needle than for a rich man to enter the Kingdom of God" (Mk. 10:25). Why? Because all economic inequality is, in the last analysis, due to man's aggression against his fellowmen. Besides, the rich end up by setting up riches as the supreme goal of life, and thus they deny the true God (Mk. 10:23-24; Mt. 6:24)

Jesus called upon his hearers to give up property and follow him, in his march toward a new economy based not on acquiring but on giving, an economy in which everything will be owned in common and distributed to each according to his need. This is in fact how the early Christians understood his massage(See Acts. 4:32-36).

Rejection of Social Inequality

Jesus of the Gospels defied all social customs and attitudes which smacked of domination of any one class over another. That he was on the side of the poorer classes, is already clear from his criticism of the rich. In other ways too, he showed his partiality to the dominated sections of society. He abrogated the practice, allowed by Moses, of sending away one's wife merely by writing her a bill of divorce, a practice based on the domination of woman by man (Mk. 10:2-9). He had no hesitation in violating the prevalent norms and taboos regarding man-woman relationships as may be seen from the fact that he allowed a retinue of ladies to accompany him wherever he went (Mk. 15:40-41). In a society, where children were considered mere items of household furniture, he proclaimed that they were the nearest to the Kingdom. For, contrasted with the adults, they were open to the demands of God (Mk. 10:14-15). Finally, in defiance of the practice of respectable classes, he consorted with the publicans and the sinners i.e. with the outcasts of Jewish society and even invited them to sit at table with him (Mk. 2:15-17).

His opposition to all man-made social barriers had, for its reverse side, commitments to the creation of a new humanity whose principle of unity will be neither kinship, nor money, nor power, but a common commitment to the will of God; "Whoever does the will of God is my brother and sister and mother" (Mk. 3:35).

No to Political Domination

No less uncompromising was Jesus' opposition to political domination. In one way or other, he was a threat to all political powers of his day. First, to Herod, who had John the Baptist beheaded because the latter undermined the moral and religious legitimacy of his rule by denouncing his marrying his brother's wife. If so, he had equal reason to get rid of Jesus, who too preached the inviolability of marriage. In fact, Luke records that some Pharisees came to Jesus to tell him that Herod was out to kill him (Lk 13:31). Jesus was a threat also to the political power of the Sanhedrin insofar as his criticism of their cult and their traditions was in substance an attack on the religious foundation of their authority. Besides, he pointed an accusing finger at the economic exploitation they carried on in the temple precincts (Mk 11:15-17). By challenging the authority of the priesthood which favoured the political status quo, he endangered at the same time the stability of the Roman rule in Palestine. Interpreted correctly, his words, "Render to Caesar the thing that is Caesar's and to God, the things that are God's" are a defiant attack on the Romans. What he meant was, "You know that God has forbidden you to make images of anything in heaven or on earth. Hence the very fact that you are using this coin bearing the image of Caesar, is an offense against God. Let Caesar, therefore, pack his coins and quit our land. But you are made in the image of God and shall be subject to none but Him alone.

Though Jesus was opposed to all political domination, he rejected the ideology and the practice of the Zealots, who were determined to throw out the Romans by force and restore the Kingdom of David. In all probability, the temptations, he overcame in the desert and the one against which he warned his disciples on the Mount of Olives, have both to do with making an option against political messianism of the Zealots.

It was therefore in the interests of all political forces in Palestine to get rid of the young prophet from Galilee. No wonder, he was brutally killed by the Romans with the connivance of the Jewish, authorities. Death was the price he paid for his commitment to a new communion of men and women in which, service, not power, will be the criterion of greatness (Mk. 10:42-44).

Freedom From False Religion

The teaching of Jesus undermined the very foundations of Jewish religion, which had become an oppressive force for the common man. Against the guardians of orthodoxy, he affirmed the primacy of man over the Law: "The Sabbath was made for man, not man for the Sabbath" (Mk 2:28). Where the law went counter to the wellbeing of man, it is deprived of all legitimacy and binding power. Of special significance is his repudiation of the rules of ritual purity. In his eyes, nothing from the world outside can defile a man; it is his heart, the common root of all knowing and loving, that renders things pure or impure (Mk 7:15). Jesus demolished the wall which traditional religion had set up between the sacred and the profane. Furthermore, he shifted the axis of religion from the domain of cult to the domain of life and love (Mk 4:35; 12:33-34). Thus he paved the way for a new religiosity which seeks to encounter God, less in the world of worship than in the domain of love for one's fellowmen.

Existential Liberation

Through his word and deed, Jesus showed the way to freedom from sin and the meaninglessness of death. He preached a God who gives and forgives, provided man repents and believes (Mk. 1:15). More, through his actions, he mediated the forgiving love of God. His meals with the outcasts of society were an offer not merely of social intimacy but also of divine forgiveness (Mk. 2:17). The miracles he performed further shows that the forgiveness of God also heals and re-creates (Mk. 2:5).

Jesus' message is also a proclamation of freedom from death. He confronted man with the God, not of the dead but of the living (Mk. 12:27). All who give themselves to God, in the service of their fellowmen, will rise up to a new life that does not succumb to the forces of death. It is in this light we have to understand his words: "For whoever would save his life (cling on to his self-centred existence) will lose it; and whoever loses his life for my sake and the Gospel will save it." (Mk. 8:35)

Our Task as Disciples of Jesus

Our task today is to continue the work of human liberation, Jesus initiated. To begin with, the challenge of cosmic liberation is today, as pressing as ever. We have to free ourselves not only from the hostile forces of nature but also from the tyranny of the forces man has released from nature. Now, we cannot rule out the possibility that man who has been completely taken hold of by God are even today able to work miracles. However, in the normal course of events, we have to rely on the means provided by science and technology in order to achieve freedom from nature. The carrying out of this task must be informed by a profound trust in God and a love that seeks the well-being of the whole man and of all men.

Discipleship demands that we commit ourselves to overthrow the economic system, which enables a privileged few to grow richer and richer at the expense of the many poor. We are bound in virtue of our loyalty to Jesus, to fight all forms of domination, whether it be of the poor by the rich, of the low castes by the high castes, of the common man by the politicians and the bureaucracy, of the masses by the elite, of women by men, of the young by the adults. We have no right to call ourselves disciples of Jesus if we remain silent in the face of oppression in any form. Nor can we, in good conscience, evade the challenge of creating a new society which, while respecting the freedom of the individual and promoting the participation of all in decision making, will not tolerate oppression or exploitation of man by man. Our criticism should extend also to those religious leaders who use religion in order to maintain their vested interests.

Finally, we should wage a constant war against the forces of sin and death, within each one of us, against self-seeking, pride, hypocrisy, and, above all, the will to violence and domination. The re-creation of the world without and the realization of wholeness within is not possible unless we take as our guiding principle these words of Jesus: "Set your minds on God's Kingdom and his justice before everything else, and all the rest will come to you as well" (Mt. 6:33).

(Findings of the AICUF National Seminar, Kerala Zone, held at Thevara, Cochin, 29 Dec. 1976 to 2 January 1977, published in The Rally, March 1977; *Ingathering*, Chapter 14)

25

Freedom From Political Domination

History is the process of man's self-creation. But man cannot create himself anew, without superseding the given conditions in which he finds himself. He has to free himself from the past and the present, to be able to mould his future. In other words, he has to negate the already, so that he may fashion the not-yet. In this sense negation is the mainspring of history. However, negativity is not to be understood in the manner of a necessary, inexorable law of nature but as instinct with consciousness and freedom. To negate is to act. And action presupposes an agent, who may be either an individual or a group. Historically it is in the prophets that negativity finds concrete, personal expression. In and through them, a community's need to go beyond the status quo becomes articulated in the form of a personal call and unconditional commitment. And Jesus of Nazareth was one such prophet, born at a critical juncture in the history of the Jews.

But no prophet negates the past without at the same time gathering it into the future to be created. The act of negating is itself conditioned by the past, as it lives on in the present. It is the memory of the past and the experience of the present that provide the stuff out of which the future is constructed. This too is true of Jesus. In negating the past, he preserved it for the future. As a total man, both the past he negated and the new model he projected encompassed the whole of human existence. It had to do not only with the structures of society — economic, political, and cultural — but also with the personal inwardness of man. In this paper, I shall deal only with his prophetic negation of political power. Here a cursory glance at the political past of the Jews is in order.

From Tribalism to State Power

The tribal past

The past, in which Jesus was rooted, went back to the days of old when Israel was but a group of semi-nomadic tribes. After settling down in Palestine, the twelve tribes assembled at Shechem and joined in a pact which made them into a nation bound together by a common faith. They acknowledged the same God, Yahweh, and worshipped Him at the same sanctuary containing the Ark of the covenant, the visible embodiment of His presence. Their life was governed by a common law, which they believed was revealed to them by God Himself through Moses. The tribal organization was like a rather loose confederation without bureaucracy, army or legislative body.[1] The tribes came together only when faced with internal conflicts or threats from other hostile tribes. On such occasions, they rallied around the person of the Judge, acclaimed as a leader for his personal qualities! They believed him to be divinely called and equipped to fulfill the role of leading Israel to victory. As the title itself signifies, the principal role of the judges consisted of adjudicating in matters concerning the observance of the law. What is important to remember here, is the fact that the democratic principle was maintained in so far as these charismatic leaders had to be acclaimed as such by the people as a whole. Besides, the office of the judges was in no sense a permanent one.

Each of the twelve tribes consisted of clans, whose members, just as in the case of the tribes, claimed descent from a common ancestor. From the time of the settlement, the clans were the effective political units at the local level. Since they settled down each in its village, the principle of common descent became subordinated to that of attachment to the land. Each clan was governed by a council of elders meaning the heads of families. In these village councils, the democratic principle was only realized in part, since slaves, aliens, and women were excluded from all official deliberations.

The economic relations did not lend themselves to the growth of class domination. In pre-monarchical days all pasture lands were held in common. Cultivated land, on the contrary, was privately owned. But even the common property outside the village was allotted in rotation to different families for use. However, the supreme ownership of all land vested in God. The land of Caanan was His gift to the people to be used as He willed. This was more than mere religious fiction. For, according to the divine ordinance, whoever had his property alienated for one reason or another was to regain its possession at the time of the Jubilee, i.e. every fiftieth year (Lev. 25: 8-17, 29-31). This prevented the concentration of land in a few hands.

Each clan in its turn consisted of families, the smallest unit of society. From the time of the earliest documents, the Israelite family was patriarchal. The head of the family wielded absolute authority — including power over life and death — over his children. The woman was but an item of her husband's property. The family included all those related by blood, extending sometimes even to three generations. It comprised also the widows, orphans, resident aliens, stateless persons and slaves whom the head of the family had taken under his protection. It was the family's responsibility to protect its members and redress any harm done to anyone of them. Herein lie the roots of the institution of blood vengeance.

It follows then that in the days of their tribal existence, there were among the Israelites no social classes in the strict sense of the term. Nor was there any State as a system dominating society as a whole. Such domination as existed was that of masters over slaves, of husbands over wives, and parents over children. All this, however, underwent a radical change with the institution of the monarchy.

Kingship and Domination

According to the original faith handed down from the days of their wandering in the desert, Israel was to have no ruler but God (Deut. 17:15). The Law alone, revealed by God, was to bind the different clans together. The idea of kingship was therefore entirely foreign to their way of thinking. The threat to national survival posed by the neighboring Philistines provided the historic occasion for the institution of kingship in Israel. The tribal organization was found inadequate to face the challenge. A central leadership that would rally all tribes together was needed. It was in these circumstances that Saul was made king both by prophetic proclamation and popular acclaim.[2]

The introduction of kingship brought about profound social changes. First, it gave birth to a bureaucracy, civil as well as military. The king made gifts of land to his officials, besides conferring on them many other privileges. Recruited from among the heads of important families, the bureaucracy, along with the elders, formed a privileged class in terms of wealth and power and were called 'the great' (2 Kings. 10:6,11; Jer. 5: 5; Jon. 3:7). Furthermore, the State appropriated a large part of the surplus product by way of taxes and levies to maintain its army of mercenaries. It held a monopoly in foreign trade. In pre-exilic days all-important economic enterprises like workshops and foundries were in the hands of the king. Production in these enterprises was carried on by slaves. The evils, Samuel predicted had come true. To quote Von Rad, "The king did conscript the young men of the country population to put them in his garrisons as regular soldiers. He laid hands on the landed property to set up estates of his own throughout the country; and from the country population too, he drew the labour forces for these estates. Other landed property he confiscated as rewards for his henchmen (1 Sam. 22:7). He taxed the whole population to defray the expenses of his court (1 Kings. 4:7; 20:15); indeed, even womenfolk were not safe from his requisition, for he needed them as perfumers, cooks, and bakers.[3] Bribery and corruption in the administration of justice were the order of the day. This was all the more reprehensible since the primary duty of the king was the proper administration of justice. He was not empowered to make laws. His role consisted solely in maintaining the law of Moses which had for its overriding concern the defense of the defenseless and the poor. The miscarriage of justice was, therefore, a flagrant violation of the law.

Prophetic Criticism of the State

From the beginning of the monarchy, there were religious leaders ready to provide it with theological legitimation. David's rule, for instance, found ideological underpinning in the prophecy of Nathan (II Sam.7). Understandably, the court theologians were the prime legitimizers of the new dispensation. The institution of the priesthood also came to its support. In contrast, there existed, also right from the beginning, a powerful current of thinking which saw in kingship a betrayal of Israel's original faith (Deut. 17:14-20; 1 Sam. 8:11-17). A poetic expression of this may be found in the fable of Jotham (Judg. 9:8ff), which highlights the futility of all expectations that kingship can promote the well-being of all, and contains the forecast that the State will prove to be an instrument of aggression and violence. It ridicules kings as good for nothings who vainly aspire to protect the rest of mankind. A more radical rejection of royalty may be seen in Gideon's refusal to be made king on the ground that it would amount to an encroachment on the exclusive rule of Yahweh (Judg. 8:22-23).

The State as an aberration

However, it is the prophets, who initiated the severest and most radical criticism of the monarchy. Amos repudiated the division of society into the rich and the powerful, on the one hand, and the oppressed masses, the little people (Amos 6:11; 8:6), on the other. He rebuked the ruling classes for the wrongs done in the administration of justice and for their failure to defend the orphans, the widows, the slaves, and the aliens. However, his criticism of the State was tempered with his belief in the sacred traditions concerning the house of David. He could think of a future only in terms of a restoration of the kingdom of David (Amos.

9:11f). The criticism of Hosea, a prophet of the northern kingdom who lived to see the fall of Samaria to the Assyrians, was directed against the growing secularization of the State and its autonomy vis a vis traditional religious moorings. The complaint of Yahweh conveyed through the prophet was, "They made kings, but not through me" (Hos. 8:4). Those who want a State without God can regain their humanity only if they are made to experience God without any State. "Many days shall the Israelites remain without a king, without officials, without sacrifice, without an ephod, and without teraphim, then the Israelites will return and seek their God"(Hosea 3:4f). Here the existence of the State and 'return' to God are presented as incompatible. Only in a stateless society can man know God. The knowledge of God is for Hosea but a synonym for the practice of justice and mercy.[4] His prophecy ends up as a definitive repudiation of the State.

Isaiah carried forward the critique of the State, initiated by the earlier prophets. His message too contains a denunciation of the status quo and the projection of a new age of justice. He attacked the ruling classes in Jerusalem, who had accumulated wealth by expropriating the small peasants of their property in land (Is. 5:8; Mic. 2:1-5). Like Amos, he criticized the miscarriage of justice perpetrated by the people's councils. Equally severe were his strictures on those who cast their hopes not on God but on the strength of arms (Is. 31:1-8). In all this, his profound concern was the observance of the divine Law. So far so good. But when we come to his project for the future, we see that he is very much conditioned by his proximity to the court and the ruling circles in Jerusalem, the scene of his activity. Unlike Hosea who preached the supersession of the State, Isaiah envisioned the future in terms of a polis, a city-state with its officials and with a messiah-king who will administer justice. Even this project should not be dismissed as merely reactionary. For it contains an element of truth, namely, that the abolition of the State is at the same time its dialectical preservation and not a mere return to primitive tribalism. In contrast to Isaiah, the negation of State comes into fuller relief in Micah who announced the destruction of Jerusalem and the return to the days of tribal organization. Each in his own way is groping towards the truth that the future can be constructed out of nothing but out of the possibilities inherent in the tribal past and the contemporary monarchy. The crucial point to remember is the fact that all these prophets preached a message that was essentially subversive and even seditious, in so far as they either wrote off the contemporary monarchy as beyond redemption or looked forward to an entirely new beginning coming from the divine initiative.

If the political criticism of the earlier prophets was in the context of the threat from the Assyrian empire, that of Jeremiah reflected danger posed by the Neo-Babylonians. Though, he fulfilled his prophetic role in Jerusalem, the roots of his message lay not in court theology but the exodus-covenant tradition current in the northern kingdom with its anti-monarchic bias. His evaluation of the State was as negative as that of the earlier prophets. He went a step further and dared to represent through a symbolic deed the utter ruin of the nation and the city. The action in question consisted of breaking to pieces an earthen flask in the presence of many (Jer. 19:11; 20:6). He prophesied the capture of the city by the Babylonians and advised the people and its rulers to capitulate before it was too late. No wonder he was condemned by the nationalists, beaten up by a royal official, and imprisoned for a night. No earlier prophet, except perhaps, Isaiah had to suffer in his person for criticizing the state and its policies. This, as we shall soon see, contains a profound lesson for all who are concerned with the liberation of man at all times and in all places.

Beyond the Law that binds

With Jeremiah, Ezekiel and the second Isaiah, prophetic radicalism reached its point of incandescence. This is particularly evident in Jeremiah's conception of the divine project for the future. The earlier prophets were ardent champions of the Law. If they attacked the State, it was because it functioned contrary to the divine ordinances. None of them had dared to question the eternal validity of the Law itself. And this is just what Jeremiah did: he announced the definitive supersession of the Law. His message from God was: "I will put my law within them, and I will write it upon their hearts, and I will be their God, and they shall be my people. And no longer shall each man teach his neighbour and each his brother, saying, 'Know the Lord', for they shall all know me, from the least of them to the greatest, says the Lord; for I will forgive their iniquity, and I will remember their sin no more" (Jer. 31:33-34).

Profound, indeed, are the implications of this prophecy. However much the law may reflect the will of God and serve to ensure the good of the community, it is something that confronts man from the outside. The very existence of the Law implies that the community has no direct access to the divine purposes, and has to depend on mediators like prophets, teachers, and priests. Besides, no law codified at an earlier stage can adequately meet the demands of mankind's ongoing dialogue with God. Therefore, the Law itself can become an obstacle in the way of man's historical self-creation. If so, no less than the State, the Law too needs to be transcended. But, what is the Law but the word of God? Hence will not the abolition of the Law also imply the abolition of God? No. For, the Law is also the word of man and, as such, is historically conditioned. Besides, the supersession of the Law is also its preservation and sublimation. The Law will be interiorized and become a norm written in the heart of man. This means that, in the new age, the community will know God in knowing the depths of its existence. This implies further, the death of the God-outside-and-above-man. The same vision of the future marked by the abolition of every mediation between man and God finds eloquent expression in the prophet Ezekiel (Ezek. 36: 24-28).

The agent of the new creation: the servant of Yahweh
The question naturally arises, Who will usher in the new age without State, without the Law? All the prophets answer, God. But not the God above but the God who has become man, or, rather the community invaded by the spirit of God. In the community, it is, above all, the prophet who is pre-eminently the bearer of the spirit (power) and the word of God. He is the one whose task it is to give the lead in the

adventure of creating a future free of State and law. But the prophet is a prophet only in so far as he gives articulate expression to the mute longings of the people, though not of all any people but only of those who long for a new order of things in which there will no more be hunger, exploitation, and aggression. Such are the slaves, the widows, the orphans, the aliens, the poor and the powerless. In short, it is with the exploited and dominated that the prophet has to identify himself. Theirs is the historic mission to fashion a better future for the family of man. I suggest that it is this profound insight that finds expression in the symbolic figure of the servant of Yahweh (Is. 42:1-4; 49:1-6; 50:4-9; 52:13; 53:12). The concept of 'the servant' has both an individual and a collective meaning: it means the slaves of all ages bent under the weight of oppression as well as those called to provide leadership to their struggle for freedom. The prophet and the people form a unity in tension. It is out of their suffering unto death that a new humanity will be born. This insight that the construction of the future has to be accomplished by the oppressed of today, in response to the challenge of God, represents a historic breakthrough in the religiopolitical thinking of all times. Prophetism thus leads up to the frightening prospect that some will have to lay down their lives so that the many may live.

The Jesuan Critique of Power

The contemporary relations of power

As far as the critique of society is concerned, Jesus is heir to the great prophetic tradition. But to grasp the full implications of his political message, it is necessary to keep in mind the contemporary relations of power. For, like the prophets of old, he too read the will of God from the horizon of history. Since the death of prophecy in Israel, brought about largely by the conservative priestly class, far-reaching social and political changes had taken place. For centuries the people had lived under foreign domination. In the time of Jesus, it was the Romans who held sway over Palestine. Judaea was directly under imperial rule, while Herod who ruled over Galilee was but a puppet in the hands of Rome.

Many were the structures of domination in Jesus' day.[5] They formed a more or less closely knit multi-tiered system. The lowest centre of authority was the head of the family. At the village level, there was the council of elders, which met only when communal problems had to be settled. It consisted of the heads of important families and a priest entrusted with the discernment of the pure and impure. Similar councils functioned also in towns, but with this difference that the elders came from the lay nobility, themselves large property owners. In these councils sat also the scribes, specialists in matters concerning the observance of civil and religious law. Of all such councils, the most important was the council at Jerusalem called the Sanhedrin, the supreme court of justice. In the first century of our era, it was the priestly class of the Sadducees that controlled the affairs of the Sanhedrin, though, among its seventy-two members, there were also scribes and representatives of the lay nobility. The Sanhedrin was the seat not only of religious authority but also of political power. It was not always in session and met only as and when the situation demanded it. The permanent seat of political power was the body of chief priests presided over by the High Priest, who in the time of Jesus was appointed by the Romans. However, the Jewish State enjoyed a certain autonomy in matters of internal government. Finally, dominating all these lower centres of power, there was Roman imperialism, which kept the people and the local rulers under control with the help of its army.

As far as the internal government was concerned, power was in the hands of the rich landowners and the priestly aristocracy who made the state apparatus serve their ends. But what the people hated most was the loss of national freedom and the presence of foreign rule. The common man had to pay twenty-five percent of his annual produce by, way of taxes to Rome. He was subjected to extortion by the tax-collectors, appointed by the Romans from among the wealthier classes. Also, twenty-three percent of all produce was to be paid to the temple, not to mention a third levy supposedly meant to aid the poor. Such were the political conditions when the young prophet from Nazareth appeared on the scene. How did he react to the evils of state power and foreign rule?

A sign of contradiction

We know little of his early youth. Admittedly, the infancy narratives in Matthew and Luke are more like legends, than of history. However, they tell us what the early community of believers thought of him. The hymn of thanksgiving, which tradition puts in the mouth of Mary, his mother, shows that they associated him with the subversive presence of God in history: "He (the Lord) has scattered the proud in the imagination of their hearts, he has put down the mighty from their thrones, and exalted those of low degree; he has filled the hungry with good things, and the rich he has sent empty away" (Lk. 1:51-53). Jesus is here presented as one sent to overthrow the existing relations of wealth and power, to be the herald of a social and political revolution. [6] The same expectation is voiced by Simeon on seeing the child, Jesus. "Behold, this child is set for the fall and rising of many in Israel, and for a sign that is spoken against." (Lk. 2:34). It is the destiny of a prophet to be spoken against, to be a sign of contradiction. Why? Because his mission is to contradict (negate) the prevalent state of affairs. As a result, he will himself be contradicted by the accredited guardians of the status quo. In this struggle of opposites, the seats of power will fall to the ground and those who were till then made to grovel and slave will rise to a new humanity. In painting such a picture, the early disciples were only being true to the self-understanding of Jesus himself, as is clear from the claim he made at his first appearance in Nazareth: "The spirit of the Lord is upon me because he has anointed me to preach the good news to the poor. He has sent me to proclaim release to the captives and recovering of sight to the blind, and to set at liberty those who are oppressed, and to proclaim the acceptable year of the Lord" (Lk. 4:18-19). Setting captives free is not possible without overthrowing the powers that be who maintain armies and prisons. From this, we may conclude that Jesus saw the political liberation of his people as an integral part of his total mission.

Beyond mastery and slavery

The conclusion we have arrived at is the only one that coheres with the general tenor and the basic thrust of his teaching. Like the prophets that came before him, Jesus too gave his people 'a future and a hope'. He looked forward to the God who was to renew the face of the earth. His was not a neutral God, who administered His blessings evenly to the oppressor and the oppressed, to the ruler and the ruled. He is partial to the poor and the downtrodden, an idea which is central to the Hebrew religion (1 Sam. 2:1-10; Job 5:8-27; 12:13-25; 36:6ff. Ps. 107:33-41; 113:7-9; 147:6). It is against this background that we should understand the saying of Jesus, "But many that are first will be last, and the last first" (Mk. 10:31; also Mt. 19:30; 20:16; Lk. 13:30). God will come to vindicate the last, the exploited and dominated by toppling those who are first in the hierarchy of power. This should not be taken to mean that there will be only a reversal of social positions, the ruled of today becoming the rulers of tomorrow. That would not do away the dichotomy between the rulers and the ruled. The future will not be a reproduction of the class society of the past, because the real interest of the last consists not in themselves becoming rulers but in overcoming all conditions of domination. Only when they seek this, their real interest, will they have God on their side. Were they to seek to attain, to positions of domination, God would have no part with them. This means that the last of today will be first in the new age, only in the sense that they will represent more than anyone else, man's authentic *being-for-others*. Similarly, the first of today will be the last of tomorrow, if they cling onto their lust for power, to the itch for domination. If so, the political revolution of the future will necessarily imply also a revolution of values.

In this context, of crucial significance is Jesus' saying, "You know those who are supposed to rule over the Gentiles lord over them, and their great men exercise authority over them. But it shall not be so among you, but whoever would be great among you must be your servant, and whoever would be first among you must be the slave of all. For the Son of man also came not to be served but to serve, and to give his life as a ransom for many" (Mk.10:42-44). According to Mark, the life situation which elicited this saying was the request of the sons of Zebedee that they be allowed to sit one on his right and one on his left when he came in glory. The request was probably based on their hope that their master would soon lead a successful revolt against the Romans and establish himself king over all Israel and the whole world, a hope which the latter had repudiated more than once both in word and deed. Quite different was the hope which Jesus himself nursed. What he envisioned was a future, when there will be neither rulers nor ruled but only sons of God and, therefore, brothers to one another (Mt. 5:9).

Seen against this hope, the above saying is nothing less than a total repudiation of power, understood as the possibility some have to impose their options, ends, and means on others. Jesus will have nothing to do with an order of things in which the rulers lord it over their subjects and make them feel the weight of their authority. Hence, his call should not be interpreted away as mere advice to use power as a means to service or service as a means to power but to radically and unconditionally renounce all exercise of power. Those who aspire to be great (that is to have slaves under them) must retrace their steps and seek to be slaves to others. Those who aspire to be first in wealth, influence, and prestige, must seek the lowest place. And in a social order in which all are slaves to one another, none is master over others. Or, rather, each man will be master and slave in one; slave, because he recognizes every member of the community as an absolute value and not a mere means to an end; master, because he, in turn, is recognized by all as an absolute value. In this sense, the future community of service is the dialectical supersession of mastery and slavery, a supersession that preserves and realizes on a higher level the truth of both, namely, *being-for-oneself* (mastery) in *being-for-others* (slavery).

Supersession of the Law

Jesus' message too contains the prophetic intuition that the law will have to be left behind as an inadequate form of man's dialogue with

God. Of capital significance in this context is his statement that the Sabbath is made for man, not man for the Sabbath (Mk. 2:27). Where the law of the Sabbath goes counter to the good of man, it ceases to have any validity. What never loses value is man, only man. More, the Law becomes irrelevant and superfluous where man stands in the right relationship to his fellow-men and thereby also to God. This will become possible only on two conditions: the re-creation of the world without (structures and institutions of society) and the re-creation of the world within (structures of knowing, loving, and being which condition the inwardness of man), a twofold re-creation that can be accomplished only in dialogue with God. The same idea is contained in the beatitude, "Blessed are the pure in hearts, for they shall see God" (Mt. 5:8). The pure in heart (those who do not harbour evil intentions against their neighbour) shall see God and in seeing God definitively transcend all law. They will then become a law unto themselves and to others, i.e. original creators of value. This is further attested by the saying, "Hear me, all of you, and understand: There is nothing outside a man which by going into him can defile him; but the things which come out of him (out of his heart) are what defile him" (Mk. 7:14-16). Here the prophetic forecast concerning the law being written in the heart of man is taken up and reaffirmed with all its revolutionary implications. But what marks Jesus out from the earlier prophets is the stupendous pronouncement that this future, without Law, is already within the grasp of man *here* and *now* if only he would go forward to meet the God who comes.

From preaching to practice

Mere hope in the future cannot change the harsh realities of the present. For the future to become present, the bearers of that hope must identify themselves with such social classes as groan under the weight of the law and the power of the State. And this is just what Jesus demanded of his disciples: "For everyone who exalts himself will be humbled, and he who humbles himself will be exalted" (Lk 14:11). Those who refuse to join bands with the lowest in the social hierarchy will have no share in the authentic humanity of the future. The same message underlies the other saying, "Truly I say to you, whoever does not receive the kingdom of God like a child shall not enter it" (Mk 10:15). Children are not here held up as models of humility or innocence. The saying must be interpreted in the light of the social conditions that obtained in those days when children were but items of household furniture, totally under the dominion of the parents. They were par excellence, the weak and the powerless in society. To become like children, therefore, involves relinquishing prestige and power, and joining the ranks of the Anawim, the subjugated masses.[7] This is what Jesus himself did when he consistently befriended the publicans and the sinners, in other words, the social outcasts of his day, many of whom were denied even ordinary civil rights.[8]

But, who is he that identifies himself with the lowly masses, raises the voice of protest against the powers that be, and in the process is tortured, mutilated, and done to death if not the prophet himself as the servant of Yahweh? The concept of the servant of Yahweh expressed the core of the prophetic self-awareness of Jesus (Mk. 1:11; Mt. 8:17; 12:18-21; Lk. 22:37; Acts 3:13). As the servant, he is what he preached: the radical repudiation of all power and the equally radical commitment to a new society based not on domination but service. He embodied in himself the supersession of all relations of power and the transition to relations of service. Here we possess the key to the very secret of his life and death.

Confrontation unto death[9]

The Gospels show that his life was a continuous struggle with the powers that be, whether familiar, religious or political. There is a hint in the infancy narratives that he experienced the conflict between loyalty to God and loyalty to parental authority. When his parents reproached him for staying back in, Jerusalem without their knowledge, his reply was, "How is it that you sought me? Did you not know that I must be in my Father's house?" He had to disregard parental authority to be true to his mission. That there is a historical nucleus in this story seems to be substantiated by the subsequent behaviour of his relatives. Mark records that once, while he was addressing a crowd, his relations came to seize him, convinced as they were, that he was out of his mind. Significantly, it was on the same occasion that he came out with the remark that his real mother and brothers are those who do the will of his Father. An echo of this may be heard in his poignant saying, "A prophet is not without honour except in his own country, and among his kin, and in his own bouse" (Mk. 6:4). May it not be that it was the domination adults exercised over the young that makes them, among other things, less fitted than the latter to enter the kingdom of God?

The Gospels also show that Jesus came into conflict also with Herod in Galilee. Luke narrates how, towards the end of his Galilean ministry, some Pharisees came to him with the warning that Herod was planning to kill him and that he should quit the territory as soon as possible. To which Jesus replied, "Go and tell that fox, Behold I cast out demons and perform cures today and tomorrow, and the third day I finish my course . . . For it cannot be that a prophet should perish away from Jerusalem" (Lk. 13: 31-33). Since the reply is in the form of a message to Herod, we may surmise that the latter himself had sent the emissaries. There is no reason to believe that the warning was not seriously meant. But, why did Herod seek to get rid of the prophet from Nazareth? I suggest that it is because be believed the latter to be John the Baptist risen from the dead. He had had John beheaded for criticizing his living with his brother's wife. Such criticism amounted to an attack on the divine legitimacy of his rule since God would not be with a ruler who violated His law. Besides, did not Jesus himself preach the indissolubility of marriage and thus undermine the moral basis of Herodian rule? Furthermore, it is not unlikely that Herod feared that Jesus would lead a popular revolt against the Romans, to set himself as king over all Israel. He could not have been uninformed of the attempt made by the people to make Jesus a king and that too in his territory (Jn. 6). He had therefore ample reason to get Jesus out of his way and this he sought to do without at the same time alienating the people.

The challenge Jesus posed to the authority of the Jewish State comes out clearly in his cleansing of the temple. He drove out the buyers and the sellers and overturned the tables of the moneychangers and the seats of those who sold pigeons. He accused the authorities, of reducing what was meant to be a house of prayer for all nations into a den of thieves, in other words, of using religion as a means for exploiting the people. Such a direct attack was bound to provoke a counter-attack from the guardians of the temple. Hence their question, "By what authority are you doing these things?" Power, when threatened, always resorts to violence. And that is just what happened. "And the chief priests and scribes heard it and sought a way to destroy him" (Mk. 11:15-19, 27-33). Yet in another way too, Jesus posed a threat to the political power of the ruling class, especially of the chief priests. He undermined the very foundations of Judaism by repudiating the separation between the pure and the impure, between the sacred and the profane, a distinction which alone provided legitimacy to the priesthood. Equally subversive of official Judaism was his radical criticism of the law. And in a society in which religious and political power reinforced and legitimated each other, any attack on the first was also an attack on the second.

Did Jesus denounce Roman imperialism over Palestine? First, we should remember that the Gospels were written by Christians living under the empire who were already subjected to persecutions. Hence it is not improbable that the writers of the Gospels have on purpose toned down the anti-Roman stand of Jesus. Be that as it may, the fact remains that he was condemned to death by the Roman procurator on the charge of sedition. Though the charge was utterly unfounded, Pilate had enough grounds to believe that the accused posed a threat to the stability of the imperial hold over Palestine. First, the Sadducean priesthood which formed the core of the Sanhedrin supported the Roman rule. Any threat therefore to the authority of the Jewish State would have acted against the interests of Rome. And we have seen that both the teaching and practice of Jesus were subversive of the religious and political power of the Jewish authorities.

But does not the saying, "Render to Caesar the things that are Caesar's and to God the things that are God's" (Mk. 12:17) show that Jesus acknowledged the legitimacy of Roman rule? Not if the saying is interpreted correctly. We must not forget that it was to entrap him in words that his adversaries asked him, 'Is it lawful to pay taxes to Caesar or not?' If he said yes, the people would have risen against him; if no, he could have been accused of sedition against Rome. Hence in replying he had to resort to coded language. To decode the meaning it must be recalled that Yahweh had forbidden Israel to make images of anything in heaven or on earth (Deut. 5:8). The very presence in Palestine of coins bearing the image of Caesar was in flagrant violation of the divine commandment. All true believers, therefore, were in conscience bound to rid the land of such coins and the imperialism they represented.[10] Man, on the contrary, was made in the image of God and, as such, belongs to Him alone. To submit to any other ruler is to reject the rule of God. Understood thus, Jesus' reply is an emphatic no not only to Roman imperialism but also to every form of state power.

If that is the case, why did he not join the Zealots who were committed to throwing out the Romans by force? Because what the Zealots wanted was not revolution but restoration. What they looked forward to was a restored kingdom like that of David and Solomon and not to a new order of things in which there will be no more state, law, army, or king. In the universalist vision of Jesus, there was no place for the nationalist particularism of the Zealots.

The conclusion imposes itself: All the political forces in Palestine had an interest in getting rid of the young prophet from Galilee. What subsequently happened on Calvary was, therefore, nothing but coldblooded political murder.

(This paper was presented to the Marxist-Christian Dialogue Forum in Madras in July 1978. Religion and Society, Vol. 26, No.3, September 1979; *Ingathering*, Chapter 15)

26

Censorship and the Future of Asian Theology

[In October 1980, the Sacred Congregation for the Doctrine of Faith, asked the General of the Society of Jesus (of which I am a member) to have my book, Jesus and Freedom, censored by a competent theologian, since it was thought to contain 'elements of a doctrinal nature that give cause for concern'. The judgment of the censor has since been communicated to me, along with instructions (1) that I should provide clarification in some form - for example by writing an article - which will show that I accept the position of the Magisterium on the points raised, (2) that I should in future submit my writings to the censorship of the Society of Jesus, and (3) that in an eventual reprint or translation of the book, I should make adequate corrections. Since censorship of this kind raises problems concerning the very future of Asian theology, I am publishing my reply to the General of the Society of Jesus for the benefit of the readers of Anawim. S. Kappen]

15th May 1981

Dear Father, This is in reply to the critical comments of the censor, appointed by you to scrutinize my book, Jesus and Freedom, at the instance of the Sacred Congregation for the Doctrine of Faith. I am writing after mature reflection, taking into consideration my responsibility both as a disciple of Jesus and a theologian. I have in all intellectual honesty tried to eliminate whatever subjective factors might color or distort my response.

Frankly, I have serious reservations regarding the very theology underlying the practice of censorship.

Censorship on the part of the Church implies that there exists a set of codified formulae, fully expressive of the truth about God and Jesus, in the light of which the truth or falsehood of contemporary theological writings may be determined. This, in my view, amounts to saying that no sooner had God 'once upon a time' fully revealed his mind than he was forced to retire from the scene, under orders never again to open his mouth before his sons and daughters. Censorship has meaning only in a world from which God has been banished, in a history purged of his presence. Underlying it all is that perverse hubris that seeks to replace God with man-made concepts. No wonder if those who consign the Almighty to the silence of the grave, feel no qualms about inflicting death on fellow humans. One has only to recall the thousands of men and women, done to death in the name of faith and dogma in the heyday of the Crusades and the Inquisition. Significantly, the age when the zeal for the integrity of faith reached its peak was also the age that saw the most brutal censorship in action in the form of witch-hunting and the burning of heretics.

I am sure the Church today disowns that lurid, gruesome past. But, how genuine is such disowning? Does she not continue to do in subtle ways, what the Inquisition did earlier in cruder ways? True, she does not kill the body. She cannot, even if she would. But she continues to kill the spirit and that through the mechanism of censorship aimed at marginalizing those who dissent and thereby silencing them.

The necro-theology, justifying censorship, goes counter to the unambiguous message of Jesus. Jesus announced the good news that God not only will come but is already coming, here and now; that he continues to speak to men and women of all times challenging them to decide. To respond to that God is the fundamental task of the disciple of Jesus. Now, the challenge of the living God and man's response to it today cannot be judged by the yardstick of petrified formulae derived from earlier ages. Rather it should be the other way round. The value of tradition must be assessed in the light of God's contemporary word. This should also apply to the traditional interpretations put on Jesus. If it is the same God who spoke to Jesus and continues to speak to us, His speech today is also revelatory of what Jesus was and what he means to humanity. If the understanding thus gained of Jesus does not conform to traditional formulations, it is these formulations that need to be called in question. To do otherwise would be letting the letter kill the spirit, dead concepts replace the living word of God, the past abolishes God's (and humanity's) present.

Moreover, if God is alive and speaks to humans of all places and cultures, there is no basis for censorship that evaluates all theology by the standard of one theology, I mean, by the standard of the dogmas and concepts developed in the western historical-cultural context. The traditional mode of thinking, in the West, is representational. It seeks to abstract the essence from the existents, thereby forming concepts meant to represent reality. By the same token, it is also analytical, bent on dissecting the real into its constituent elements. In the process, it disrupts the primordial unity of being and knowing. In essence, this way of thinking is technological, its goal being the domination of the given world. By elaborating concepts and systems it strives to gain mastery over the earth. Knowledge thus becomes a means to power, if not itself power. Thinking rooted in, and spurred on by, the will to power ends up by becoming an instrument for the domination of human beings, as is borne out by the history of colonialism, fascism, and the on-going technocratic manipulation of the masses. This kind of thinking can only beget a theology that strives to gain mastery over God by reducing him to manageable concepts. The spirit that split the atom and the spirit that dissects God into concepts is at the bottom the same. It is through this mold of thinking as it had developed in the Greek-Roman world that the prophetic life and message of Jesus was destined to pass. Naturally, what came out of it was no longer the live Jesus but dead, ossified concepts. These concepts, further elaborated in the course of the cultural history of the West, are today used to measure the truth or falsehood of the theological discourse of people who do not belong to that cultural context, who do not share that history. As Asians, our mode of thinking is unitive rather than analytic, experiential rather than representational, existentialist rather than essentialist. The dichotomies western thought has thrown up - matter and spirit, faith and reason, nature and grace, temporal and eternal, human and divine, and the like - are foreign to us. For us thinking is communing, not conquering; is being present to what presents itself, not re-presenting it through concepts; is being one with the oneness of all, not exploding the one into the manifold. Our ancient seers would have questioned even the 'and' in the customary formulation, God and man if taken in the additive, disjunctive sense; so finely attuned were they to the underlying oneness of the many. These cultural specificities are ignored by the Church when she compels us, Asians, to think as do people in the West. What is this but cultural imperialism and colonization of the mind?

Further, whereas theologians in the West live among people sharing more or less the same Christian tradition, the Asian theologian finds himself inserted into a world of religious pluralism. Confronted with followers of other religions who are morally or culturally in no way inferior for not sharing the Christian faith, he is forced to ask questions regarding tradition which those in the West dare not raise. To give but one instance, if I tell a non-Christian that salvation is only through Jesus, I alienate him once and for all and erect an insuperable barrier in the way of common action for the Kingdom of God. For by my words I have reduced all those, who do not believe in Jesus, to the level of second class children of God. This raises the question, How could a belief be true that is harmful to the interests of the Kingdom? Thus a theologian who takes his discipleship seriously has no other option but to radically rethink what tradition teaches. Such rethinking is not just a matter of expediency but is dictated by that which theology is about: God encountered in history. If the central command of Jesus is to seek the Kingdom of God and its justice first, praxis in response to that command should be the main controlling factor in all theological reflection. Only that theological thinking is valid which is carried on in the broader context of living and working with people of other religions and persuasions, not excluding atheists and Marxists. The primary locus of theology, therefore, cannot be the closed community of Christians but the open community of all those who hunger and thirst for justice and freedom. And if the theology that emerges out of dialogue with the Lord of history bursts the old wineskins of tradition, none need shed a tear over it except the makers of old wineskins!

Finally, the very nature of authentic theological reflection precludes blind conformity to any rules of censorship. The theologian's task is to conceptually articulate the dimensions of faith as a human response to God's word here and now. He is not free to write what he wills but is bound by the reality of God he has seen. He is under orders, never his own master. Hence he is essentially also a prophet, constrained to bear witness to what he believes to be the call of the Kingdom as vehicled through his history and culture.

This does not mean that the theologian, Asian or otherwise, is a law unto himself. Sharing the human condition, he is liable to err, His formulations may be one-sided, his views immature. Hence he too needs to "be censored, if not censured. But who is to do that? The living God speaking through his people, through all those who believe in his final coming. It is God's history with his people that will censor away the false from the true, winnow the chaff from the grain. If what the theologian propounds is false, God will disown him. And his theories will eventually find a place in the dustbin of history where they belong - even if they have the support of the official Church. If, on the contrary, they are true, they will have a future - even when disowned by the same Church. Has not God reinstated values like religious freedom, freedom of conscience, and democracy, all of which the Church at one time condemned? On the other hand, has not God repudiated "many an earlier notion which the Church fiercely clung to such as "Extra ecclesiam nulla Salus"? Nor is it only in the long run of history that God's judgment through his people reveals itself. Rather it is under its shadow that the theologian articulates his faith. His discourse about God takes place in the context of continued dialogue with people and is constantly subjected to their criticism. Which, when internalized, becomes self-censoring, the only kind of censoring that respects the freedom of God and man. The traditional practice of censorship has meaning only where theology has become a mere academic exercise cut off from the mainstream of history where man meets his destiny with God.

It is in this spirit of seeking the Kingdom of God and its justice first that I have tried to engage in theological reflection. Nor have I done so in isolation but in dialogue with all those trying to remold society according to the demands of the Kingdom: theologians, priests, pastors, social activists, laypeople. And the book, Jesus and Freedom, is the crystallization of my basic convictions regarding Jesus and his message. So much so, for me to deny its central message would amount to sheer intellectual dishonesty and a betrayal of my mission as a disciple of Jesus. This does not mean the book is flawless or perfect. No human work is. But, as of today, I am fully convinced that whatever limitations it may have concern only matters of style and details of minor importance, and not the substance of my methodology and interpretation.

This being my position on theology and censorship, it serves no purpose answering point by point the judgment of the censor. He judges my work by the standard of traditional theology, which in my view needs itself to be evaluated by the more fundamental criteria of the original message of Jesus and man's historical encounter with God today. If still, I put down my reactions, it is not so much to defend my book as to show how the current practice of censorship fails to do justice not only to the theologian but also to Jesus and his God.

After complimenting me on the stress I have laid on the human values of Jesus, the censor writes: "These (human) values are attributed to the Jesus of history as distinct from the Christ of faith while other values about the Christ of faith remain unsaid or passed under silence." Significant here is the use of the term, value. It points to the specifically western approach to reality. Jesus is viewed as a subjectum or substance in whom inhere certain values. Now, values are things evaluated by human beings as objects "worthy of appropriating. Thus, Jesus is seen as an object of human striving, not as a subject who calls and "challenges. Having thus transmuted him into stereotype concepts, the censor can now employ the same to assess the truth of my reflections-reflections which refuse to dissolve Jesus into representational concepts.

I have approached Jesus mainly by way of that thinking which is akin to loving, the only thinking that can gain access to a person as a person: "Nemo cognoscitur nisi per amicitiam" (St. Augustine). Leaving aside my objection to the concept of value as applied to Jesus, I would ask what the 'other values' are which the censor attributes to the Christ of faith. From the context, it would appear he has in mind 'divine values'. These he attributes to the Christ of faith as distinct from the Jesus of history, implying there are no divine values in the latter. Since he admits the validity of the distinction, if not of the contrast, between the Jesus of history and the Christ of faith, this amounts to denying the divinity of the former. As though Jesus was a man who subsequently became God through the faith of the community. This is much more out of keeping with "the constant teaching of the magisterium" than anything I have ever written. And you too must find it ambiguous, if not dangerous. I reject this dualist, architectural conception of a superstructure of divinity "resting on an infrastructure of humanity. For me, the humanity of Jesus is the revelation of the divine. The censor goes on to say: "the book does not sufficiently make the transition from the point of departure of recognizing Jesus as a member of the human family to a more explicit and complete vision of faith, also found in the New Testament." The problem of transition is a typically western problem. The western mind first divides what is whole and then tries to recover the same whole out of the disparate parts. In the process wholeness escapes it; for reality resents the rape of reason. The censor, who separates the divinity (which he attributes to the Christ of faith) from the humanity of Jesus, has now to find a transition from the one to the other. This is his problem, not mine since I see the divine in the human. However, I agree with him that there is already in the New Testament, on the level of interpretation, a transition from the Jesus of history to the Christ of faith; but the transition is not to be viewed solely as one from the implicit to the explicit, from the inchoative to the full, as the censor seems to think; it is also one of alienation and distortion, as I have again and again pointed out in my book. From the earliest times, tradition has sought to tone down the radical stance of Jesus to suit the interests of the ruling classes. Such being the case, to attribute uniform value to all the statements in the New Testament is to flout all canons of biblical scholarship and sound theological reflection.

Now to come to the 'particular instances' noted by the censor: He thinks my reflections on the Eucharist give "the impression of reducing to a merely symbolic meaning the words of the institution of the Eucharist and their significance for the Jesus of history." On his admission, the censor is going by an impression. Impressions are conditioned by the way a person is attuned to reality and will vary from person to person. I wonder whether it is fair to make the fallible impression of one theologian the infallible norm for another theologian. More importantly, the censor has missed my fundamental concern which is precisely to salvage the Eucharist from that empty symbolism and conceptualization which neutralizes its revolutionary significance. A true Asian and a Hebrew, Jesus did not think in scholastic categories. His thinking was concrete, holistic. In his mouth, 'body' and 'blood, taken singly or conjointly, meant not separate substances but his whole being. Nor did the 'this' of "This is my body" and "This is my blood" point to the material elements of bread and wine but to the collective gesture of eating and drinking at the same table in anticipation of the festal meal of the end-time. To interpret the Eucharist, along these lines, is to bring it down from the rarified realm of vacuous symbols to the historical context where it truly belongs: Jesus' table-fellowship with publicans and sinners. It is the western penchant for reducing reality to abstractions that is responsible for the current manner of celebrating the Eucharist where there is no real eating and drinking, not even real bread and real drink, let alone any real commitment to, and anticipation of, the Kingdom to come. If the censor thinks otherwise, it might well be because constant dwelling among, and conversing with, mute symbols have made him mistake the same symbols for reality.

The censor considers my reflections on the death of Jesus ambiguous since they "can be interpreted as denying the sacrificial value in Jesus' own mind of his death on the cross". It is impossible for me to adequately answer him, since he does not say what, according to him, is Jesus' sacrificial understanding of his death. If laying down one's life in the cause of the Kingdom is a sacrifice, Jesus' death is a sacrifice. Not, if sacrifice is understood as a symbolic offering representing man's self-surrender to God, or as ritual suicide. For Jesus of Nazareth did not die a natural death nor did he commit suicide in honor of his Father. He was murdered for the sole crime of protesting injustice and domination. This indeed will be found disturbing. And what better way to neutralize the disturbing challenge of the cross than to label it 'sacrifice' and reduce it to a particular instance of a universal concept. To thus conceptualize the cold-blooded murder of Jesus is to condemn him to death a second time, and I refuse to be an accomplice if that is what the censor wants me to do. He further comments that the fact of Jesus' offering his life out of love "should not be made a pretext for reducing the significance of Jesus' death to that of any man offering his life for other". This is logic run amuck. To compare the death of Jesus to that suffered by many others in the struggle for a more humane world is not to reduce the one to the other. The comparison would, of course, be galling to those for whom discipleship is just the opposite of what it ought to be - a comprehensive system of insurance against death, made doubly sure through a tacit alliance with the powers that be.

Finally, the censor remarks that my "insistence on the horizontal dimension (of the content of liberation in the mind of Jesus) seems to overshadow the vertical dimension". Here too he has drawn upon his arsenal of ready-made concepts. 'Horizontal' and 'vertical' are spatial concepts. And spatial thinking is derived from the Greek conception of nature as a closed system (cosmos) governed by immanent laws. As such, it is alien to Jesus' mind which shared the Hebrew view of nature as open to God's action and gathered into God's history with mankind. Not space but history was where Jesus encountered God. Hence too my emphasis on man's meeting with God in history. It is the kind of theology the censor represents that does violence to the mode of knowing and viewing the world germane to Jesus.

The charge that my insistence on the horizontal, overshadows the vertical dimension, tallies with the earlier criticism of my 'one-sided' emphasis on the Jesus of history and his humanity. This raises some fundamental questions: Where is that danger-line where a given stress ceases to be legitimate and becomes censorable? Besides, if the allegedly one-sided stress on Jesus and his humanity is censorable, how much more censorable is the two thousand year's history of one-sided insistence on the divinity of Jesus to the neglect of his humanity! If the criterion of one-sidedness is strictly applied, would not most preachers and teachers of religion have to be silenced, and most books, written on Jesus withdrawn from circulation? Yet nothing of the sort is done. How is it that the criterion of one-sidedness is itself applied one-sidedly? Could it not be because the human Jesus makes disturbing demands on a Church and a theology that has come to terms with the principalities and powers of this world?

Enough has been said to show that the censor has not done justice either to my book or to its central theme which is the liberating word and deed of Jesus. And this because he has approached the work intending to determine how far its content and manner of discourse fit into his thought-forms whose validity he takes for granted. He thinks with the tools of representational concepts, whereas my thinking moves on the plane of life, death, and man's encounter with God in history. His theology is centered upon the Church; mine upon the Kingdom. If my book were scrutinized by any Indian theologian who lives his hope in the Kingdom and has made a definitive option in favor of the poor, the judgment would have been quite different. The best Indian Jesuit theologians have welcomed my book and have gone out of their way to make it known. Which shows how unfounded is your remark about the work containing opinions that "are dangerous or ambiguous - to say the least". I have propounded nothing dangerous to the true interests of God and his reign, which is all that matters as far as I am concerned. If it poses a danger to vested interests in the Church and the Society of Jesus, I cannot help it, and I intend to tender no apology. As for the Society's rules of censorship, I had made it clear to my Provincial that, though I consider them obsolete and in need of radical revision, I am prepared to submit whatever books I may write to the criticism of any Jesuit theologian acceptable to him and me, provided no demand is made on me to sacrifice my fundamental convictions. Seeking such criticism is not possible in the case of articles and papers which are often written under pressure and at short notice. If still, you insist, "we have a law; and by that law..." what answer can I give but the silence of Jesus.

Yours fraternally,

Sebastian Kappen S. J.

(Supplement to Anawim, No. 29, 1-10; *Ingathering*, Chapter 16)

Notes

Chapter 1

1. On this question, see Bornkamm 1961, pp.13-27; Perin 1967, pp.207-248; Robinson 1959.

Chapter 2

1. Meghnad Desai, 'India: Contradictions of Slow Capitalist Development,' in Blackburn 1975, pp.28-30. **2.** Dandekar 1971, pp.31-33. **3.** Ibid, p. 68. **4.** Blackburn 1975, p.29. **5.** Ibid, p.19. **6.** Myrdal 1968, vol.2, p. 819. **7.** Hoda 1972, p. 26. **8.** Dandekar 1971, pp.124-126. **9.** Gadgil 1974, p. 97. **10.** Srinivas 1974, p.90. **11.** Gray, 'The Problem,' in Desai 1969, p.537. **12.** Myrdal 1968, vol.1, p.286. **13.** Kuitenbrouwer 1973, p.7. **14.** Gadgil 1974, p.308. **15.** Myrdal, vol.2, p.1057. **16.** Srinivas, 'Changing Attitudes in India Today,' Yojana, Delhi, Oct. 1961. **17.** Weiner, 'Political Leadership in West Bengal,' in Desai 1969, p.733. **18.** Gadgil 1974 p. 306. **19.** Report of the Santhanam Committee, I, Government of India, New Delhi, 1964, p.108. **20.** Gadgil 1974, p.306. **21.** Report of the Santhanam Committee, I, p. 10. **22.** In writing this part of the chapter, the author has drawn largely upon his article, 'Values in Crisis' in Kappen 2002b, Chapter 12.

Chapter 3

1. Jeremias 1971, p.170. **2.** Perrin 1967, pp.68-74.

Chapter 4

1. This knowledge of the common realities permits him to contrast them with the kingdom he is revealing. cf. Matt. 6:19, 25; 7:27; 11:28; Luke 5:1-11. 2. Sometimes there were nameless crowds: "He saw a great crowd; his heart went out to them, and he cured those who were sick" (Mark 14:14). At other times the occasions are fully described; cf. Mark 1:21-28, 29-31, 40-45; 2:1-12; 3:1-16; 5:25-34; 8:22-26; 9:14-29; Matt. 9:32-34; Luke 13:10-17. 3. Nineham 1973, p. 45. 4. See references in note 2 for healings and exorcisms; raisings from the dead: Mark 5:35-43; Luke 7:11-15; John 11:43-44; nature miracles: Mark 6:45-52; 11:12-14; Matt. 17:24-27; Luke 5:1-11; Mark 6:35-41; John 6:1-13; 2:1-11. 5. Fuller 1963, pp.24-39. 6. Ibid., p.41.

Chapter 5

1. On this point see Jeremias 1969, Chapter 6. 2. Modern versions use servant rather than a slave for Doulos in such texts as Matt. 24:45-51; Luke 12:42-48; and 17:7-10. A domestic slave could become a manager or steward. 3. Jeremias 1971, pp.112-13. 4. Cf. the Beatitudes, Matt. 5:3-10, and Isaiah's text that Jesus applies to himself, Luke 4:18-21. 5. Belo 1975, pp.233-237.

Chapter 6

1. Jeremias 1969, Ch.14 to 18. 2. Jeremias, 1971, p. 266. 3. Ibid. (For a fuller discussion on the position of women in Jewish society, see Jeremias 1969, Ch.18. 4. Jeremias, 1971, p. 117. 5. Ibid, pp. 289-290. 6. Willi Marxen, 'The Lord's Supper: Concepts and Developments' in Schultz 1971, pp. 106-114.

Chapter 7

1. Richardson 1973, pp. 41-44. 2. Paul Winter, 'Sadducees and Pharisees,' in Schultz 1971, pp. 47-56. 3. Jeremias 1971, p.71 4. Belo 1975, p.217. 5. Ibid, p. 243 and footnote. 6. Ibid, pp. 287-289. 7. Ibid, pp. 250-255.

Chapter 8

1. Bultmann 1964, p. 7. **2.** For example, in reading from the scroll, "The Spirit of the Lord is upon me " (Isa. 61:1 ff), he omits what follows "the year of the Lord's favour"; "a day of vengeance of our God." Compare Isa. 35:4, "See, your God comes with vengeance, with dread retribution he comes to save you," and what follows: "Then shall blind men's eyes be opened, and the ears of the deaf unstopped," and so on, and the message to John the Baptist, "The blind recover their sight" (Matt. 11:2-6). See Jeremias, 1971, pp. 206-207. **3.** Jeremias, 1971, p. 211.

Chapter 9

1. Rad 1968, p. 200. **2.** Jeremias, 1971, p. 120. **3.** Ibid, pp. 116-117. **4.** Ibid, p. 201. **5.** Robinson 1966, p. 14. **6.** Ibid, p. 15.

Chapter 11

1. *Bhagavad Gita*, VIII, 17-20. *2. Katha Upanishad.* II, 20-23.

Chapter 12

1. Lawler 1971, n. 35.1. **2.** Ibid, n.57.2. **3.** Ibid, n.38.4. **4.** Edward Schillebeeckx, O. P, 'The Church and Mankind', in Lynch 1965, p.82. **5.** Ibid, n.38.4. **6.** Lubac 1967, p.94. **7.** Lawler 1971, n. 9.5. **8.** Ibid, 37.1 **9.** Ibid, n. 39.4. **10.** M. D. Chenu, 'Les signes des temps', in Congar 1967, pp.111-112. **11.** Lawler 1971, n. 42.2. **12.** Pastoral Constitution on the Church in the Modern World, Gaudium et Spes, 1965, (PCC), n.5. **13.** Lawler 1971, n.43.3. **14.** Ibid, n.43.1. **15.** Lubac, p.29. **16.** Ibid, n.42.2. **17.** Ibid. **18.** Pius XII 1956, p.212. **19.** Lawler 1971, n.42.2. **20.** Ibid, n.40.4. **21.** Ibid, n.42.3. **22.** Lawler 1971, n.26.4. **23.** Schillebeeckx, 'The Church and Mankind' in Schillebeeckx 1965, p.95. **24.** Decree on the Apostolate of the Laity (DAL), n.24.7. **25.** Lawler 1971, n.43.5. **26.** PCC, n. 31.3. **27.** DAL, n. 7.5. **28.** Rahner 1967, p.76. **29.** DAL, n. 8.1,3.

Chapter 13

1. Lumen Gentium, 1. **2.** A. Sievers, 'Die Christengruppen in Kerala, ihr Lebensraum und das problem der christlichen Einheit', in Zeitschrift fur Missionswissenschaft und Religionswissenschaft, Juli 1962, Heft 3, p.173. **3.** Ibid. **4.** Ibid, p.185. **5.** Ibid, pp.170-171. **6.** Ibid, p.172. **7.** Ibid, p.175. **8.** Ibid, p.176. **9.** Tisserant 1957 p.185. **10.** Ibid. **11.** Ibid.; Also, see Appendix II; Liturgy of the Syrian Catholics of Malabar, pp.175 ff. **12.** Sievers, art. cit, p.186; The difficulties created in Kerala, as elsewhere in the East, by overlapping multiple jurisdiction were brought to the notice of Vatican II, which, however, failed to provide a satisfactory solution; cf. Commentary on the Documents of Vatican II, Ed. H. Vorgrimler, 1967, Vol. 1, p.316. **13.** This was the case already in pre-Portuguese days. At the Synod of Diampur a vain attempt was made to persuade the Syrians to give up their caste privileges which stood in the way of missionary work among the lower castes: Tisserant 1957, p. 63. **14.** J. A. Jungmann, 'Wirkende Kraefte in liturgischen Werden', in Cott in Welt, Herder 19 64, Band II, p. 233ff. **15.** Ibid, p.244. **16.** 1 Cor. 11:26. **17.** Constitution on the Sacred Liturgy, 2. **18.** Ibid. **19.** Lumen Gentium, 13. **20.** Constitution on the Sacred Liturgy, 40. **21.** Ibid, 4. **22.** Gaudium et Spes, 4 and 11. **23.** See the significant contribution of Robert Antoine, S. J, "Kommt eine indische Liturgie?", in Die katholischen Missionen, Heft, 2, Maerz-April, 1968, pp. 49-53. (In quoting documents of Vatican II, the numbers indicate articles.)

Chapter 14

1. Abraham 1969, pp.9, 32. **2.** Chap.13. **3.** This is just one instance among many, of certain unethical means, employed by Fr. C. A. Abraham in the leaflet 'A Matter o Rite' (MR). (See Abraham 1969). He has apparently no qualm of conscience in misquoting and manipulating my original statements. For instance, the reader is invited to compare the views attributed to me on p.2, with my original assertions. **4.** MR, p.1. **5.** Ibid, pp.1, 4, 20. **6.** Chap.13. **7.** MR, pp.5-6, 8-9. **8.** Chap.13. **9.** MR, p.1. **10.** MR, p.3. **11.** Ibid, p.4. **12.** Ibid. **13.** Ibid, p.5. **14.** Chap.13. **15.** MR, p.8. **16.** Chap.13. **17.** MR, p.1. **18.** Ibid, p.7. **19.** Ibid, p.10, 12. **20.** Ibid, p.31. **21.** MR, p.12. **22.** Ibid, p.7. **23.** Ibid, p.12. **24.** MR. pp.26-28. **25.** Joseph Ratzinger, "Zur Frage Nach dem Sinn des priesterlichen Dienstes," in Geist Und Leben, Oct. 1968, pp. 347-376. **26.** MR, p.27 **27.** Ibid, p.1. **28.** Chap. 16. **29.** MR, p.33. **30.** Ibid, pp.14-32. **31.** Ibid, pp.11-31. **32.** MR, p.19. **33.** Chap.13

Chapter 15

1. Figures according to National Sample Survey as quoted by Editorial, Sunday Standard, Madura Edition, April 6, 1969. **2.** Census of India, 1961. **3.** Report on the socio-economic Survey on Castes and Communities in Kerala, 1968, (Bureau of Economics and Statistics, Trivandrum, 1969) Vol. I, pp.11-15. **4.** Ibid, p.10. **5.** Ibid, pp.22-23. **6.** 33.75% of the population is illiterate; 31.95% literate but possessing below primary education. Those who have finished their High School education total only 4.22 %. Those with College education (Pre-degree, Graduation or Post Graduation) constitute another 1.31% (Ibid, p.18). Of this last group, the vast majority come from the upper or middle classes. **7.** On the problem of secularization in India, cf. Srinivas 1966. **8.** Aiyappan 1965, p.169. **9.** Ibid. **10.** Damodaran 1967. **11.** Seminar Digest, Reports and Proceedings of the Kerala Regional Seminar on Church in India Today, December 1968, Manjummel, Kerala, 1969, p.118. This Seminar was conducted in preparation for the National Seminar on the Church in India Today which was held later in Bangalore in May 1969. **12.** Ninan Koshy, "Role of the Church, a Historical Survey and Prospect for the Future", Paper read at the Seminar on the Political Situation in Kerala, held at Adoor, September 1969, under the joint sponsorship of the Christian Institute for the Study of Religion and Society, Bangalore, and the Kerala Christian Council. **13.** However, the bourgeois character in question is not a uniform phenomenon. It becomes less and less pronounced, especially in respect of material conditions of life, as we move away from centres of power, secular or religious, in the church. **14.** See relevant articles in Concilium, Vol. VI, No.4, June 1968 **15.** Gaudium et Spes, 29. **16.** Ibid. **17.** For a detailed discussion of this question, see my article "The Role of the Church in National

Development", Clergy Monthly, India, Vol.33, No. 2, Feb. 1969, pp. 59-75. **18**. This agrees in substance also with the conclusions reached by the Adoor Seminar. **19**. Gaudium et Spes, 21. **20**. The Kerala regional Seminar in its official report has recommended that surplus property should be utilized for the rehabilitation of the poor: Seminar Digest, p.151

Chapter 16

1. Catholic Directory of India,1964 (CDI). **2**. Directory of Catholic Secondary Schools and Secondary Training Schools in India, 1964, published by the Xavier Association of Secondary Schools, Bombay (DCSS). **3**. Dickinson 1967. **4**. CDI. **5**.Valerian Cardinal Gracias, "The Role of Christian Colleges in Indian National Development", in The Christian College and National Development, The Consultation of Principals of Christian Colleges, Tambaram, 1967, published by The Christian Literature Society, Madras, 1967; (Tambaram Consultation). **6**. Dogmatic Constitution on the Church (DCC),1. **7**. DCSS. **8**. The available sociological data would suggest that in educational institutions all over India, the traditionally underprivileged are poorly represented. See Srinivas 1964, p.92. **9**. Tambaram Consultation, p.24; cf. also Dickinson 1967, p. 45. **10**. Tambaram Consultation, 40.3. **11**. Dickinson 1967, p. 63. **12**. G. Kalapurakkal, "Christian Colleges in Kerala", in Tambaram Consultation, p.189. **13**. "The Role and Problems of Private Enterprise in Education", Tambaram Consultation, p.123. **14**. Valerian Gracias, art. cit, Tambaram Consultation, pp. 24-25 **15**. Lubac 1967, p. 29. **16**. Pastoral Constitution on the Church in the Modern world. (PCC), 5.4. **17**. Ibid, 42.2. **18**. Ibid, 39.4. **19**. M. D. Chenu, "Les Signes des Temps", in L'Eglise dans le monde de ce temps, pp.111-112. **20**. PCC, 42.3. **21**. Decree on Lay Apostolate, 24.7. **22**. PCC, 43.8. **23**. Ibid, 43.5. **24**. Decree on Lay Apostolate, 7.5. **25**. DCC, 31.2. **26**. Decree on Ecumenism, 12.2. **27**. Dickinson 1967, p. 61. **28**. Rahner 1967, p.76.

Chapter 18

1. For an understanding of the social relevance of the Beatitudes, see Dupont 1969, pp. 65-90. **2.** Cullman 1963, pp. 12-42. **3.** Gandhi 1963, p. 68.

Chapter 19

1. Marx 1963, p. 52. **2.** The National Sample Survey, 1969. **3.** The Illustrated Weekly of India, Nov. 9, 1969, p. 11. **4.** Srinivas 1964, p. 90. **5.** Ibid. p. 93. **6.** Myrdal 1968, Vol. 1, p. 293. **7.** Ibid. p.286. **8.** Ibid, pp. 262-275. **9.** Devanandan 1961.p. 46. **10.** Swami Nikhilananda, in Moore, pp.238-240. **11.** A. B. Shah, in his introduction to Shah 1965, p.11. **12.** Damodaran 1967, p.480. **13.** Chap.12. **14.** Marx-Engels, Gesamatusgabe, Vol. 4, p.200.

Chapter 22

1. Jeremias, 1971, p.162. **2.** Perrin 1967, pp.102-103. **3.** Nineham 1972, pp. 44-45.

Chapter 25

1. On early Israelite tribalism see Vaux 1974, pp.4-15. **2.** Here we have two parallel narratives of the institution of the monarchy, one favourable to it (1 Sam. 9:1-10, 16; 10: 1-11, 15) and another opposed to it (1 Sam. 8: 1-22; 10: 18-25 continued in cc. 12 and 15). **3.** Rad 1962, p.59. **4.** Miranda 1974. **5.** On this, see Belo 1975, pp.98-102. **6.** Grundmann 1974, pp.63-65. **7.** Hoffmann 1976, pp.211-212. **8.** Jeremias 1969, pp.311-312. **9.** In writing this section, I have drawn heavily upon my work, Kappen 1977, pp.107-117. **10.** Belo 1975, pp.253-255.

Bibliography

Abraham, C. A. (1969), *A Matter of Rite: An Examination of the One-rite Movement*, Indian Institute for Eastern Churches

Aiyappan, A.(1965), *Social Revolution in a Kerala Village, A Study in Culture Change*, Bombay

Belo, Fernando (1975), *Lecture Materialists de l'Evangile de Marc*, CERF, Paris

Blackburn (1975), Robin, ed., *Explosion in a Subcontinent*, Penguin, London

Bornkamm, Gunther (1961), *Jesus of Nazareth*, Harper, New York

Bultmann, Rudolf (1964), *Primitive Christianity in Its Contemporary Setting*, Fontana, London

Congar, Yves; Philippe Delhaye; Michel Peuchmaurd (1967), *L'E´glise Dans le monde de ce temps:* Constitution pastorale 'Gaudium et Spes.', Le´s Editions du Cerf, Paris

Cullman, Oscar (1963), *The State in the New Testament*, London

Damodaran, K. (1967), *Indian Thought, A Critical Survey*

Dandekar (1971), V. M. and Nilakantha Rath, *Poverty in India*, Krishna Raj, Bombay

Desai, A. R., ed. (1969), *Rural Sociology in India*, Popular Prakasan, Bombay

Devanandan, P. D.(1961), *Christian Concern in Hinduism*, Christian Institute for the Study of Religion and Society, Bangalore, India

Dickinson, Richard and Nancy Dickinson (1967), *Directory of Information for Christian Colleges in India*, The Christian Literature Society, Madras

Dupont, Jacques (1969), *Les Beatitude*, Tome II, Paris

Fuller, Reginald H. (1963), *Interpreting the Miracles*, SCM, Westminster, Philadelphia, 1963

Gadgil, D. R. (1974), *Planning and Economic Policy in India*, Gokhale Institute of Politics and Economics, Poona

Gandhi, M. K. (1963), *The Message of Jesus Christ*, ed. Anand T. Hingorani, Bombay

Grundmann, Walter (1974), *Das Evangelium Nach Lukas*, Evangelische Verlagsanstalt, Berlin

Hoda (1972), Mansur, ed., *Problems of Unemployment in India*, Allied Publishers, Bombay

Hoffmann, Paul; Volker Eid (1976), *Jesus van Nazareth und eine christiliche Moral*, Herder, Freiburg

Jeremias, Joachim (1971), *New Testament Theology*, Scribner, New York

————————— (1969), *Jerusalem in the Time of Jesus*, S. C. M., London

Kuitenbrouwer, Joost (1973), *Growth and Equality in India and China: A Comparative Analysis*, Institute of Social Studies, Hague

Lawler, Michael G., Todd A. Salzman, and Eileen Burke-Sullivan (1971), *The Church in the Modern World*, Liturgical Press, Collegeville, Minnesota

Lubac, Henri de (1967), *The Religion of Teilhard de Chardin*, New York

Lynch, Kevin A, ed. (1965), *The Church and Mankind*. Dogma Vol. 1, New York

Marx, Karl (1963), *Early Writings*, Trans. T. B. Bottomore, London

Miranda, Jose (1974), *Marx and the Bible*, Orbis Books, N. Y.

Moore, C. A., ed., *The Indian Mind*, Honolulu

Myrdal, Gunnar (1968), *Asian Drama: An Inquiry into the Poverty of Nations*, 3 vols., Pantheon, New York

Nineham, Denis E. (1973), *Saint Mark*, Penguin, London

Perrin, Norman (1967), *Rediscovering the Teaching of Jesus*, SCM, London; Harper, New York

Pius XII (1956), *Acta Apostolicae Sedis*, Vol. 48

Rad, Gerhard von (1969), *The Message of the Prophets*, S. C. M., London

————————— (1962), *Old Testament Theology*, I, Study Edition, SCM Press, London

Rahner, Karl (1967), *The Christian of the Future*, New York, Herder and Herder

Richardson, Allan (1973), *The Political Christ*, S. C. M., London

Robinson, James M. (1959), *A New Quest of the Historical Jesus*, Studies in Biblical Theology, 25, SCM, London

Schillebeeckx, E. ed. (1965), *The Church and Mankind*, The Catholic University of America Press

Schultz, Han Jurgen, ed. (1971), *Jesus in His Time*, SPCK, London

Shah, A. B., and Rao C.R.M., (1965) *Tradition and Modernity in India*, Bombay

Srinivas, M. N. (1964), *Caste in Modern India, and Other Essays*, Asia Publishing House, New York

____________ (1966), *Social Change in Modern India*, Bombay

Tisserant, Eugene (1957), *Eastern Christianity in India: A History of the Syro-Malabar Church from the Earliest Time to the Present Day*, Longmans, Green, and Co

Sebastian Kappen's Books

- *Jesus and Freedom* (1977), intr. Francois Houtar, Orbis Books, Maryknoll, New York, Edition 2: Notion Press, Chennai, 2019

- *Marxian Atheism* (1983a), self published, Bangalore.

- *Jesus and Cultural Revolution - an Asian Perspective* (1983b), BILD, Bombay

- *Jesus Today* (1985). AICUF, Madras

- *Liberation Theology and Marxism* (1986), Asha Kendra, Punthamba

- *The Future of Socialism and Socialism of the Future* (1992), Visthar, Bangalore.

Posthumous Publications

- *Tradition Modernity Counterculture – an Asian Perspective* (1994), Visthar, Bangalore.

- *Spirituality in the New Age of Recolonisation* (1995), Visthar, Bangalore

- *Hindutva and Indian Religious Traditions* (2000), ed. Sebastian Vattamattam, Edition 2: Notion Press, Chennai, 2019

- *Divine Challenge and Human Response* (2001), ed. Sebastian Vattamattam, CSS, Tiruvalla

- *Jesus and Society* (2002a), ed. S Painadath S. J., ISPCK, Delhi.

- *Jesus and Culture* (2002b), ed. S Painadath S. J., ISPCK, Delhi

- *Towards a Holistic Cultural Paradigm* (2003), ed. Sebastian Vattamattam, CSS, Tiruvalla

- *Marx Beyond Marxism* (2012), ed. Sebastian Vattamattam, Voice Books, Manjeri.

- *Ingathering – Autobiographical Writings and Selected essays* (2013a), ed. Sebastian Vattamattam, Jeevan Books, Bharananganam

- *What the Thunder Says – A poem and selected Essays* (2013b), ed. Sebastian Vattamattam, Jeevan Books, Bharananganam

Books in Malayalam

- *Viswasathil Ninnu Viplavathilekku* (1 9 7 2) , e d it i on 3 : Pusthaka Prasadhaka Sangham, Kozhikode, 2019

- *Nalathekku Oru Laingika-sadacharam* (1973), Edition 3: Pusthaka Prasadhaka Sangham, Kozhikode, 2019

- *Paristhithi Samskruthi* (1988), (Co-author: Sebastian Vattamattam), Edition 2: Ascend Books, Kottayam, 2014

- *Marxian Darsanathinu Oramukham* (1989), tr. of Marx Beyond Marxism by Sebastian Vattamattam, Edition 2: NBS, Kottayam, 2012

- *Kalasrushtiyude Uravidam* (1991), tr. of Martin Heidegger: Der Ursprung Des Kunstwerkes, DCB, Kottayam

- *Pravachanam Prathisamskruthi* (1992), Yatra Publications, Kottayam

- *Socialisathinte Bhavi* (1993), Manusham Publications, Ettumanoor

- *Akraistavanaya Yesuvine Thedi* (1999), Current Books, Kottayam, 2005

- *Irupathonnam Noottandinoru Prathisamskruthi* (1991), tr. of Tradition Modernity Counterculture, Yatra Publications, Kottayam

- *Yesuvinte Mochanam Sabhakalil Ninnu* (2012), Dr. Bishop Paulose Mar Paulose Foundation, Thrissur

- *Daivathinte Maranavum Manushyante Jananavum*, (2015), tr. of Marxian Atheism, Media House, Calicut

About the Editor

Sebastian Vattamattam is a retired professor of mathematics and a writer. In Malayalam he has authored the books: *Ecology and Culture* (with Fr. Kappen), *Language and Power, Unconscious Travels of Language – From Freud to Lacan, Ideology and Symbolic Revolution, Sigmund Freud*. His books in English are *Book of Beautiful Curves* (Math) and *What Dreams Tell Us – Lacanian Interpretations*. Vattamattam has compiled, edited, and published many books of Fr. Kappen.

Contents of the Six Volumes

Volume I

Part 1: Jesus and Freedom

Part 2: Essays

Volume II

Part 1: Marxian Atheism
Preface of the First Edition

Part 2: Essays

Volume IV

Part 1: Liberation Theology and Marxism

Part 2: Essays

9. The Spirit Descended Upon Him

10. Jesus beyond Jesus

11. The Man Jesus: Rupture and Communion

12. A Lesson in Socialism

13. Table-fellowship as Socialist Praxis

14. Christians and Class Struggle

15. Church a People's Movement

16. Between the Church and the Reign of God

17. Church as the Bearer of New Values

18. The Asian Search for a Liberative Theology

19. Towards an Indian Theology of Liberation

20. A New Approach to Theological Education

Volume V

Part 1: Hindutva and Indian Religious Traditions

1. The Materialistic Conception of History and the Indian Religious Tradition

2. Religious Ideologies and Political Change

3. Hindu-Christian Relations in India

4. Whither Religion? Whither Democracy? 1990

5. Religious Pluralism and the Survival of Indian Democracy

6. Hindutva Emergent Fascism?

Part 2: Essays

7. Response to Comments on Chapter 1

8. Towards a Strategy of Socialist Reconstruction

9. Socialism Through Community Action

Volume VI

Part 1: Tradition Modernity Counterculture

Preface

Part 2: Essays

9. Beyond the Cult of the Dead God

10. The Dialectic of Faith and Unfaith

11. Spirituality in the New Age of Re-colonization

12. The Prophetic Role of the Christians in Contemporary India in the World of Art

13. Jesus and the Elections

14. Towards an Indian Model of Socialism

15. The Future of Socialism and Socialism of the Future

Part 3: A Poem and Autobiography

16. What the Thunder Says

17. Ingathering